And Then They Were Gone is a mind-blowing
the utopian dreamers who died at Jonestown
The story honors in particular the adolescents
and taught as students full of promise, childr
their classes at Opportunity High School in
before the bizarre events that are variously referred to as "the Jonestown
massacre" or, simply, "Jonestown."

—CATHARINE LUCAS, Professor Emeritus, San Francisco State University

A moving portrait of the high school students who lost their lives in
Jonestown. Through documentation, personal memory, and in many cases,
the teenagers' own poetry, Judy Bebelaar and Ron Cabral show us the real
young people behind the grim headlines.

—AUTUMN STEPHENS, author of the *Wild Women* book series

The book ends with a passing moment during which two of the survivors —
sons of Jim Jones himself — return to their high school, the place where their
innocence once thrived, to stop in and see an old teacher. In this moment the
book ultimately nails what it set out to do: to show the humanity of the people
of Peoples Temple, and to do so from the students' and teachers' perspectives.

—CRAIG FOREMAN, educator, "One Teacher to Another: A Review of
And Then They Were Gone," *The Jonestown Report*, 2018

…Thankfully Bebelaar and Cabral do not put Jones as the center of their
narrative, but rather as a shadow of what is to come. Instead they are smart
and focus on the teenagers themselves: Mondo Griffith, a sixteen year old
who shared his poetry the first day of class. Dorothy Buckley, who also took
Bebelaar's creative writing class, and was featured on the school's radio show
where she played songs from He's Able; and Wesley Breidenbach, who was
well liked by his teachers for his intelligence and his ability to draw others into
class conversations. And then there's Stephan [Jones] who has a world weariness that didn't seem right on a seventeen-year-old boy. Little did they know
the weight Stephan was carrying, dealing with family and church pressures…

—JENNIFER KATHLEEN GIBBONS, prize-winning author,
"That Championship Season Before the World Turned Gray,"
The Jonestown Report, 2018

....Through the chapters about their time at the school, we get an interesting glimpse of teenage life outside the Temple, according to their teachers, although the Temple youngsters mostly kept to themselves and were more guarded about their personal lives than the other pupils. Through the poetry they wrote in Bebelaar's creative writing class, we learn about their dreams, hopes and ideals.

The book follows the Temple children as they migrate from Opportunity II to Guyana. We hear about their daily lives in Jonestown as well as the general development, or rather deterioration, of the Peoples Temple organization and Jim Jones' corresponding decline. This part of the book brings interesting new details and personal perspectives to situations many will have heard of before, through interviews with Stephan Jones, among others....

—RIKKE WETTENDORFF, writer and co-editor, *The Jonestown Report*, "From High School to Jonestown," *The Jonestown Report,* 2018

And *Then They Were Gone* provides fresh information about the teen members of Peoples Temple, filling a vast gap in our overall understanding of Jim Jones and his (mostly) doomed followers. I'm grateful to the authors for these insights.   —JEFF GUINN, author of *The Road to Jonestown: Jim Jones and Peoples Temple*

A heart-breaking tribute to a group of San Francisco teens who were sent to Jonestown, as recounted by two of their former high school teachers. This book humanizes such a horrific tragedy by inviting readers to become well acquainted with these teenagers—so many of whom were killed in the mass murder-suicide. Before they were victims of a crazed religious leader, they were just kids—with the hopes and dreams common to children everywhere. By reading about them, we honor their memories.

—JULIA SCHEERES, author of *A Thousand Lives: The Untold Story of Hope, Deception, and Survival at Jonestown*

Seen through the eyes of two of their high school teachers, this book is a work of love and fond memories, a testament to how youth and innocence can be hijacked. The dead cannot speak, yet Bebelaar and Cabral have allowed us to hear their voices once more.

—DEBORAH LAYTON, author of *Seductive Poison: A Jonestown Survivor's Story of Life and Death in the Peoples Temple*

And Then They Were Gone

Teenagers of Peoples Temple
from High School to Jonestown

Judy Bebelaar and Ron Cabral

2018
Sugartown Publishing
Crockett, California

And Then They Were Gone Honors and awards 2019, 2020

1 Ron and Judy named *San Francisco Library Laureates, 2019*
2 Nominated (1 of 5 nominations, General Nonfiction) for the *Northern California Book Awards, 2019*
3 *Northern California Publishers and Authors* first prize General Non-fiction, 2019
4 *Non Fiction Authors Association* silver award, United States, Sociology, 2019
5 *Royal Dragonfly Book Award* first place Historical Nonfiction, 2019
6 *Royal Dragonfly Book Award* first place, Other Nonfiction, 2019
7 *Book Excellence Awards* (*A Celebration of Global Literary Excellence*) winner, Young Adult Nonfiction (chosen from "among hundreds")
8 *Chanticleer International Book Awards* semifinalist, *Nelly Bly Award for Narrative Nonfiction* (winners to be announced July, 2020)

Sugartown Publishing
1140 Solano Ave., #140
Albany, CA 94706
sugartownpublishing.com

Book cover and interior design by Jannie Dresser and Margaret Copeland (*terragrafix.com*)
Photo identifications for book cover and interior, and credits on page 293.

Contents

Foreword

had a hard time writing this foreword—not because of this first-rate and moving book, but because each time I sat down at my desk and began to write, my mind became overwhelmed with thoughts of the many mass killings that have occurred during my seventy-nine years. Each has troubled me and contributed to a generalized grief and mourning that has been part of the ambience of my life. Just a few minutes ago I heard that there was a spate of murders in Chicago over Christmas and, the report added, more than seven hundred gunshot deaths in that city during 2016.

I cannot accept these sad horrors without pushing back on murderous intent and action, without searching for hope that seeps through the cracks and insists that love too has a central place in even the most tragic of circumstances.

The authors of this book, in telling the story of their Peoples Temple students, provide a humane and complex portrait of the decency, sensitivity, and creativity of youngsters caught in a sinister web constructed for them in Guyana.

This is a teachers' perspective on the tragedy, one that conveys not just the complexity and hope of these trapped young people but also the loving concern of educators dedicated to nurturing their students' growth and providing them with tools for having a fulfilling adult life. In the case of Jonestown this effort was tragically thwarted, but that does not diminish the commitment and admirable efforts of caring others.

The specific and concrete portraits presented in this book are central to personalizing the Jonestown killings; they can help us understand and memorialize those caught up in other mass killings. Many people have forgotten these Jonestown deaths and many others have never learned about them in the first place.

This book is an antidote to that forgetfulness by putting a face and giving voice to some of the victims. It teaches us how not to forget, but instead to bear witness to these interrupted lives and to honor them—and by doing so to honor other victims of human aberrations and crimes. Perhaps in this way we may be able to redeem some modicum of love, the driving force of what is best in ourselves, from the slough of despair created by so many terminated lives.

—HERBERT KOHL, educator and author of more than 30 books
including *36 Children*

PEOPLES TEMPLE
OF THE DISCIPLES OF CHRIST
DENOMINATIONAL BROTHERHOOD
JIM JONES, PASTOR
Services
FRI. 8 P.M.   SUN. 11 AM-7 P.M.

Preface

They came so suddenly, and left too soon, the teenagers from Peoples Temple. Most Americans knew nothing about the Church in 1976.

The young people entered Opportunity II High, the small public alternative school where Ron Cabral and I were teaching in September of that year.

Beginning in spring of 1977, some of these students—whom we had just started to get to know—began to leave San Francisco to join their church's utopian agricultural community in South America. By summer's end almost all of the 120 students from the Temple who had enrolled at Opportunity had joined the settlement in Guyana, a small South American country tucked between Brazil and Suriname.

The first reports of the tragic events that took place on November 18, 1978, stated—incorrectly—that 400 people had been found dead in a jungle outpost, Jonestown, Guyana, apparently a mass suicide following the assassination of Democratic Congressman Leo Ryan of California. We feared some of the dead might be our students.

That first number, 400, gave us a grim kind of hope. We knew there were far more than that in Jonestown. Many of the teenagers we knew *must* have survived the catastrophe. Strong and vibrant—they would be the ones to make it through. Then we saw the pictures, aerial photographs of bodies—facedown, arm in arm or cradling children—spread in fans of bright color against dark grass and earth. Almost all who had gone to Jonestown died there, we read, by drinking a sugary fruit drink, a generic Kool-Aid, laced with cyanide. The final toll: 918 lives.

At Opportunity, we searched for those we knew in the lists of the dead being published in San Francisco papers. We found too many. A few of the more athletic young people did survive, not because of their superior strength, but because they had been participating in a basketball tournament in Georgetown, Guyana's capital, 140 miles from Jonestown, when Reverend Jim Jones gave the suicide order.

Only ten days later, on November 28, 1978, two more inexplicable murders rocked the Bay Area and the nation. The victims were San Francisco's handsome, affable, progressive mayor, George Moscone, and Harvey Milk, the first openly gay member of the city's Board of Supervisors. Both men were determined and optimistic, and both were shot in cold blood in their offices in City Hall. The deranged gunman, Dan White, no stranger to his victims, was a former police officer and member of the Board of Supervisors.

Dianne Feinstein, then president of the Board, announced the assassinations from City Hall. Her tense, grief-filled voice reflected the shock we all felt that sad November.

The impact of these tragedies threatened to drain what dim hope survived from the turbulent 1960s with the assassinations of John F. Kennedy in Dallas, Martin Luther King Jr. in Memphis, Malcolm X in New York City, and Robert "Bobby" Kennedy in Los Angeles. All over the world, those dedicated to positive social change seemed to have been methodically exterminated by a few madmen.

To quote popular San Francisco newspaper columnist Herb Caen, the world had gone gray. The cynics had it right. The fact that so many of the teenagers we knew were being brought home in caskets, that one-third of those who had died in Jonestown were children, underlined the horror. The hopelessness was palpable, colder than fog off the Bay.

❧

Many people today—especially those born in later decades—have never heard of Jonestown and what happened there, despite the more than fifty books, a play, two movies, and at least three television documentaries. As for those who received the terrible news firsthand nearly forty years ago, there are many who have dismissed the Peoples Temple members as mindless followers of a cult leader. The real story is not so simple—in fact, it is far more interesting and complex, especially as far as the students we knew were concerned.

Ron asked me to collaborate with him on a book about the Temple teenagers who were our students at Opportunity after seeing Leigh Fondakowski's play, *The People's Temple*, at Berkeley Repertory Theatre in 2005. Ron had known well the Temple boys who made Opportunity's baseball team possible, and I knew many Temple kids from my Creative Writing class. I had even saved their work. After I saw the play, we met to talk.

Both of us admired how Fondakowski's work centered on the *people* of the Church (thus the apostrophe in her title, *The People's Temple*, which is not in the official Church name) rather than chronicling the story of Jim Jones. We felt our students' story needed to be told, as no other work has focused on the teenagers who went to Jonestown. We wanted to honor them in the way the play did its characters.

Berkeley Rep production of Leigh Fondakowski's play
(courtesy of David Allen)

I became lead writer while we both collaborated on research and revision. Ron began a collection of relevant photographs and began to reach out to former Opportunity students. I made connections with Jonestown survivors, including Stephan Jones, Jim Jones's son, who was enormously helpful, and learned much from Tim Reiterman's and John Jacobs's book, *Raven: The Untold Story of the Rev. Jim Jones and His People*, as well as from Lawrence Wright's 1993 article, published in the *New Yorker*, based on an interview with Stephan and his brothers. (As only Stephan has been in touch with us, we can only speculate about Tim's and Jimmy's thoughts, beyond what we've read.)

Once we began our project, in 2005, we quickly learned that many people would clearly prefer not to think about Jonestown. The mere name often triggers an instinctive look of repulsion. There is often a taint of judgment as well, which not only condemns Jones but also conveys condescension toward his victims. We don't like to think people are capable of dying this way, apparently duped by a madman. But the people who went to Jonestown were caught in a situation that became nearly inescapable. This was especially true for the young who were sent to Jonestown—in some cases against their will—by guardians or parents who were members of Peoples Temple and followers of Jones.

This is their story, drawn from dusty memory; from yellowed newspaper articles; from faded books of poetry and ragged copies of the school paper; from class lists and baseball statistics; from papers in boxes in a Mission Street library, the repository of Peoples Temple papers; from conversations with those who were our students and colleagues long ago; from videos, books, and articles; from the Web, especially the Jonestown Institute at the San Diego State University site, *Alternative Considerations of Jonestown and Peoples Temple*; and partly from imagination—what we think probably happened—knowing as we do the places, the times, the people. Over the course of forty years even the keenest memory can erode or inadvertently alter facts. The book's dialogue is an amalgam of what we can piece together from our notes and our memories. All of the baseball game statistics are true, and all of the poems were written in the form that you see here, as published in our magazine, *In Small Dreams*. The same is true of excerpts from articles published in the school newspaper, *The Natural High Express*. In my classes I often quoted Joseph Conrad, who said good writing endures, and depends on truths "as old as the hills," that each writer's job is to find a new way to remind people of those time-honored values we always seem to forget. Honor. Truth. Compassion. Love. Jim Jones may have perverted those ideals, but the sincere words these kids wrote survived.

We hope the dozen teenagers whose stories we follow from San Francisco to Guyana will take you on a journey with them, and give you a deeper understanding of the tale that has been too often sensationalized—or pushed out of mind and forgotten. We hope our book memorializes the young people we knew who died and pays tribute to the courage of those who lived—and kept on living, in spite of the collapse of utopian dreams, haunting nightmares, and unimaginable grief and loss. We also hope their experiences will serve as a cautionary tale to young people today and in the future, and to those who love them.

There is a reason people tell stories about tragedies. Tragedies remind us of the complicated nature of life, of the ways faith and fallibility, idealism and delusion, noble aspiration and disastrous defeat are often inextricably linked. The tragedy of Peoples Temple and Jonestown, in particular, reveals the shaky ground between doubt and fervent belief.

We would like to think that the teenagers we knew, some of those who died and the few who lived, can help make Jonestown more than a barely remembered story of people who perished in a faraway jungle, a tale often reduced to the dismissive phrase coined from the tragedy: "To drink the Kool-Aid." We hope this story about our young students—their hopes, their poetry, their efforts to help make a better world—will bring some light to the dark story of Jonestown.

—JUDY BEBELAAR, Berkeley, California
January 2018

Acknowledgments

We never would have embarked on this project if not for Leigh Fondakowski's play, *The People's Temple*. For this we thank her. Our gratitude also goes to Fielding McGehee III, who has been a friend and guide throughout the writing of this book. The Jonestown Institute website he oversees, *Alternative Considerations of Jonestown and Peoples Temple*, http://jonestown.sdsu.edu, was an invaluable resource.

We are especially grateful to Stephan Jones for generously sharing his time, his remembrances, and his own eloquent writing. Without him, this book in its present form would not have been possible. Many other former students offered us guidance as well: Raymond Berrios, Jesús Berrios, Manny Blackwell, Hugh Dinneen, Bruce Dixon, Michelle (Di Quattro) MacClellan, Dean Marcic, Cary McClellan-Maki, Valerie McGraw, Cynthia McGraw, Linda Mertle, Darryl Phillips, Terry Preston, Carl Ross, Ronnie Ross, and Junior Siufanua.

And special kudos to Mary (Delema) Guitron for saving and sharing with us some rare photographs she took at Opportunity II High.

We wish to thank the following teachers from Opportunity and other schools who offered their memories of the turbulent seventies we experienced together: Hal Abercrombie, Carroll Covey (Colin Covey's wife), James Dierke, Fong Ha, Danny Hallinan, John Liu-Klein, Tina (Kollias) Johns, Mary McCrohan, Marcia Perlstein, Jeff Thollander, Norman Vogel, and Anna Wong.

Tim Reiterman kindly read our first draft of the book, a collection of memories of our students, their baseball games and their poems, and gave us good advice: Make it a story. The book he coauthored with John Jacobs, *Raven: The Untold Story of the Rev. Jim Jones and His People*, first published by E. P. Dutton, gave us a larger understanding of the Temple and Jonestown. Their hard work doing research, conducting interviews, and putting together the best and most comprehensive book on the subject gave us a solid foundation for our story of the Temple youngsters we came to know. We thank them, and we especially thank Reiterman for his continued support of our project as well as his wise counsel.

We also thank reporters Charles Krause and Ron Javers, who, like Reiterman, reported what they saw in Guyana. Without their courage and careful reporting, our book would not have been as accurate and detailed especially about the last days leading to the tragedy of November 18. Lawrence Wright's *New Yorker* article, "Orphans of Jonestown," was also an invaluable resource, and we are grateful to him. Deborah Layton, author of *Seductive Poison: A Jonestown Survivor's Story of Life and Death in the Peoples Temple*, gave us additional insight into a young person's experience in Jonestown and personally reached out to help us get details right. Julia Scheeres, author of *A Thousand Lives: The Untold Story of Hope, Deception, and Survival at Jonestown*, told us more about the Bogue family's part in the story. Sheeres also generously offered her support.

We were also inspired by some of the documentary films about Peoples Temple and Jonestown, especially Stanley Nelson's *Jonestown: The Life and Death of Peoples Temple*.

In addition, we would like to thank Denise Stephenson, former librarian in charge of Peoples Temple papers at the California Historical Society, for her encouragement and help in researching our project. Mary Moriganti, director of library and archives at California Historical Society, Debra Kaufman, reproductions and reference associate, and Marie Silva, archivist and manuscripts librarian, were also most helpful.

Our heartfelt thanks go to all the people who spoke with us in person, online, or on the telephone. Their firsthand experiences fleshed out significant parts of the story. Mark Sly's mother, Neva Sly-Hargrave, shared stories about her son. Thom (Tommy) Bogue, our student Marilee's brother, helped us with important details about his experiences in Jonestown," as did Eugene Smith, husband of our student Ollie. Dakota Lane, a former student and now published writer, helped us develop the voice we wanted to use in the book.

Kathryn Barbour, author of the photographic memorial book, *Who Died*, was generous with her time, providing support and helpful information. Laura Johnston Kohl, author of *Jonestown Survivor: An Insider's Look*, has created a Peoples Temple Flickr photo site, a wonderful resource for us. Photographer Nancy Wong has posted photos related to Peoples Temple on her Wikimedia site, another important source. We thank all three.

Also thanks to those who, in various ways, aided our quest: Don Beck, Philip Blakey, Langston Cabral, Jerry Garchik, Ana Gregoriu, Jennie Horn, Joan Gelfland, Sue Noyes, Michelle Morales, Noel Panganiban, Gay Marie Powell-Cabral, Mike Sadek Jr., Ralph Solonitz, Kimberly Spina, Stephen Stept, Karen Summerly, Mike Touchette, Jordan Vilchez, and Chloe Zirbel.

Tom Centolella's and Clive Matson's writing workshops gave us helpful feedback. Early editors Catharine Lucas and Autumn Stephens started us on our way. Developmental editor Stephanie Baker, a fellow teacher and writer, understood our project from a special perspective and helped us hone and clarify. Kirsten Janene-Nelson with her broad experience in editing and publishing, helped us take our book farther down the road, and Holly Cooper, with a keen eye and a caring heart, wore many editors' hats and helped us to the end of the journey. Margaret Copeland did a beautiful job designing and laying out the book, and Doug Williamson of Minuteman Press in Berkeley oversaw the final printing. Jannie Dresser of Sugartown Publishing, felt our book was important and ushered it into the world, and we are most grateful.

Writing this book has been a learning process for us—saddening, but encouraging too. Along the way we learned of courageous acts of resistance, large and small, against unfairness and cruelty, and moments of youthful joy in spite of the conditions. We treasure the connections and reconnections we have made with those whose willingness to share with us helped get the story right.

Finally we want to thank our spouses, Rita Cabral and Alan Jencks, for their loving and patient support over the past ten years.

The student poems and excerpts in this book originally appeared in one of Opportunity's publications, *In Small Dreams* or *Fire*. The newspaper articles written by students are from Opportunity's *The Natural High Express*. All can be found in the Peoples Temple Collection at the California Historical Society in San Francisco. Poems by living students appear by permission of the authors.

If there were a window in the sky
    I would see
    spirits of dead in dreams,
    gossiping gods,
    spirits of dead deeds,
    spirits of war gods, thunder gods,
    spirits of mothers who have lost their babies,
    weeping like
    spirits of seeds unplanted,
    spirits of weeping willow trees,
    spirits of giant redwoods,
    sacrificed to man's greed,
    spirits of all the helpless things,
    spirits of brown grizzly bears,
    spirits of infants taken before their time.

*— Group poem written by Creative Writing
students at Opportunity II, 1976*

Part I
San Francisco

The Times, Opportunity High, and Peoples Temple

he times were turbulent, the nation still reeling from President Kennedy's violent death in 1963. The threat of a nuclear war hung like a pall. In the midst of the Cold War, the world's two superpowers, the United States and the former Soviet Union, took their battles into regional conflicts and outer space. Throughout the mid-sixties and on into the seventies, sparks flew between opposite poles. The young, along with many older activists, were determined to make changes. "Ain't gonna let nobody turn me 'round," declared one gospel song-turned-civil-rights-anthem. Many older Americans were firmly against those in the youthful protest movements and tried to hold back the tide, fearful they would find themselves living in an America they could not recognize.

When Dr. King was assassinated in Memphis in 1968, riots flared in more than one hundred cities.[1] Alice Walker's novel *Meridian* (published in 1976) later made vivid the painful division in the Civil Rights Movement, with some insisting Dr. King's nonviolence was the only way, and others believing the time had come for a more aggressive stance. Malcolm X's phrase "by any means necessary" was cited by some as justification for rightful action, by others as damning evidence of violent rebellion.

Many groups joined in to demand their own rights. Women and those championing the gay rights movement were part of the chorus of voices. Civil rights was not the only issue. Americans took opposite sides over the draft and Vietnam, over the birth control pill and gender roles, over the three *R*s ("reading, writing, and 'rithmetic") versus relevance in education.

Throughout the 1970s, more and more students were leaving school before they could graduate. By 1976 the number of high school dropouts had reached almost five million nationwide, and was on the rise.[2] One book in particular struck a chord with teachers: *Summerhill: A Radical Approach to Child Rearing*, by A. S. Neill, first published in 1960. It gave many teachers—particularly those who taught in inner cities—ideas about creating their own ideal schools.

In the middle of this social context, a few teachers launched an innovative public alternative school, Opportunity High, in San Francisco's urban center.

Marcia Perlstein and Opportunity I

Marcia Perlstein, who could make even a group of strangers in an elevator laugh and whose political savvy equaled her sense of humor, came to Berkeley from New York with her college roommate in 1965. She had learned about a new teacher-training program, part of the School of Education at the University of California's Berkeley campus, and applied. Perlstein, more often seen in sandals, arrived for her interview "in tottering high heels and nylons" and was accepted. The Graduate Internship Program was originally meant to draw working professionals into the world of teaching. But Perlstein and many young people like her were attracted to the program because they wanted to help change America by transforming education practices.

Marcia Perlstein

Many of those young people, like Perlstein, chose to focus on what were then labeled "Academic Non-Achievers." True products of the idealistic 1960s, Perlstein and her fellow educators wanted to make a difference in the lives of kids who had tuned out and turned off. Their vision and efforts formed the seed of what would become the first Opportunity High. After finishing the summer segment of the program, which included student teaching, the aspiring teachers were required to find teaching jobs as well as to continue attending seminars during the year.

Perlstein invited her teaching colleague, Judy Bebelaar (whose husband, John, had also become a teacher through the program in 1964), to join her in applying to teach at Samuel Gompers High School, and the next year two others from the Berkeley program joined them.

Gompers was San Francisco's "continuation" school for kids who were not making it in the regular schools and were in danger of dropping out. Its student body included those who had been suspended for more than ten days, girls who had become pregnant (their folders were labeled PWOP for "pregnant without official permission"), as well as recent immigrants whose

English was so poor they would have fallen behind in the regular high school curriculum. These students were sent from a wide swath of San Francisco neighborhoods to the dun-colored Gompers building in the Mission District.

Most kids did not want to be at Gompers—it carried a taint of failure—and neither did some of the teachers. In two years the school had three principals. Teachers and students do not do well under a constantly changing administration. There was no English as a Second Language training for teachers who taught the "Americanization" classes at that time. One teacher, nicknamed "the Colonel," wore the same red Mount Rushmore tie to school every day and rudely snatched hats off the heads of black kids who were covering up unruly hair damaged by chemical straighteners (a new "do" cost too much money). The Colonel's method for teaching a Work Experience class was to toss a bundle of newspaper want ads on a desk. Another teacher, put in charge of the supply room, passed out masking tape to teachers in three-foot segments.

The head counselor and the Work Experience coordinator, though, welcomed the energy of the new teachers from Cal (U.C. Berkeley), and worked with them, giving them counseling duties and assigning Perlstein and Bebelaar to teach in the morning program, for students who had jobs in the afternoon. Still, achievement scores at Gompers were low and truancy ran high. The situation was impossible.

Perlstein saw that a new school was needed. She enlisted the three teachers who had migrated with her to Gompers to help craft a proposal to present to the San Francisco school board. They wanted to launch a new alternative high school that students would *want* to attend, where a counselor was always available, and where students had a choice of classes among relevant topics taught by passionate and understanding teachers. They briefly pursued the idea of a privately funded school, but decided a public school was what was needed—and there was new state funding for such "Opportunity" schools.

To everyone's amazement except Perlstein's, the school district agreed: Opportunity I would be launched in a small office building in downtown San Francisco. The four teachers were to plan the new school in the district administration office while the Mission Street site was renovated and other teachers and a principal were hired. After a month or two Perlstein and her crew were tired of waiting. They wanted to teach! So they convinced the powers that be to let them begin. In the fall of 1967, while workmen finished the second-floor classrooms, eight teachers moved into the downstairs open space with two large tables, some chairs, a couple of desks and file cabinets, a portable blackboard, and thirty students. People passing by would often stop and peer in through the big plate glass windows at the unlikely group of "hippies" and teens.

The school expanded quickly—the teachers had done active outreach while they were planning Opportunity from the district offices, going out to district high schools and asking students wandering the halls or the streets nearby if they would like to come to the counseling office to hear about a new school. This was Perlstein's idea as well.

That first experiment, Opportunity I, had some successes. To encourage students to "buy in" to their education, all who applied were interviewed to be sure they understood the school's goals and their own responsibilities. During the interview, they were given a short reading test and shown their results, after which they could choose their own reading class—or decline to take one altogether—rather than be assigned to what students would invariably see as a "dumb class." In every case the students who needed extra help *did* choose reading; many were shocked at how low their scores were.

Students were accepted in order of when they applied and with an eye toward reflecting San Francisco's demographics. In some "emergency" situations, such as a requirement that a student be enrolled in school in order to be accepted into a group home, someone could be bumped up on the list.

The school offered an array of "hyphenated" classes (Psychology-English, Sociology–Social Studies), as well as other innovations: a cooking class in a small kitchen in which students prepared an entire meal, karate in the downstairs room. Special guest speakers (poets, therapists, anyone who might inspire the kids to find and follow a passion) were invited to talk to the kids, and teachers frequently took their classrooms outdoors on walking field trips to expand learning opportunities. In addition, each teacher had counseling responsibilities for fifteen students.

Many kids decided that coming to school was a good idea and could even be fun. Still, in spite of the best intentions and efforts of the staff, too many students still failed or dropped out. It didn't help that the ideas of the by-the-book principal hired by the school district contrasted sharply with the teachers' ideas about pedagogy.

In 1970 a core of interested teachers decided, at Perlstein's urging, to revise the plan and create a new school—they wanted to get it better this time, to reach more kids. Once again the plan was accepted. A few early Opportunity graduates, bright and motivated, were invited to become teacher aides. College students at the new Antioch College campus, Antioch West, were approached to be part of the staff as well.

The selling point that secured approval from the school district was that the new school didn't require paying a principal's salary. Instead, a teacher would serve as a Coordinating Teacher for no extra pay for one or two years. With this rotating—rather than hierarchical—structure, teachers could be more autonomous, free to implement their innovative, often wonderful, and sometimes crazy ideas.

Opportunity II

Opportunity II launched in the fall of 1971 in a small office building at 739 Bryant Street, in a warehouse district south of downtown San Francisco, "right between the freeway and the railroad tracks," as the student-composed school song rang out. Perlstein was elected the first Coordinating Teacher. A Coordinating Student, usually one who had made important changes in life and school choices, was invited to give input as well. Amenities at Bryant Street included a good-sized kitchen where Bebelaar and co-teacher Tina Kollias helped students prepare meals from different cultures. John Liu-Klein, who taught science, photography, and gardening, helped students build a vegetable garden on the rooftop. (You can no doubt imagine what else some students tried to plant there.)

Most importantly, the teachers were able to retain control over the school's budget and hiring. The staff could now take learning beyond school boundaries with extended field trips to Berkeley, Monterey, and Yosemite—an exciting prospect for many kids who had never ventured from their own neighborhoods, let alone traveled beyond San Francisco. Once, when students from the Natural History class went on a field trip to Tilden Park in Berkeley, some of the boys were unimpressed when they looked out the window to see only dirt paths rather than a city with lots of action. A few would not budge from the bus, but sat there in their platform shoes, fancy shirts, and leather jackets. Teachers better prepared students for a trip to Yosemite, where they all stayed in cabins, hiked, and rode horses. But the teachers were dismayed to learn, on the bus home, that one student was selling jewelry lifted from the gift shop. (Thankfully no charges were filed after teachers contacted both the shop and the student's parents.)

The cooking class took an inexpensive trip to the beautiful oceanside conference grounds at Asilomar, near Monterey, and ate at a nice restaurant in an old Victorian—a first for many of the students, who had never eaten out except at fast food places.

Students even put on their own concerts with the help of rock star Country Joe McDonald (a friend of teacher Ron Cabral's) and music impresario Bill Graham, at Friends and Relations Hall near Ocean Beach and at Bimbo's 365 Club, a popular North Beach nightclub. Teachers bought a used Volkswagen bus with school funds; when the district refused to insure it, Bebelaar added it to her own insurance policy. (To her eventual relief, the bus was finally stolen and discovered in a junkyard sans wheels, roof, and motor.)

Ron Cabral, Yvonne Golden and "Country" Joe McDonald

Yvonne Golden Comes to Opportunity II

In the summer of 1973, Superintendent Tom Shaheen, whose support had made the school possible, asked Opportunity to hire teacher Yvonne Golden.

Yvonne Golden

Golden, a black woman in her forties, had come to San Francisco from Daytona Beach, Florida, with her husband, a retired military man. Yvonne had a contentious relationship with her own school's administration at Lincoln High in San Francisco. She had alienated them by organizing protests over the issue of school busing. The City's schools, built as old neighborhood schools, were by default, segregated. There were largely black schools, like Wilson; mostly Latino-Chicano schools, like Mission; and mostly white schools, like Washington and Lincoln.

The Opportunity teachers agreed to hire Golden. Her left-liberal politics were in line with their own beliefs and they admired her fearlessness in confronting administrators and the school board. She had fought vociferously for school busing, opposed banning books, and challenged any action she perceived as racist. At first, it seemed, their new teacher was "one of them."

Golden made her first major impression at Opportunity II during a school board meeting in early 1974, where busing and racial integration of San Francisco schools were being debated. A group of men and women suddenly stood in protest, shedding overcoats to reveal Nazi uniforms. Golden took over the microphone, screaming for their removal. Then, members of the communist Workers' Action Movement and the Progressive Labor Party came in and started slugging the Nazis, who slugged right back. Eventually the police broke up the fight, but a few days later Golden was arrested and charged with "inciting a riot." The following month, California State Assemblyman Willie Brown and African American activist Angela Davis came to Golden's defense. The charges were eventually dropped after a mistrial.[3]

A Visit from Reverend Jones

In the spring of 1975, Perlstein, still serving as Coordinating Teacher, received a startling visit from a minister, Reverend Jim Jones. He sought the immediate admission of all the high-school-aged teenagers from his church, Peoples Temple. Perlstein explained the policy at Opportunity II, that new students were admitted one by one after completing personal interviews. This interview process was not a simple formality—the teachers had designed it as a careful strategy to win each student's

Tina (Kollias) Johns and Hal Abercrombie interviewing students

heartfelt commitment to the school's goals. Although Opportunity was the last chance for many to obtain a high school diploma, teachers wanted students to feel that their enrollment was a personal choice.

Jones persisted, continuing to lobby Perlstein. He wanted all the Temple kids to enter together, and promised that the teenagers of Peoples Temple would comport themselves perfectly. Perlstein suggested to him that anyone who could guarantee impeccable behavior from a large group of teenagers must be doing something manipulative to elicit that behavior, something she wanted no part of. Jones was out of luck—for the time being.

Meanwhile there was growing friction between two strong personalities: Perlstein and Golden. Perlstein was smart, savvy, and diplomatic, although she never hesitated to speak her mind. Golden was also politically astute, but she tended to be impatient, and her passionate temperament ran hot. Easy to anger, she had already alienated some teachers.

For the 1975–76 school year, Opportunity II was moved to a block-shaped, vaguely Art Deco cement office building on South Van Ness, near a freeway overpass. Larger and more centrally located, it was near San Francisco's Civic Center. This time the cooking class had a large kitchen with three stoves. The first-floor lobby could be used as a meeting area. Its garage was perfect for a shop.

Opportunity II High looking up South Van Ness

New students continued to apply to the school, often urged to do so by their counselors, social workers, or parole officers. On the whole, Opportunity seemed to be on the right track. Still, at the end of the spring semester Perlstein decided to leave her brainchild of a school to become a full-time therapist. Bebelaar—who had been Perlstein's trusted sidekick and friend from the beginnings of Opportunity I—would miss her friend dearly. The two had made a good team.

Golden was elected Coordinating Teacher in the fall of 1976. When rumor had it that Golden was taking courses toward an administrative credential, suspicions grew that she was also planning to take the reins of school leadership, thus ignoring Opportunity's traditionally democratic and consensus-driven model for making decisions and implementing policy. Some feared they were losing control of their dream school, while others thought Golden was just the type of leader needed to fight downtown school administration. Whatever their opinion was on this matter, most Opportunity teachers were reluctant to say anything negative about Golden to those outside the school. Teachers felt that school district officials, in particular, criticized Golden unfairly—not because of her job performance, but because of her outspoken manner and leftist political beliefs.

ঌ

Without warning, the school district sent a principal to "shape up" Opportunity's unconventional staff and align the school with the rules and regimen of other San Francisco high schools. Downtown administrators were particularly upset that students at Opportunity were allowed to smoke in the building—an idea that made sense to teachers at the time. Their goal was to do whatever worked to keep the kids attending school. Later, all the teachers agreed that the idea of allowing smoking on campus was an incredibly bad one.

Some staff protested the new principal by noisily marching into the office of the assistant superintendent in charge of high schools. After registering their outrage, the teachers struck a bargain with the district. They would stop the on-site smoking if Golden, who had by then acquired her administrative credential, could serve as Opportunity's principal—something, not surprisingly, Golden herself had proposed. Up to this point, even though Golden was Coordinating Teacher, the school still practiced leadership on key issues by a consensus process. In spite of a few mild misgivings, most teachers thought they had won the day when they accepted that one of their own should take over as principal instead of bending to the school district's imposition.

A New Number One

At one of the first weekly staff meetings in the fall of 1976, Golden announced that she had just met a new "Number One." Previously she had acknowledged her admiration and loyalty to Reverend Cecil Williams, the

charismatic African American pastor of the growing multicultural congregation of Glide Memorial Church in San Francisco's Tenderloin district, which had been losing its mostly white and older members until Williams arrived.

Reverend Williams had

Cecil Williams and Jim Jones at a protest January 1977 given the commencement talk at Opportunity's 1973 graduation ceremony, held in the impressive theater at Lowell High School, the district's college preparatory school. (At the time, Opportunity had no room big enough for a ceremony.) Before Williams spoke, he turned to face the graduates behind him, some in their purple gowns and caps, some in tuxes or fancy dresses, and one student dressed all in black with elaborate face paint. With a big smile on his face, Williams turned back to the audience and announced, "Now this is a group with *style!*" The audience laughed and applauded.

Dean Marcic with diploma

But in the fall of 1976, Golden declared that the Reverend Jim Jones had replaced Cecil Williams in her top spot. Most of the staff admired Williams, but had never heard about Jones. Over the next few weeks and coming months, all of San Francisco would hear about Jones a great deal.

Jim Jones was a dynamic white minister from Indianapolis where he had established his largely African American church in 1955. In 1965, he convinced most of his congregation to move with him to Ukiah in Northern California. By 1969, they had built a church in Redwood Valley, complete with swimming pool, vineyard, gardens, and an animal shelter. In 1970 an expanding congregation began meeting in the auditorium of Benjamin Franklin Junior High in San Francisco, and also began to hold services in Los Angeles. In 1972 Peoples Temple bought a building on San Francisco's Geary Street that ultimately became its official headquarters.

Golden announced that Jones was a socialist like herself. He taught about the evils of racism and capitalism and described his Church as one that encouraged political activism.

Without a Marcia Perlstein to oppose the en masse enrollment of surprisingly impeccably behaved teenagers, Jones finally succeeded in bringing 120 high school kids from Peoples Temple to Opportunity. In the fall of 1976, they entered the school—and Golden had made it happen. Most were transferred from Washington, a large district high school. It later became clear that Jones had long planned to make Opportunity his Temple's school. Undoubtedly, he favored the avowedly socialist principal—one he could count on, not only to allow Church field trips, but to support his political goals.

Although student interviews had been a cornerstone of Opportunity's program, these were swept aside for the Temple youngsters. Even though some teachers had their doubts about the imposition of a large new student population without the usual protocol, they were by no means unanimous in their dissent; many still greatly admired Golden and were comfortable with her leadership. Others did not want to abandon the school and the principles they had worked so hard to establish; neither did they want to neglect the kids they originally wanted to serve. However, as the Temple kids began to attend and the teachers started to get to know them—all the Opportunity teachers liked them and saw them as bringing a special spirit to the school.

Judy Bebelaar and student

Chapter 1

Peoples Temple
Comes to Opportunity

September 1976

Stephan

tanding at over six feet tall, thin and fit with fine, regular features, the boy was handsome and dark-haired. Neatly dressed in a sports jacket, shirt, and tie, he could have been any age from sixteen to twenty.

Some of the teachers had seen Stephan's father, Jim Jones, in a recent television newscast featuring interviews of civic leaders about the upcoming presidential election; others recognized him from various newspaper articles and photos. He usually wore a light-colored leisure suit, black shirt, white tie, and aviator glasses, and resembled musicians Roy Orbison or Johnny Cash.

Mark Sly, a Temple kid who had enrolled at Opportunity earlier, brought a copy of the Temple newspaper, the *Peoples Forum*, to show to Ron Cabral, who taught a journalism class. There on the front page was Jones—again in his dark glasses—and a smiling First Lady Rosalynn Carter. The caption announced, "Rev. Jim Jones, by invitation, dines with Mrs. Jimmy Carter."[1] It was discovered later that the two had met for only fifteen minutes over coffee, but there was no reason to doubt the story at the time.

❧

John Liu Klein

"You must be Stephan," John Liu-Klein said, reaching out to shake Stephan's hand. Liu-Klein was Opportunity's head counselor who kept track of records and student entries, as well as their often mysterious exits—when phones were disconnected and letters returned.

Students liked the tall, easygoing Liu-Klein, with whom they had near-instant rapport. He had added his wife's name, Liu, to his own when they married, and the kids thought it was cool that Carol was Chinese;

they knew of few interracial marriages at the time. Liu-Klein joined the Opportunity staff in 1974. When Bebelaar and her family moved into the same Berkeley neighborhood, the Liu-Kleins and Bebelaars saw each other often. After John and Carol divorced, he and the Bebelaars built a cabin together on a hillside near Ukiah, their gesture toward joining the "back-to-the-land" movement. Bebelaar's husband's name was also John, so when she talked about him with her students she called him "John B" to differentiate him from John Liu-Klein. Opportunity students often called teachers by their first names.

Now he turned to Bebelaar. "Jude, meet your new counselee." To Stephan he said, "You and Judy can talk here in my office, Stephan. I'm going over to the Cone for coffee." The Pine Cone was the greasy spoon up tiny Plum Alley, the back street adjacent to Opportunity's building on South Van Ness (though the teachers found it hard to imagine a plum tree had ever grown in that grimy alley). Both teachers and students frequented "the Cone" for breakfast or burgers.

Judy Bebelaar

Stephan followed Bebelaar into the office, waiting until she was seated before taking a chair himself. "I hope you'll like it here if you decide this is the school for you, Stephan," Bebelaar said. "Is there anything you want to ask about Opportunity?"

Stephan shook his head. "I will definitely be coming here." He didn't return Bebelaar's smile, but she didn't sense a hostile teenage barrier either. He looked tired—maybe he had just had a late night, she thought. She explained her role: "I'll keep you on track for graduation, and you can come talk to me if you have any problems or questions. I'm also the one you should call if you're sick. Here's my phone number." Bebelaar fished for a card in her purse and handed it to him. Stephan took it and placed it in his shirt pocket.

Opening a desk drawer, she pulled out one of the pink school district attendance cards and wrote his name on it. "If you'll fill out this card, it will give me a way to contact you if I need to. We always call if you're out and you haven't let us know why. Have I spelled Stephan correctly?"

"Yes, you have," the young man replied politely. "And you won't need to call. Tim, the counselor from the Temple, will let you know if we're absent. Sometimes we're called to go on Church trips."

Jim Jones was providing two counselors, a man and a woman, to lighten the load for Opportunity teachers, who each taught four classes as well as provided counseling. The influx of new students meant that each teacher would be adding six or seven counselees to the fifteen they already had. Stephan filled out the pink card and handed it back.

"Say, does Opportunity have a basketball team? I played on the Ukiah team with my brothers, and last year at Washington."

Bebelaar noticed his eyes held a sudden glimmer of teenage enthusiasm. "Our school is so small it's hard to get a team together, especially one that can compete with the regular schools." Then she thought of Cabral, who had been trying to organize a baseball team for two years. "Do you like baseball?" she asked. "How are your grades? There's a teacher here, Ron Cabral, trying to put a team together."

Stephan looked disappointed for a moment, then recovered. "Yeah, I like most sports. I kept a B average so I could be on the team at Washington."

"I have a feeling you could do better than a B average. Am I right?"

"Probably." He looked a bit embarrassed. "My brothers and a couple of others are pretty good at baseball. I'll talk to them. Where can I find Mr. Cabral?"

"His room is on the second floor, 8—next-to-last one on your left. And Stephan, we really want to be sure you want to be here. That's an essential part of how the school works."

"I understand, but my dad wants me to attend Opportunity."

"Your dad won't be attending; you will. We want to be sure you'll feel comfortable here." Usually it was a probation officer or a social worker, not a parent, who referred a kid to our school. Otherwise kids chose the school themselves, drawn by its relative freedom and unusual curriculum.

Stephan shrugged his shoulders. "Sure. It seems like as good a school as any."

"We can't offer as many choices as the regular high schools, but we have some pretty interesting classes. For social studies credit, you can take Hal Abercrombie's Sociology class. Last year they went on a weeklong trip to do a survey of farm workers in Delano and then of people in Palm Springs. Kids like his karate class too. Or you can take my course on Native Americans, created at the students' request."

Stephan said, "That's pretty cool. They didn't have classes like that at Washington."

CARLOS CASTANEDA
THE TEACHINGS OF
DON JUAN: A YAQUI WAY
OF KNOWLEDGE

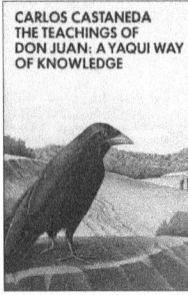

"I think so too. We even got a letter from Carlos Castaneda a couple of years ago when the students wrote to him after we read *The Teachings of Don Juan*. He thinks Americans often take drugs in a very self-indulgent way, just for the 'high' without self-reflection or thought. He said he's worried about kids and drugs. The Yaquis took a drug for a spiritual purpose, then stopped when they achieved their goal."

Stephan had a look on his face that Bebelaar couldn't quite decipher. Was it the subject of drugs? Couldn't be. He and the other kids from the Temple looked more like well-scrubbed country kids than hardened urban teens. Then Stephan's expression became noncommittal again. Bebelaar wasn't used to such reserve. She wondered if it was simply self-confidence, or unusual maturity.

"Or you could take Colin Covey's U.S. History. Just ask any of the kids what his classes are like." Bebelaar thought of how Covey's booming voice resounded through the hallways when he really got going about capitalism, or that "vicious capitalist game," football. Kids were fond of "Covey"—everyone called him that, or sometimes "Cubby." Bebelaar sensed that Stephan would probably not wind up in Covey's class. Judging from Stephan's reserve, she did not think he'd be comfortable there. "You can choose among different social studies classes to get the credit you need for graduation requirements."

She paused, leaving a space for a question or comment—most teenagers would have something more to say by now. She had not been able to elicit as much as a smile. Stephan looked seriously at her; he was difficult to read. At least he seemed interested in baseball. She decided to talk to Ron Cabral about Stephan. She administered the short reading test. No problem there.

Pulling a class list from the upright file on Liu-Klein's desk, Bebelaar placed it in front of Stephan. "Same for English. Your choices are Creative Writing, Journalism, Psychology, Book Reports—that's if you like to read and then write about the books—Speech, or Letter Writing and Composition. Here's the full schedule of classes. Radio Production does a real radio show on KALW, and in Cooking class students make a meal and sit down and eat it together. It's a three-hour class that I co-teach once a week with Tina Kollias, and we both love to cook. Any of those sound good?"

Stephan finally smiled politely, but again didn't say anything. He seemed—Bebelaar thought for a moment—*weary, maybe that's the word*. Yet, he sat upright. Most teenagers found a way to lounge, even in a small metal office chair. She wondered how she could get him to open up. Maybe that was how it was with a minister's son; maybe they were just serious. As Stephan studied the class choices, Bebelaar imagined that perhaps he hadn't wanted to come to Opportunity. Maybe he had wanted to stay at Washington with his basketball team. As Jones's son, he probably had no choice if all the other Temple kids were being sent to Opportunity.

Once he got to know some of the teachers and met the kids, she thought, perhaps he would be happier here. And maybe he wasn't unhappy, just careful. She remembered the minister's daughter in the small town where she had grown up. Town kids wondered why, in her senior year, she went to live with her aunt, so far away. Then they figured it out. She hadn't been careful enough. Pregnant girls were often sent away in those days.

Liu-Klein opened the door. "Better wrap it up, guys. Golden has the kids from the Temple collected for a little introduction to Opportunity, and we all better be there."

Stephan stood and handed Bebelaar his transcript and report card, which was unusual. Few kids came in with their records. Gazing down, he reached to shake her hand, "Thank you very much, Mrs. Bebelaar."

"The kids usually call me Ms. B or Judy. I hope you'll like it here. Check off the classes you'd like on that list, and I'll see what you need. You can drop by my room after school. Maybe you'll have some questions by then."

"Thanks, but I have to get back right after school. I'll pick up my schedule tomorrow."

The three of them walked down the short hallway to the lounge area, where Raymond Berrios, another student, approached them. "Hi, Ms. B." Bebelaar introduced Stephan to Raymond, hoping they would connect. If anyone could make Stephan feel more comfortable, it was Raymond. Maybe Raymond would convince him to take Creative Writing. The two said hello, but Stephan quickly excused himself and headed toward the folding chairs set up for the Temple kids who were gathering in the lounge.

Raymond moved toward the windows that overlooked Plum Alley. It was the favored spot for the Latino and Chicano kids from the Mission District, and where the girls liked to cluster, in their long black leather coats worn over hooded sweatshirts, big hoop earrings, dark lipstick, eyeliner, and platform shoes. The boys joined them in their bell-bottoms and wide-lapelled polyester shirts, their hair worn long or slicked back.

Old Kids and Newcomers

The 250 "old" Opportunity students (as they came to be known after the arrival of the Temple kids), from neighborhoods all over the city, were children of the times: the optimistic sixties of their childhood folding into the more pessimistic seventies.

As she walked through the lobby toward where Temple students had clustered for Golden's introduction, Bebelaar was aware, once again, of the divisions among the students. Like Raymond and the Latino students, each group had its favorite gathering spot: The black kids from the Fillmore, Potrero Hill, Visitation Valley, and Hunters Point liked to lounge in easy chairs near the rear entrance, next to Shop class. They sported teased-out 'fros or beauty parlor 'dos. The boys wore wide-brimmed hats with fancy bands, porkpies, or knit-watch caps. The girls wore jeans or miniskirts over fishnet stockings.

The white rock 'n' rollers gathered near the stairs at the front of the building. Both boys and girls had the post-Haight Ashbury look; they were young versions of old hippies, bell-bottoms now fashionably giving way to boot-cut jeans. Most had long hair, and sometimes wore beads and headbands, and T-shirts emblazoned with band names: Led Zeppelin, AC/DC, Blue Öyster Cult, Lynyrd Skynyrd, Rush, the Sex Pistols, or the Ramones. Worn sneakers, Keds, or Converse All-Stars and workmen's suede or steel-toed boots completed the look. Their favorite hangout after classes—or sometimes during—was the site of the closed-down Mel's Drive-In next door to the school site.

The few Asian kids who attended Opportunity had long hair, wore denim jackets, and divided themselves between the rock 'n' roll crowd and the Mission District kids. Everyone was cool and casual with an urban edge. Opportunity had been designed to reflect the ethnic groups of the city, and admission was partly based on maintaining that kind of diversity. The arrival of the Temple students changed that.

Many of the old students were troubled youngsters who had been referred to Opportunity because of truancy, pregnancy, or problems with the law. A few had tough shells and exhibited a determined, sullen resistance. The teachers found, however, that the ones who were frequently the most troubled were often the friendliest. Most were open-minded teenagers, glad to be at Opportunity for its progressive policies and freedoms relative to the regular schools. They were a loose-knit student body, hanging out with their own ethnic groups, with a few who acted more or less as free agents who treasured their independence.

The first thing the old students seemed to notice about the newcomers from the Temple was that they kept to themselves. The Peoples Temple kids were mostly African American with a few white and Asian kids. They carried themselves more like family, sharing a closeness that reflected their lack of racism. The teachers first admired that about these very likable kids—that and the fact that they were so attentive, how they always raised their hands to speak in class, and remembered to say "please" and "thank you." The teachers agreed that the Peoples Temple newcomers were a group of good kids who, unlike so many of the other students, actually showed up every day. Later, the staff realized their always-good behavior might have had something to do with Tim Carter, the Temple counselor who regularly visited the school.

Carter, who seemed to be in his early to mid-thirties, had served as a Marine in Vietnam but had come to feel the war was wrong. After he returned from the war, he found the Temple and joined. He liked the spirit of the group, how people, black and white, worked and had a good time together. By joining them, he felt he was making a positive contribution to society.

Carter had a lot in common with the Opportunity teachers, all of whom had marched against the war. They had made a choice to work with inner-city kids as a way of participating in social change. The activist spirit of the 1960s with its marches and protests had evolved into one inspired by Gandhi's idea to "be the change" in the 1970s. Many young people in college changed their major to one that would involve them in a life's work that would help change the world.

Like many Temple kids, Carter kept his brown hair cut short and wore a sport coat with jeans. Sometimes he could be seen at Opportunity taking roll or talking seriously with one of the Temple children. Jones was perhaps concerned about the effect that Opportunity's wilder bunch—most of whom knew well the ways of the streets—might have on these model young people who were polite, punctual, and hardworking. Opportunity teachers wondered how this new group of students would ultimately fit in with the old kids who were, for the most part, open with their classmates and teachers. Even though the Temple kids seemed color-blind, they mostly kept to themselves.

In retrospect, it may have been that the old students had come to think of Opportunity as *their* school and may have been jealous of the Temple newcomers, not to mention a little distrustful of their "straightness." Still, despite their diverse backgrounds, all the students were looking for a different kind of education, a different kind of teacher. This was particularly true of the rock 'n' rollers who identified with the hippies who had come before them (including staff members). One student, Hugh Dinneen, later told Bebelaar and Cabral, "Here's a group of teachers who've had their chains taken off. They're free to teach!"

The Welcoming

The chairs set up for the orientation were nearly all taken. Stephan sat next to two boys about as tall as he was, one pale with curly blond hair, the other handsome with dark skin. These were his adopted brothers, Tim and Jimmy. Near them, a small wiry boy with a short Afro and a shy smile sat in the back row. Liu-Klein sat next to him, sipping his coffee. He motioned to Bebelaar to join them. "This is Teddy McMurry," he said. She smiled at the boy, who wore a brown plaid shirt and brown slacks. "He's your counselee, too. That brings you to eighteen, but you can handle it, kid. And I don't think Teddy here is going to give you a single problem. Right, Teddy?"

"No, sir, no ma'am. I sure won't." John had intended to make a joke, but Teddy looked a little worried.

"Nice to meet you, Teddy. Don't pay attention to John. He likes to tease—he teases me too. My next class is Creative Writing. Come sit in for a while, and then I'll find someone to take you around the school."

Golden, in her first year as principal, came out of her office, hurrying toward the folding chairs and the big brown vinyl couch opposite the windows to the alley. Small but solidly built, she wore jeans, a blue flowered blouse, and gold hoop earrings that hung below the blue bandana tied over her close-cropped Afro.

As she walked through the lobby, Golden addressed one Temple kid, then another. She spoke warmly to them. She had a charming side, and genuinely seemed to like kids. It was adults with whom she usually lost her cool.

Terry Preston

"Sit down, kids, right over here by me and Terry. Pull those chairs closer," Golden instructed. Three of the Temple girls sat on the couch near the wall, hands in their laps; the rest of the Temple kids, maybe a dozen or so, quietly pulled the folding chairs into a neat semicircle. In contrast, most old

Opportunity students would have made a noisy show of sitting down.

Terry Preston was a tall slender young man whose Afro made him appear even taller than his six feet as he stood next to Golden. In his white shirt with fashionably long lapels worn under an oversized army jacket and Ben Davis work pants, he looked like a revolutionary businessman, dignified but hip. Terry was one of the few boys in the school who sported a

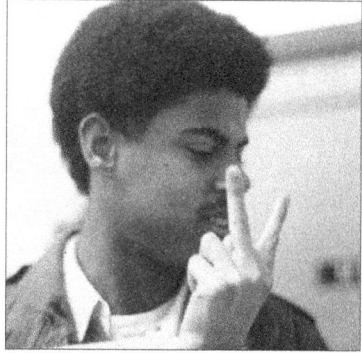

Terry Preston

mustache; his was luxuriant and well-groomed. He smiled at the students, then grew more serious.

"Hi, everyone. I'm Terry Preston, your Student Coordinator. That's part of how our school works. The Student Coordinator is elected every year. Now Yvonne here is our Coordinating . . . ah, our principal."

Terry turned to smile at her and she smiled back, obviously proud of him.

"The Student Coordinator works with Yvonne to make the school better, make sure everyone's voice is heard. I'd like to read a piece from our school newspaper, *The Natural High Express*. I'm the editor, and I invite you to submit stuff, maybe think of signing up for Journalism. Ron Cabral teaches it, and we can pretty much write about whatever we want to. Anyway, here's my 'Message to the Students' from the latest issue."

He held up a mimeographed magazine, stapled in one corner, with a drawing of a blissed-out bird floating up through clouds on the blue cover. Terry opened the paper and began to read in a measured, serious voice. From time to time, he looked up at his audience.

> *One of the basic foundations on which Opportunity High was founded is the equality between students and teachers. Now, we all know it doesn't always turn out that way. Why? Maybe because students here show such a lack of concern about the direction and organization of our school. For example, when the more stringent rules regarding attendance were adopted, how many of you raised your voices? How can I as Student Coordinator and the rest of the Student Committee supposedly represent you if you don't care? . . . Remember, you're not at Balboa, Lowell, or McAteer now . . .*

He looked up and added, "or in you guys' cases, Washington," then went on: "Here, what you say can make a difference. It's my job to see that it does, to take student participation and representation at Opportunity High to where it could and should be. Don't sit on your butt like a wart on a frog's … "

Again, he paused and looked at his audience and without reading he addressed them directly: "Excuse my language, but you see, we honor freedom of speech here—'like a wart on a frog's ass.' It's time we students exercised some voice around here. The Student Committee meets at one thirty in room 5 on Mondays. Let us hear what you think!"

Dorothy Buckley

The students applauded enthusiastically. One of the girls on the couch raised her hand. Dorothy Buckley was one of those teenagers who still retained a child's round face—she had large brown smiling eyes and a sweet mouth. Her hair was pulled back into a ponytail and tied with a ribbon. She wore a red dress and a style of coat that no style-savvy San Francisco kid would wear: brown, with a simulated fur collar, the hem just at her knees. She stood.

"Is there going to be a meeting today?"

"Yes," Terry answered, "and room 5 is just up those stairs, not that you're likely to get lost in this school. There's only 250 of us—well, more like 350 when all of you are enrolled. It's a pretty sad fact, but a lot of kids don't come to school every day. They don't seem to realize they're never going to graduate if they don't come and do the work. You can come to any of us old Opportunity students if we can be of help, if you're having problems at home or anything. And you can always talk to your counselor or Yvonne or John."

Terry continued, "Now I don't think any of you will be among the students I'm appealing to in the next article." He held up the paper and pointed out the piece titled "To All the Residents of Plum Alley."

"You should know that dope is definitely not allowed there, though some ass … excuse me, idiots—I know you guys go to church and all—think it should be. As I say in the article, 'the police don't like us, Downtown'—that's what we call the administrators at 135 Van Ness—*they* don't like us, and all some kids are doing is giving them a reason to put us out on the streets."

He looked up, very serious now, and there was another round of appreciative applause.

Peoples Temple Comes to Opportunity

"Anyway, welcome to Opportunity. Catch me in the hall or down here in the lobby if you have any questions." Dorothy and Willie, who sat next to Golden on the couch, both had wide eyes.

"Thanks, Terry," Golden said. "You go on to class now."

Terry threw a smile at the newcomers and headed up the stairs. The principal continued, "I want to tell you babies about our Lyceum Series. Who knows who Vincent Hallinan is?" She placed her hands on her hips and looked around the room, challenging them to come up with an answer. Dorothy met her gaze and raised her hand. Golden nodded.

"Yes, baby?"

Dorothy stood. "Father—I mean Reverend Jones—told us about Mr. Hallinan. He's a San Francisco lawyer. I think he's ninety-something, a true elder. Reverend Jones always says our elders are our treasure, our book of knowledge. Anyway, in something like 1952, Mr. Hallinan ran for president of the United States on the Progressive ticket, which is kind of the same as being a socialist. And when two young hoodlums tried to beat him up and take his wallet on his way to his office—he walks there every day—he took his cane to them and they took off running!"

The other kids laughed and applauded. Dorothy smiled and sat down.

"You are absolutely right, Dorothy. He's come to speak at our Lyceum meetings, which we hold right here, for the entire school. We've also listened to Dolores Huerta—who can tell me who she is?"

An athletic-looking African American boy with soft, large, wide-set eyes raised his hand. "My name is Amondo, Miss Golden; kids call me Mondo. And Dolores Huerta"—he pronounced her name carefully and correctly—"works with César Chávez and the United Farm Workers to help get rights for the people who pick our food."

Mondo Griffith

"Right on, Mondo, except kids call me Yvonne. We've also heard the words of Dr. Angela Davis and Margo St. James, founder of COYOTE, who believes prostitution should be legalized. And who has heard of Delancey Street and John Maher?"

Willie's hand shot up. Golden called on her. "I'm Willie, Miss Golden. That's a place where drug addicts

Willie Thomas

can go to get off drugs, and John Maher is the head of it. Reverend Jones has helped a lot of people get off drugs too." Willie—short for Willieater—was tall, elegant, with a neatly rounded Afro and a warm smile. She wore a blue dress and black cardigan that looked too small for her, a little worn.

"You got it, baby! And how about Dennis Banks?"

All the hands went up—except Stephan's. Golden shot up a power-fist salute and laughed her deep-throated laugh.

"Yes, babies, you all are going to be a great addition to our school! And your minister is going to come speak too, and what's more, he said he was sure the new mayor would come." She said this with a questioning look, gazing around the room, eyebrows raised expectantly, and several kids chorused, "George Moscone!"

"You got it. Ain't nobody putting nothing over on you babies. Now I want you to follow John here, our head counselor, and he'll take you around to classes. You can sit in on one if you like, then come back down here when class is over and we'll try to get you together with your counselor. And this is how you know it's time for class." Golden rang the brass bell, a relic one of the teachers had found in the school district warehouse.

The teachers had agreed they didn't want a regular bell system, a decision in keeping with their overall intentions to have an alternative school. For the most part, the teachers were as rebellious as many of the older group of students. They too wore their hair long and wore jeans to class. The men sported long sideburns, mustaches, beards, or all three, and the women teachers, after years of being denied the right to wear even tailored slacks instead of below-the-knee skirts, now dressed in miniskirts, platform shoes, or boots like Bebelaar's purple cowboy boots with brass toes. Paul, one of the poets who had come to her class, called her boots "a mean pair of shit-kickers," which made her like them even more.

Liu-Klein was definitely not a slave to seventies fashion, but that day Bebelaar noted he wore the jacket that matched his khaki shirt, maybe in honor of the new students.

"Welcome to Opportunity, guys and ladies," Liu-Klein said with a smile, standing. "First we'll take a look at the art room and the kitchen, where we have a cooking class, then we'll stop by Judy's class, Creative Writing." Golden circled the room, scolding each group of old students, who were hanging out toward the front of the downstairs area, away from the orientation gathering, to hurry up the stairs.

"Get your butts up to class. Now. I want you to set a good example for our new students!" She rang the bell more insistently. Kids began heading up the stairs. Liu-Klein and Bebelaar and the new group of Temple kids followed, talking in low, excited voices.

COMING YOUR WAY BY MEANS OF OPPORTUNITYS

NATURAL HIGH EXPRESS

14TH ISSUE MAY~JUNE 1977, OPPORTUNITY HIGH S.F. CR.

EDITORS ~ LINDA WALKER AND DEBBIE LIATOS ART~GuL~RUTHERFORD

YVONNE GOLDEN INTRODUCES

DENNIS BANKS TO OPPORTUNITY

DENNIS BANKS, an American Indian Movement Leader (AIM), has been one of the people we have been fortunate to have speak here at Opportunity this school year. Some of the other Activists we have had speak here are BIG BLACK, a brother who was involved in the Attica uprising, and JIM VENERIS', an ex-Korean POW who has been living in China for 26 years. Harry Edwards, Sociology professor at U.C. Berkeley, Don Morton, a white South African ex-Missionary, and two Black South African exiles Sukosa Mji and Tsietsi Mashinini also have spoken at Opportunity.

COURT ORDERS DENNIS BANKS
TO BE EXTRADITED!!

DENNIS BANKS, a leader of the American Indian Movement and a teacher at an Indian and Mexican-American college near Sacramento, has been ordered by a court to be extradited; Governor Brown has been ordered to extradite him to South Dakota for sentencing on an assault conviction. Brown announced he will appeal the ruling to the California Supreme Court for a definite ruling. South Dakota Attorney General William Janklow first sought extradition for the militant Native American leader 14 months ago following his flight to avoid sentencing on a conviction of assault with a deadly weapon during the 1973 Custer Courthouse demonstration.
CONT'D ON PAGE 8

Natural High Express

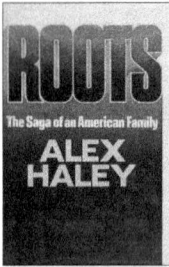

ROOTS
The Saga of an American Family
ALEX HALEY

MALCOLM X SPEAKS

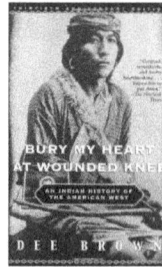

BURY MY HEART AT WOUNDED KNEE
AN INDIAN HISTORY OF THE AMERICAN WEST
DEE BROWN

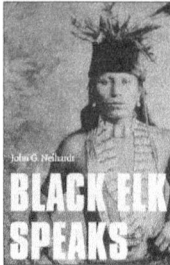

John G. Neihardt
BLACK ELK SPEAKS

LEAVES of GRASS
Walt Whitman

THE COMPLETE WORKS OF WILLIAM SHAKESPEARE

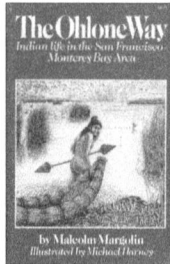

The Ohlone Way
Indian Life in the San Francisco–Monterey Bay Area
by Malcolm Margolin
Illustrated by Michael Harney

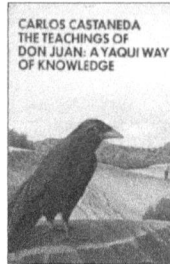

CARLOS CASTANEDA
THE TEACHINGS OF DON JUAN: A YAQUI WAY OF KNOWLEDGE

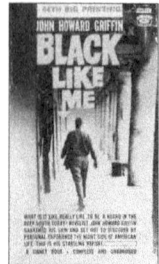

JOHN HOWARD GRIFFIN
BLACK LIKE ME

Chapter 2

Of Poetry and Baseball

September 1976 and a few days after

Creative Writing

A ll the classrooms were upstairs except for the tiny music room and the woodshop, located in what once had been the building's garage. The former offices were now fitted with chalkboards, the metal student desks used in every San Francisco school, and battered teachers' desks. Bebelaar's room was to the left as kids came up the stairs. The window of the small room looked out over grimy Plum Alley. A Navajo dream-catcher made of twigs and yarn hung from the ceiling. A large willow basket woven by a student in Native American Studies sat on a table by the window. An assortment of novels, poetry, and other books filled three cases: *Roots, Malcolm X, Bury My Heart at Wounded Knee, Black Elk Speaks, Leaves of Grass, The Complete Plays of Shakespeare, Cool World, Black Like Me, The Way We Lived*. Posters covered the walls: John Lennon, Bruce Lee, Frida Kahlo, Jimi Hendrix, and Paul Robeson, as well as reprints of photographs taken from Edward Curtis's books of Indian photographs. A small schefflera plant sat on a small table by the window where it could catch a little light.

The door stood open and a lively buzz emanated from the room full of teenagers, fifteen of them, the class size designated by the original school proposal. Bebelaar walked in with Teddy, her newest Temple counselee, who followed her to the teacher's desk.

She shut her purse in the bottom desk drawer—she had learned to leave her wallet in her car. Gesturing with the stack of papers she'd pulled out of her book bag, Bebelaar said, "Teddy, why don't you have a seat over there by Scott. He comes all the way from Berkeley every day—well, almost, but starting today, it *will* be every day, right, Scott?" Scott nodded, giving Teddy a right-hand peace sign. Bebelaar asked the class, still chatting animatedly, to settle down and introduce themselves.

"Each of you say your name and tell Teddy the color that's the best metaphor for how you feel today—and, if you like, something about Opportunity."

She wasn't surprised that Raymond spoke first. Kids were used to his being a genial class host. He'd helped Bebelaar type and mimeograph the most recent edition of the class poetry magazine, *In Small Dreams*. She would never have had an issue out so soon in the school year if it hadn't been for his help after school.

"I'm Raymond, Raymond Berrios. Today I'd say I'm kind of blue, not sad blue, but blue like the sky today, a nice sunny blue. Most teachers here are pretty cool. Welcome, man." Teddy said "hello" in a quiet voice. He didn't look up at the class, though he gave Raymond a tentative smile.

Dean Marcic, a student who often helped Bebelaar carry the groceries upstairs for cooking class, entered as she stood at the blackboard writing down phrases from the kids' introductions. Dean was typical of many of Opportunity's old kids. He was bright, but with terrible school records: failed classes, poor attendance, and stints in juvenile hall—in his case, five years in group homes, beginning when he was twelve, and transfers out of five schools. Opportunity seemed to work for Dean, who much later told Bebelaar about his time at the other schools:

> *I wasn't there every day. I wasn't there a lot. And I guess you'd say because of altercations. Seemed like I was the only white kid, especially the only blond white kid, in most of those schools. O'Connell was okay, but the only open job-training program was shoe repair. . . . I'd learned not to like school by then. At Galileo, there weren't so many fights. But I didn't like any of my classes. Sort of got out of the habit of going at all.*

When Dean had first come to Opportunity, he told Bebelaar about writing anonymous love notes to a girl in one of the group homes. The notes were apparently so poetic and inspired that another boy claimed them as his own—and he and Dean got into a fight. After Bebelaar heard his story, she told Dean about *Cyrano de Bergerac* and suggested he take Creative Writing.

Now in class, she turned to Dean and asked him to introduce himself with a metaphor. He glanced at a poem on the wall beside him and said, " 'The color of a window in the sky,' like the poem we wrote together says here."

Next Marty Emmons rose. Tall, his long hair drawn back in a ponytail, he looked like the proud Sioux he was. An old student, like Dean, Marty was the artist for *In Small Dreams*. The current cover featured a headshot drawing of Jim Jones—though it bore a good resemblance to the reverend, it also looked like Superman—surrounded by smaller faces of teenagers of all shades and racial groups. Bebelaar had given Marty the canvas tipi cover the kids had made in Native American Studies class after the poles were cut up for another project. Marty was going to paint it in the old style, with a story of a famous battle, maybe take it to the nearby Native American Center.

In Small Dreams *poetry magazine cover by Marty Emmons*

"I'm Marty. Turquoise blue, like the sky in North Dakota on a good summer day. That's where I'm from."

Next, Ronnie, whose face resembled that of one of the kids on Marty's cover drawing: "Ronnie Ross. I'm ebony, like on the piano keys."

A long-haired boy with blue-green eyes stood next. "Carl Lucania. I'm gray, like clouds, 'like heavy drapes hinting the cleanness above them.' That's from my last poem in our magazine." Carl then walked across the room to give Teddy a copy of the latest issue.

A slender, tall boy with a close-cropped Afro stood next. "You know me already, Teddy. I'll just say I'm a grain of sand. But every grain counts, right?" It was a reference to his poem, also on the wall, which ended:

> *Let the light search your heart*
> *To find the right way*
> *It's hard to conceive the light*
> *Because the light in reality is you and me*
> *The nations built today*
> *Are built on guilt of yesterday*
> *The world goes by the master plan*
> *Some say "keep your head to the sky"*
> *It might just tell you why*
> *Can we understand*
> *We are but grains of sand*
> *In lost time?*

Manny Blackwell was the class philosopher-poet. He and Marty were best buddies and always sat together. Everyone liked Manny, who had an athlete's carriage and an easygoing manner. He seemed to know all the Temple kids, but he had come to the school earlier than they had. He had entered Opportunity after trouble at another school.

"Definitely wasn't his fault," Liu-Klein had explained. "Bum deal for a nice kid. He was defending himself from a bunch of bullies much bigger than him. He was trying to climb through a hole in the fence to get to school on time, and blam! You know I like most kids, but some of 'em . . ."

The teachers didn't know then that Manny had been a member of the Temple; Bebelaar and Cabral would learn his story later.

"Hi, Teddy. You should take this class." Joyce Polk Brown, a Temple kid, pointed to the small piece of tan parchment paper over the blackboard bearing an anonymous sixteenth-century poem:

O western wind, when wilt thou blow
　That the small rain down can rain?
　　Christ, that my love were in my arms
And I in my bed again!

"That's my favorite poem. Ms. B said a sailor wrote it on a ship back when it took maybe a year to cross the ocean. You just had to hope the wind would come up to take you home."

Joyce was a beautiful girl with soft brown eyes that held a quiet, confident intelligence. Today she wore a red blouse, a black scarf around her neck, and a black skirt. On several mornings she'd brought Bebelaar a little bundle of her poems to read.

Joyce Polk Brown

"Ms. B, okay if I read my poem from our book?"

"Sure—any of you can do that." Joyce reached for a copy of the magazine.

"Well then, I guess I'm the color of the trade wind," she said:

O trade wind, when the nice breeze blows,
As the rain tingles on the roof of the tropic island,
Birds fly to the nest in the tropic trees,
Little creatures hiding from
The small rain.

Next, Bebelaar turned to Scott Roberts, an accomplished musician. She knew from his mother that when he wasn't in school, his love for music was the reason. He composed and had a band. There were many kids at Opportunity who, like Scott, felt the pull of something beyond the school walls, and for some it seemed that magnet was stronger than their parents' wishes or teachers' pleas and admonitions through phone calls and one-on-ones. "Why don't you read your Coltrane poem," Bebelaar urged, knowing he wouldn't volunteer.

"Sure, Judy . . . You know 'Trane, Ted?" Teddy nodded. "This is for him." Roberts read his poem:

> *John Coltrane*
> *from the fiery town of New York*
> *the soft beauty of his gold tenor*
> *is like a thousand rainbows*
>
> *he rises from his gray and grim life*
> *and creates*
> *tranquility*
>
> *but does he please*
> *himself?*

The other kids had finished their introductions when Mondo and Willie came in with Liu-Klein.

"Hi Jude, hi kids." He put one hand on the shoulder of the handsome, athletic boy to his left and one on the shoulder of the tall slender girl at his right. "Mondo Griffith and Willie Thomas. They wanted to check out your class."

"Come on in, Mondo, Willie. You can sit over there by Joyce," Bebelaar said. "Later, kids," Liu-Klein threw over his shoulder, and disappeared back through the open doorway.

Bebelaar was glad to see new faces, and hoped some new students would sign up for Creative Writing. The magic often dissipated, even disappeared, when only three or four kids showed up for class—which also meant that she would have to make phone calls to kids or parents that night. Bebelaar asked Mondo and Willie to introduce themselves with a color too, then explained the writing assignment.

"See all the words and lines I've written on the board? I took them from what you said, and that's your start for writing today. Let them take you someplace. We'll write for seven minutes. Maybe just rearrange the words so they please you. Try to fill a page. No rules except there's no talking. If you're stuck—raise your hand." Heads bent. There was a wonderful silence as kids scribbled away—or almost all of them. Bebelaar noticed Ronnie's head was on his desk. She went over to him and whispered, "What words or lines do you like, Ronnie?"

He mumbled, head still on his desk, "None of 'em. I don't feel like writing. I can only write when I'm in the mood."

By now, uncooperative students didn't faze Bebelaar. She took remarks like Ronnie's as challenges, and this class, she felt, was her best chance of meeting that challenge, to get the students to *want* to cooperate. In a month or two the kids would feel they knew one another—could trust one another—enough that they could start to remove their teenage armor. Ronnie might need a little more time than some. Though he came to school every day, he didn't always do his work, and often missed class—sitting in the principal's office for trouble of one kind or another.

Bending low by his desk, Bebelaar said, "Here's a pen, and paper. Remember, to get credit, you have to write, every day. Maybe something up there on the board makes a picture in your mind. Maybe you like the sounds of the words. There's no wrong answer. It's what feels right to you." His head was still on the desk when Bebelaar went over to Marty, who had raised his hand. Soon the room was quiet except for the scratching of pens and pencils. Ronnie had not yet lifted his head.

Judy Bebelaar

It was more like fifteen minutes later when kids were beginning to look up from their papers—Bebelaar asked if anyone felt like reading what he or she had written. Mondo raised his hand. His eyes were wide-set, clear, serious. "We were talking about the colors of feeling, so I wrote about feeling. Is that okay?"

"Sure, Mondo." She was astonished. His first day in a new class, new school, and he was ready to share his poetry?

"Okay. Here goes nothing," he said launching into his poem:

Feeling—can you feel?
Can I feel?
Yes I can feel.
I can feel the tree right beside me.
I can feel my hand on my face.
Is this the feeling you are talking about?
Or is it the feeling that we have within?
Is that the feeling you are talking about—
Feeling for people like my mom or dad or sister?
Do you mean feeling for all people?
I get the point—starving people.
Not just one race, but all of them.

Now I got the feeling.
The feeling is love.

The kids were quiet.

Ronnie had raised his head halfway through the poem. Now he exclaimed, "Man, you've got the touch, Mondo!"

Mondo said, "I've got another too, here in my pocket. Okay if I read it?"

"Of course," Bebelaar said. "There's just one thing: You *have* to sign up for this class."

"I'm already in! Here we go."

I was sitting in the dark
not waiting for dark
the dark is like no sound around
it's quiet
very quiet
once in a while
I look up and down and all around
to make sure I am by myself
I do not like anybody to see
me talk to myself
because I might say
the wrong thing.

For a moment Bebelaar wanted to smile at what seemed like the tongue-in-cheek silliness in the last lines. As Mondo's words sank in, she wondered: Had the Temple kids been told to be careful about what they shared with outsiders? Was there some Church secret they had been forbidden to reveal? As quickly as these thoughts arose, she pushed them away. After all, these teenagers all seemed so happy, so self-confident.

Joyce said, "Can I read another one of mine?"

"Of course," Bebelaar said.

Joyce explained, "I remembered that poem we read the other day, by Joyce Carol Thomas, 'Paint Me Like I Am.' So I kind of used that."

Paint me with my head up looking proud
Paint me with a big happy smile on my face.
Paint me with beautiful colored beads,
With my hair corn-rolled in an African style.
Paint me with the animals of the jungle,
Like a colorful bird and a brown soft
Monkey jumping tree to tree.

Paint me with all the nationalities of people.
Paint me with a gorgeous colored dress . . .
Paint me beautiful.
PAINT ME. PAINT ME. PAINT ME.

Bebelaar didn't know then that Jones had already begun to create a beautiful picture of a jungle paradise for his flock, that two of Joyce's poems probably described her romantic idea of life in Guyana. She must have thought she would have time for plaiting cornrows and decorating her hair with beads, for watching animals, for boyfriends and laughter.

As for that monkey jumping from tree to tree, Bebelaar would later be startled to learn that Jim Jones once peddled pet monkeys door-to-door, fundraising for his new interracial church in Indiana. Mr. Muggs, the pet monkey who would be loved by many children in Jonestown, would make the trip from California to Guyana.

Willie raised her hand. She had a fluffy Afro and an easy, graceful carriage.

"I wrote something, Ms. B, about the color black, and prejudice."

"Let's hear it, Willie." The Temple newcomers were making their presence felt! Willie stood.

Young, old, poor and black
Shot, burned, killed, beaten,
For what reason?
Our dark skin?
Prejudice
Please help
They're laying down a little black child . . .
Who killed that little boy?
Somebody tell me
Who killed him?

The class was silent again. Bebelaar asked Willie if she'd sign up too. "Yes, I plan to," Willie said.

Then Golden rang the brass hand bell and admonished kids to go to their next classes. As students began to head for the door Bebelaar did too, to collect their papers. Ronnie was the last one out. He handed her a page—he'd written after all.

Room 8

After having brought Mondo and Willie to Creative Writing, Liu-Klein had continued to escort his group of Temple kids around the school, dropping a few in each class. The last small group—Stephan, his brothers Tim and Jimmy, and Johnny Cobb—told the counselor they'd like to check out Ron Cabral's class and ask about the baseball team Ron was organizing.

Peering in the small window down the hall, Liu-Klein saw Cabral in his class talking on the CB radio, so he told the students to go in and introduce themselves. After having seen several of the classrooms, the boys probably weren't surprised to see that room 8, dominated by a huge photo of the Beatles and another of Jerry Garcia, more closely resembled an adolescent's bedroom than an institutional classroom. The walls were plastered with pictures of spaceships and psychedelic post-

Ron Cabral at KALW radio station

ers from shows at the Fillmore and the Avalon Ballroom—even a Country Joe and the Fish placard signed by the entire band. Cabral, with long black hair, sideburns, and longish moustache, was an unlikely looking coach. He played trombone and had managed a rock 'n' roll band, Gold, with his brother. They'd played at Winterland and Fillmore West, and Cabral was a friend of Country Joe's.

The teacher perched on a desk near the rear window helping a student understand how the CB worked. The two were radioing a trucker on the nearby freeway overpass. The other students were writing or talking.

After they finished, the Temple boys introduced themselves, Stephan taking the lead. Cabral looked up at the tall foursome quizzically. "So, you're all brothers?" Tim was fair with blond curly hair cut to look like an Afro; Stephan had straight dark hair and skin a shade or two darker than Tim's; Johnny's complexion was brown; and Jimmy's was dark.

"Yes, except for me," said Johnny, smiling, "though in a way I am too."

"I was a good friend of Stephan's, way back when we were kids," explained Tim, a tall, broad-shouldered, muscular kid. "Finally, Mom and Dad—most people in the Church call them that—adopted me. They treat me just like I was really one of their own. So yes, I'm a brother. Jimmy's adopted too—but I guess you could tell that."

After a pause, Tim said, "We heard you're trying to start a baseball team."

"Yeah," Jimmy continued. "You know, sometimes Dad preaches against sports and how it's all about competition and capitalism and bashing in people's heads and stuff. But Stephan and me and Jimmy and Tim and a couple of other kids, we love sports anyway. Can't help it. Mom, now, she doesn't mind. She comes to our games, football or basketball or track or whatever, and she roots for us." Jimmy spoke easily. He seemed to be comfortable communicating with adults on an equal level. Many of the Temple kids were more mature than other high schoolers.

Tim nodded his head, "She's a good lady, my mom. And you don't have to worry about us," he added. "We'll show up, and keep up a B average, do whatever we have to do. And we can get more guys to sign up."

Cabral gathered himself, a little stunned. His attempts at starting a team before had always failed. He said, "Tim, I think I saw you with the Sporting Green in your back pocket downstairs."

"Yes sir," Tim replied.

"I just put out a sign-up sheet for the baseball team. It'll be great to add you to the list." "I can pitch," Tim volunteered.

"And I can play outfield," Jimmy said.

"And you, Stephan?" Cabral asked. Stephan shook his head.

"I'm just rooting them on," he said. "Basketball's my game."

Cabral looked at the four athletes. Back in '74 he'd accumulated a list of prospective players, but somehow interest faded before the team could be organized. He'd pretty much given up hope over the past year that enough kids would show up regularly.

Johnny Cobb summed it up: "Let's do it!"

Within a few days, seven kids from the Temple had signed up: Tim, Jimmy, and Johnny; Billy Oliver, six foot three and 240 pounds, who had been catcher on a youth team; Mark Sly, who wanted to play outfield; Teddy; and Mondo, the poet, who had just come over from Mission High where he had been a standout infielder on the Junior Varsity team.

It was beginning to look as if little Opportunity, the school the district saw as a place for misfits, might field a team to play against the big schools.

Chapter 3

In Small Dreams

The Following Week

Secrets

San Francisco sent kids who were in trouble with the law to two juvenile detention centers: Youth Guidance Center, which the kids called "YGC" or "The Green House," at the top of Market Street near Twin Peaks; or Log Cabin, far down the Peninsula in the countryside. The poem Ronnie handed Bebelaar after class his first day was about his stay at Log Cabin, but he had apparently spent time at both.

I expected log cabins
instead, big blue and brown dorms
trees everywhere
quiet flowers, no fences
even a swimming pool
I flashed to the city
and YGC
narrow dull green halls
always dark
locked up
nasty hard oatmeal
but back at cabin
it was open
though days went by
and time went slow
six months
no green halls, but locks all the same
then I was out
free of feeling
free of doing
free of coming
free

The following day Bebelaar asked if Ronnie would like to read the poem to the class. He did, with style, and received applause. Ronnie was popular with kids, outgoing and friendly. He had a Honda 305 motorcycle that he had bought in bad shape and repaired. He gave kids rides after school—sometimes even Temple kids, who were not supposed to spend time out of class with the other students—something teachers did not know was a Temple rule.

Ronnie was a favorite with many of his teachers—especially math teacher Joe Bailey and Colin Covey, the social studies teacher who ranted about capitalism and took kids on sailboat rides. Ronnie was one of those kids who loved Opportunity's free-wheeling ways. He still got in trouble, but students and teachers alike were fond of him, partly *because* of his irrepressible spirit.

One day Ronnie walked to class with Bebelaar. "You know, Ms. B, before the kids came in from the Temple, Yvonne told us there was a big bunch of them coming and she wanted us to show them respect. Well, we tried. But they don't really seem to want to talk to us much. I feel like this is our school. Know what I mean? I don't mind sharing it with them, but I say, *talk* to us!"

She responded that he should take it easy on them, that some were from the country and maybe found city life—and city kids and their ways—a little foreign.

"Well," he said, "I'm not gonna give up on 'em yet."

As they reached Bebelaar's classroom Ronnie's younger brother Carl came out of the darkroom, heading their way. Liu-Klein and another of his photography students, Mary Delema, were also approaching them, from the stairwell. Liu-Klein and Mary were talking animatedly; Carl, quiet, was seemingly in his own world.

Mary, with curly dark hair and fair skin, was a foot shorter than Carl, who had a thin but athletic frame and mid-size Afro. Carl came to Opportunity later than Ronnie had.

Mary Delema (by John Liu-Klein)

Then someone else exited the darkroom: Kimberly Fye, a Temple girl. Her face flushed, she looked down at the floor as she passed Bebelaar and Carl. Was she hiding a smile? She hurried down the stairs.

Liu-Klein and Carl stopped at the classroom door. As Mary turned to head downstairs to her next class, Liu-Klein bent to give her a brief kiss on the top of her head. "You be good, now, girl," he admonished. "Go to all your classes today." Mary was another old kid who was very bright and loved the school, but still didn't attend regularly.

"Hey, Mary," Ronnie called out, half-teasing and half-serious, as she headed downstairs. "Is John your dad? That's what some of the kids said."

Mary looked pleased as she turned back and shook her head. Bebelaar suspected the girl wished John *were* her dad.

Kimberly Fye

"Hey Ms. B, Ronnie," Carl greeted them. Carl was head of the school welcoming committee. He was more subdued than his brother Ronnie, but friendly like him, and well-spoken. He never missed a class, and was never in trouble—as Ronnie often was. Despite their differences, the two brothers were obviously close.

Carl was at school early, every day. It was rare that a teacher arrived before him. He had his reasons for finding the school a kind of sanctuary. Lots of the kids did, arriving early and staying until teachers had to chase them out to lock up. "Home" was often not an easy place. The normal tension between teenagers and parents might be exacerbated by a harried single mother, an abusive father, or the influence of drugs or alcohol.

Ronnie continued his teasing, giving his brother a friendly punch in the arm, "You know what else I heard? That big blond kid—Tim, the minister's son—they say the Giants want to recruit him soon as he graduates—but his dad won't let him play ball. Has other things in mind for him, I guess. Man. Kids say he can throw a ball 85, 86 miles an hour!"

Bebelaar told Ronnie that Tim and some other Temple kids had signed up for the baseball team, and that Tim had just signed up for Creative Writing too.

"That's pretty cool. Can't wait to see him pitch a game," Ronnie said. "But you know, I can't get that guy to talk to me." He turned to his brother. "I was just saying to Ms. B how these Temple kids, they sure keep to themselves."

"Yeah, I know what you mean," said Carl. "I think the church has something to do with it. But some of them . . ." He suddenly looked a little embarrassed. "Anyway, Ronnie," Carl continued, "not Mondo at least." He explained to the two teachers, "Ronnie and me know Mondo, from way back when. We grew up with him. He doesn't shut people out. I say just give 'em a little time. And maybe a ride on your Honda, big bro. Say, you guys hear that their minister is going to talk at Lyceum today?"

"You mean that guy who always has dark glasses on in the newspaper pictures? I saw him down at the principal's office the other day. Had 'em on then too. Wonder what's up with that? One of the Temple kids told me if he takes 'em off and looks straight at you, you'll go to hell when you die."

"Oh, Ronnie, they were just pulling your leg," Bebelaar said.

"Anyway, I'll be there. I want to hear what he has to say for himself."

They heard Golden ringing the bell. Bebelaar said goodbye and went into her room to get ready for Creative Writing. Ronnie and Carl remained outside the door, talking.

❧

Joyce had convinced Dorothy to join Creative Writing. Dorothy, born in Mississippi, had lived in Ukiah before she came to San Francisco. She, her mother, and her older sister Loreatha had all relocated with Jim Jones in the Church's move from Indiana. One of Dorothy's first poems expressed nostalgia for a simpler world and a sense of foreboding about the future. Bebelaar invited her to read it to the class. Dorothy seemed pleased, even touched, but said she'd rather not have the class hear it. "It's kind of personal, you know, Ms. B. I don't think I want to read it."

"Well, think about giving me a copy for the next issue of *In Small Dreams*, okay?" she said. "It's a good poem."

As kids began to drift in, Bebelaar pulled out her poem to read it again. Something nagged at her, but she wasn't sure why. Dorothy always had a smile on her face; she must be okay.

Walking down a busy wide street
  Seeing many people pass by me,
I'm happy with my friends,
Like a bluebird when it sings its happy song,
The smell of the biscuits cooking in my friend's house
The streetlights on my face like the stars,
Looking down on the earth, my earth mother earth,
Now home, looking down on the busy cars
Wanting my brother to come home,
  But he won't never come back . . .

She hadn't wanted to tell Bebelaar more about her brother. Was he the reason Dorothy's mother had joined the Church in Indiana? Opportunity kids often wrote about traumas in their lives. Bebelaar had always made it clear that what someone shared in class was just between those in the class, that the writer's trust deserved everyone's respect. Nothing would go into *In Small Dreams* without the writer's permission.

At first some kids wrote about their troubles obliquely. Once other students showed understanding for what a writer was trying to express, he or she almost always began to write more directly. In the end the poems improved, and the burden the poet carried seemed lighter. Often someone else in the class shared an experience similar to the one in the poem. It seemed fairly obvious that many of these kids were moving through the stages of grief or recovery from trauma, and that the opportunity to write in a supportive atmosphere offered them some steps toward healing.

Bebelaaar looked at Dorothy's poem again to add a few more comments before she put it in the "Return" folder. Dorothy had a good sense of the power of language. "My heart grasps me." Bebelaar had hoped that Dorothy would continue to write poetry: her words, like Joyce's, went right to Bebelaar's heart.

Lately, Joyce, the Temple girl who had written her own "Western Wind" poem, seemed preoccupied with something outside of school, outside of writing. *Probably a boy,* Bebelaar thought, *handsome, smart, maybe an older guy, since Joyce is so much older than her years.* As Bebelaar set out the day's handouts, she decided to ask Joyce and Dorothy to attend a poetry reading with her. Poets noticed the teenagers in the audience and always made it a point to speak with the young people. She would have to remember to ask them after class: the Temple kids often disappeared right after school every day instead of hanging around as so many of the old students did. Did they have duties at the church? Did they want to spend free time with each other, rather than with the other kids?

When most of the kids were in their seats Bebelaar announced, "Okay guys, today we're going to listen to this." Bebelaar held up the wild cover of a record she had discovered: *The Zodiac: Cosmic Sounds* was a psychedelic rock album, featuring, among other instruments, a Moog synthesizer, and a musical interpretation of each sign of the zodiac with a voiceover of poetry. Bebelaar asked the kids to listen for ideas, then to write about their own signs. Knowing that teenagers are fascinated by the new selves they are becoming, the Opportunity teachers tuned their antennae outside of class to find any hook they could to pull students into class and into their lessons.

At the end of the writing session, some of the kids read their pieces. Raymond's ram "was contented with the sound of silence." Marty, the Sioux artist, wrote about running, feeling clean dirt under his feet, going fishing. Sandra was a crab with "claws like castanets," and Rory, the new Temple kid, a wiry African American boy with a huge smile, was:

The twin of an eagle
Flying over the jewel blue seas—
Here is some of the fruit
I smell the flowery aroma of oranges and lemons
The king flies on

A black panther in his brown trees
An olive green jungle
A king pacing slowly in his land
Watching the stone flowers growing

"Gemini, right?" asked Scott. Rory nodded. His smile showed he was pleased. Looking back, Bebelaar wished she had asked more about the jungle imagery both he and Joyce had used. At the time, she knew nothing about the Church settlement in Guyana, then in its nascent stages.

Tim Jones had gone his own way with the poetry lesson, becoming a camera and focusing on a young lady. The color of her face, he said, reminded him of night:

Rory Bargeman

night that comes
and settles down
over the world.

The kids applauded both poems. "Great imagery!" Bebelaar told Rory. "And Tim, what makes yours so good is how simple and beautiful it is. You can really feel the softness of night, as if it were a black bird."

Tim apparently had talent for more than baseball and—like most teenagers—was in love. Bebelaar read out loud some poems from the previous two class lessons. Joyce's were lovely; detailed, romantic, as usual, and, like many of her poems, featured an animal.

I am thinking about redecorating my room,
An autumn kind of scene on my walls,
Colors of brown, orange-rust, light yellowish-green leaves.

There would be a very beautiful stallion,
Standing by a clear blue stream,
Leading to a little white cottage

Another could have been a beautiful song.

How do you get from
the ghetto to the sparrow,
How in the corner of a ghetto
a sparrow grows lips, and
remembers how to sing

And one made Bebelaar wonder:

When will the violins stop and
Hear only drums?
When will I stop feeling half
And feel whole?
When will I stop crying and
Start laughing?
When will I change?
WHEN? WHEN? WHEN?

Why would Joyce want to change? She was sweet, sensitive, talented, hard-working, and lovely as well. Maybe her feeling of incompleteness was the teenage angst of wondering if she'd ever find her true love. After class, Bebelaar invited her and Dorothy and Willie to a poetry reading the next week. All three said they were busy.

Sick with Love

In Native American Studies, Bebelaar's class was reading "High Horse's Courting," a chapter from *Black Elk Speaks*. Kids always loved the story about a young man so "sick" with love that he steals a few horses as a bride price. When that tactic does not work, he sneaks into her parents' tipi to steal her away. The story is funny, exciting—and with a happy ending. *Sometimes*, Bebelaar thought, *teaching is a predictable, enjoyable breeze.*

Junior, a likable kid whose terrible attendance worried her, had signed up for this class—but he kept disappearing. He'd been out of school for a week and his phone was disconnected. She feared he was in the detention center again. It was sad that such a nice kid kept getting into trouble.

Marty, Manny's good buddy, entered the room. "Hey Judy, what's up today?"

Bebelaar held up *Black Elk Speaks*.

"Hey, he's Sioux too, Ms. B., Oglala Lakota." Marty often wrote about being Indian, both for this class and in Creative Writing.

"Right, and after today, you'll want to read the whole book—guaranteed! And someday, Marty, I'd like to see what you've done with that tipi cover. Maybe you could bring it to class and tell us about the story you've painted."

"I'm still working on it, Judy. I'll bring it one of these days."

More kids ambled into the classroom—Junior too, Bebelaar noted, pleased. She pulled out stacks of handouts and displayed the book on the blackboard ledge. She had bought three or four used copies that could be loaners for kids who—she hoped—would want to read the entire book. Many kids' attendance was sporadic, and they often disappeared without explanation—the school district called this "LWT" or "Left Without Transfer." Bebelaar learned to create stand-alone lessons so no one would feel lost, while continuing to reinforce skills she wanted to teach. Unfortunately, buying extra books didn't always help. Students in the class were supposed to, on their own, read and write a report on one book per grading period—"supposed to" being the applicable term for many. Some had decided long ago that homework was not for them. And for many, home was not an environment conducive to quiet reading or thoughtful writing.

"Okay, guys, settle down so we can start. Here's the book we're reading from." Bebelaar held up the display copy. "I'll pass it around so you can look at the pictures at the end of the book. You can see Black Elk as a young man, and as he looked when he told the story to John Neihardt, the man with white hair standing next to him. Black Elk's son was forced by the authorities to go to a boarding school to learn English, and, the plan was, to become a Christian."

Bebelaar went on with Black Elk's history. "Many Indian kids were taken away like that, and forbidden to speak their language. The idea then was that Indians should 'assimilate.' " She wrote the word on the board and explained it. "As you can imagine, that didn't always work. Black Elk's son did learn English in the missionary school, but he didn't forget his native Sioux, so he could later translate what Black Elk said. Then Neihardt's daughter took down in shorthand what Black Elk's son had told her—girls often took shorthand in school back then—and she went home and typed it up. And that's how we got this beautiful book."

She gave the stack of handouts to Marty, who passed them out. "We'll do the reading game. Remember, you only *have* to read one sentence, but you can read as much as you like, and you get a point for starting in the right place." This game encouraged the lesser-skilled kids to try and follow along. "I'll start, and when I toss you the reading ball, it's your turn."

You know, in the old days, it was not so very easy to get a girl when you wanted to be married. Sometimes it was hard work for a young man, and he had to stand a great deal. Say I am a young man and I have seen a young girl who looks so beautiful to me that I feel all sick when I think about her. I can not just go and tell her about it and then get married if she is willing. I have to be a very sneaky fellow to talk to her at all, and after I have managed to talk to her, that is only the beginning.[1]

She tossed the ball to Marty, who continued. No one missed a beat, even when two kids came in late. They were too intrigued with High Horse's bold venture, the girl's mother screaming when she saw a strange creature—High Horse in war paint—lying next to her daughter. He had lain in the dark until it was safe to steal the girl away, but had fallen asleep. Then he had to run for his life.

Fortunately, someone thought the creature in paint and feathers might be a spirit, so no one shot at him. The class had just reached the satisfying ending, where Black Elk and his friend come back with one hundred horses, stolen from the Crow, to offer to the father, who had refused first two, then four, as the bride price for his daughter. Bebelaar read the last few lines.

It was not the horses that he wanted. What he wanted was a son who was a real man and good for something.
So High Horse got his girl after all, and I think he deserved her.[2]

"What do you guys think?" Laughter and nodding heads and a few "right-on"s answered Bebelaar's question. Just then there was a knock on the classroom door—a student with a phone message.

"Hang on, guys. I'll be right with you." A few minutes later Bebelaar re-entered to find Junior and Marty standing by their desks, pumped with adrenaline, glaring at one another. Junior was as proud of being Samoan—in fact the son of a village chief—as Marty was of being Sioux, and both were tall and strong.

There weren't many fights at Opportunity. When one occurred, a male teacher usually intervened. Bebelaar had never had a fight in her classroom before.

She took a stand between them, looking up at each in turn—they were both taller than she was. They didn't seem aware of her, obviously all too ready to start swinging, their jaws and fists clenched.

With the most determined, in-control look she could manage, she commanded, "Calm down. Sit down and let me go on with the lesson. Remember how Black Elk said High Horse had to be very clever? Clever works better."

To her huge relief, both boys sat down and stared straight ahead. The rest of the class was quiet, wide-eyed. Bebelaar turned to read from the Author's Postscript.

> *After the conclusion of the narrative, Black Elk and our party were sitting at the north edge of Cuny Table, looking off across the Badlands ("the beauty and the strangeness of the earth," as the old man expressed it).[3]*

Glancing at the boys, Bebelaar read on. In the Author's Postscript, Neihardt describes how Black Elk asks to be taken to the mountain where he'd had his first vision. Black Elk tells his son, Neihardt, and Neihardt's daughter that if the spirits will listen to him one more time and hear his request, the thunder beings will bless him with a little rain.

Although Black Elk is worried—the sky is clear and they are in the midst of a terrible drought—his prayer that his people live is answered with "a scant, chill rain" and thunder. "For some minutes the old man stood silent, with face uplifted, weeping in the drizzling rain."[4]

Bebelaar could never get through reading that passage without feeling her own tears welling up. Though kids were always kind if they noticed, she was relieved to hear Golden ringing the bell for Lyceum.

As Marty and Junior left, they both apologized with a nod and a "Sorry, Ms. B." When she asked if they would shake hands they obliged, though neither looked the other one in the eye.

Reverend Jones Speaks at Opportunity

The chairs were set up in the first-floor lobby used for gatherings. Many Temple kids were sitting in the front rows, with a few adults who were likely from the Temple. Golden stood at the podium, ringing her bell, the minister beside her with his dark glasses.

Ronnie and Carl sat together near the middle of the audience. Bebelaar looked around for Stephan. He was nowhere to be seen, though his brothers were sitting near the front.

Golden cast a glance around the room that said *quiet down*. The buzz of talk began to abate. She introduced the minister as a great man, a true revolutionary, someone they were fortunate to hear, and added that she expected respect and perfect behavior. "Now please welcome the Reverend Jim Jones!" The old students applauded politely while those from the Temple, students and adults, clapped enthusiastically—and for a surprisingly long time.

Although Jones quoted frequently from the Bible, he had a very modern take on the old stories. Eve had gotten a bad deal, having been blamed for death and sin in the world. Things hadn't changed much as far as he could tell. All the women and girls responded with applause.

Jones talked about Christ as an agent for change, about how early Christians had to be courageous to follow their beliefs, how they lived communally, giving what they had to support the small group that lived together. He said he was a white minister of a mostly black Church because he could take his black parishioners where they might not be able to go themselves.

Golden beamed throughout the whole presentation, and added her affirmations and responses loud and clear. When Jones finished his spirited talk—punctuated by appreciative laughter and occasional cheers from the audience—there was more applause, the loudest again from the Temple members in the audience, though by now everyone clapped enthusiastically. Then Jones said he hoped to hear thoughts or questions from the young people in the room, and that old people and youngsters are "our treasure."

Ronnie stood, and next to him Carl did too, knowing that what Ronnie was about to say would get him in trouble again, and in this case wanting to stand with him.

"Reverend Jones, why don't you take your shades off?" Ronnie asked—in a tone somewhere between a demand and a question—"So I can see your eyes." The room became quiet. Ronnie removed his own dark glasses. There was an audible chorus of gasps. Ronnie was about to continue when Golden and the security guard headed through the crowd to stop him. They hustled Ronnie and Carl toward the principal's office as Golden scolded angrily: "How dare you? You've embarrassed us!" To the minister she said, "Please go ahead. I apologize for this terrible, disrespectful behavior."

The minister seemed to smile, unperturbed.

He didn't take his glasses off.

Peoples Temple buses

Chapter 4

Freedom of Expression

Into October

The Fresno Four

little before eight o'clock one Thursday morning, Golden stood, hands on hips and eyes on the door, in the center of the lobby. A few students sprawled on the couch; others gathered in clusters talking, laughing, flirting, doing their best to appear cool or entertainingly goofy. A group of Temple kids sat in chairs near the Formica-topped table used for teacher meetings and interviews, talking quietly or doing homework. On the table were scattered the brown paper bag lunches they brought every day. The old students never brought lunches from home—either because no one provided them, or because paper bag lunches were way un-cool.

Norman Vogel, the young social studies teacher, and his buddy, music and reading teacher Bob Morrow, came through the school's front door. Golden called out to them, "Come on in here to my office, guys. I want to tell you about a great chance for you two!"

Vogel was a long-haired, bearded young man who favored jeans and Frye cowboy boots. He had come to San Francisco from Los Angeles after being accepted to San Francisco State. Like many of the teachers at Opportunity, he was from a conservative background but had been drawn into the Bay Area's lively music scene, the politics, the protests. He was what the school district called a "long-term substitute," a label that allowed the district to hire a new teacher who perhaps hadn't completed all the requirements for a credential—giving the district license to pay less and avoid providing benefits. Like many young teachers, Vogel was eager to teach in an inner city school and had agreed to help Cabral coach the newly formed baseball team.

Morrow was a slender black man with a neat Afro and horn-rimmed glasses. A jazz musician with an impressive musical background, he played the bass, sax, and clarinet. John Coltrane was his favorite musician. With Morrow on bass, Cabral on trombone, and students on sax and drums, the combo jammed together at school sometimes; Bob and Ron had played together a few times at

Ron's house. The first time they drove to Ron's suburban home across the Bay, Morrow had asked, deadpan, "Hey Ronnie. Where you takin' me? How far out into the fuckin' boondocks are we goin' and where's all the black people?"

Morrow had apparently had some difficult financial times and held a quietly pessimistic view of the world. He often spent the night in the old Bryant Street building where the school was formerly housed. He didn't reveal much about himself to anyone except Vogel, Cabral, and Kollias. When Vogel described a particularly bad time in a class or shared some personal trouble, other teachers would try to be supportive and encouraging. But when he expressed his woes to Morrow, his friend instead painted a vivid picture of just how bad things would probably get. Even so, Vogel was one of the few people who could make Morrow laugh.

That morning Morrow and Vogel followed Golden into her office. "Listen," she said, "you guys believe in freedom of the press, right?"

Vogel nodded while Morrow gazed at her with his usual enigmatic, slightly sardonic look. She continued. "Well, you must have heard about the Fresno Four? The editor, Gruner, the City Editor, and two other reporters for the *Fresno Bee* were jailed for refusing to reveal their sources for some articles. Jailing reporters trying to tell the truth! What the hell is that all about?"

Golden told them that the next day, Friday the seventeenth, Jim Jones was taking some Church members on Greyhound buses to protest at the newspaper offices. "Jones asked if any of our teachers might want to go, and I thought of you two."

Golden said she would get their classes covered, and instructed them to be at the church at four the next morning, sharp. Norm told her he was game; Bob said he would go as long as he didn't have to take a sick day. Apparently all the kids from the Temple would be going.

Golden had asked Kollias and Mary McCrohan, another teacher, to go as well.

Bus Number Seven

When Vogel and Morrow arrived at the Peoples Temple on Geary, two tall, burly men at the entrance asked their names. One said, "We've been expecting you," and ushered them in.

The seats inside—the church had folding chairs rather than pews to allow space for dancing—were nearly full; young and old, black and white—everyone interspersed, just as the Temple kids were at school. Black children sat on the laps of white men or women, white teenagers sat next to elderly black people. Some of the old people and the smaller children looked tired, but most of the congregation was bright-eyed and alert despite the early hour.

"Well, we fit right in," Vogel whispered to Morrow. "Blackie and Whitey." They couldn't help but notice the group was at least three-quarters black—again, like the Temple kids at Opportunity.

Morrow spotted Kollias and McCrohan sitting with a group of kids who attended Opportunity. He and Vogel were about to sit next to them when a woman asked them to follow her to the row of chairs in the front. Marceline

Marceline Jones

Jones, Jim Jones's wife, was sitting there, looking elegant in a simple but stylish blue dress, her gold-blond hair piled high on her head. She smiled and shook their hands warmly. She said that Jim Jones wanted them to ride with him on the trip, in bus number seven.

Jones strode to the podium at the front of the church. He nodded and smiled at the teachers, then addressed the crowd. He told them this was a special day: they were going to stand up for the rights of reporters, for Constitutional First Amendment rights; they would be a part of American history. When the crowd stood and applauded wildly, cheering and stamping their feet, Jones smiled broadly.

The teachers exchanged glances. They were not used to this kind of overwhelming enthusiasm, especially so early in the morning. They felt out of place even though they had been welcomed by Jones and his wife. What in the world were they doing here at 4:00 AM? What were all these other people doing here this early, especially the children? There was no turning back, so the two men followed the smiling people out to board the waiting buses.

Jones shook their hands as they entered bus number seven and told them how happy he was that they were joining the protest. After he headed down the aisle to the back of the bus, Vogel said to Morrow, "I feel like we're on our way to summer camp. Or maybe we joined the military. Everything certainly goes by the schedule." Breakfast rolls and coffee were passed out as bus number seven pulled onto the freeway.

Morrow replied, "It's all okay by me, as long as they keep feeding us. Think I'll take a little snooze."

A few rows back the two women teachers sat with some kids they knew, sipping coffee. About a half hour before the bus reached Fresno, Jones stood and addressed the passengers, speaking into a microphone. The four later learned later that the sound system was connected to all the buses so all the protesters heard his talk. Vogel gave a good imitation of Jones when he recounted the adventure later:

> Good morning, good morning, good morning. It's going to be a great day, a great day for the First Amendment. But I want you to be prepared, brothers and sisters, for what may happen today. I do not want you to walk into the trap that may be set for us. You may be spat upon. You may be taunted. You may be abused, with words, or with physical abuse. We are the soldiers of freedom today. We must not fall prey to people who want to mess up this demonstration. We must take what comes, whatever comes, with dignity and strength. I know I can count on you. I know you are a strong people, filled with love, filled with the love of freedom.

The bus broke into loud and enthusiastic cheers. Vogel said, "He's like a general. A god-damn fucking five-star general."

Though they didn't cheer, Vogel and Morrow felt compelled to join in the clapping. They were guests; they were the kids' teachers. It was kind of like open house night at school, but instead of just a few sets of parents, here were busloads: parents and grandparents and the minister too.

McCrohan and Kollias also joined in the applause, then went back to talking to the Opportunity kids sitting with them. They hoped that by going on the trip they would be able to get the kids to open up. Though the Temple youngsters were polite and responsive, neither woman felt they had succeeded. "I guess they're just different from the let-it-all-hang-out city teenagers we're used to," Kollias said. "But they sure are nice kids—every one of them."

Jones sat at the back of the bus after his speech. There seemed to be some sort of special compartment behind the last row of seats. (They discovered later it was Jones's private compartment.[1]) The buses reached Fresno at eight in the morning, parking a few blocks from the newspaper's offices, and everyone seemed to know exactly how to line up as they disembarked. The teachers followed Jones and the protesters. Temple members distributed neatly lettered picket signs with messages about freedom of speech and First Amendment rights from a large bundle.

The teachers took the signs and dutifully marched around the newspaper office building, chanting and singing along with "We Shall Not Be Moved" and "We Shall Overcome." After an hour or so, Morrow and Vogel stepped aside, handing their signs to some Temple kids they recognized. They headed across the street to a shady park, and sat on a bench in their shirtsleeves. From a brown paper bag given to them on the bus, Vogel pulled out a peanut butter and jelly sandwich. They noted that Temple members made up most of the *Fresno Bee* protesters.

Vogel did his best to make Morrow laugh, pointing out and commenting on the attire of people as they walked by. People in Fresno looked decidedly different from those in San Francisco. At about noon they found a café, had a burger, and headed back to where the bus was parked. The driver let them climb in to relax and talk.

Later in the afternoon the others joined them. Some of the buses went on to Los Angeles, where the Temple had another church. For the others, the ride back to San Francisco was quiet, and Jones was nowhere to be seen. Later that day, however, the Fresno Four were released.[2]

When the Temple kids returned to school, Bebelaar asked Kollias if Stephan had been on the trip. She said she hadn't seen him in the group.

Testimonial

At their Monday faculty meeting a week later, Golden told the staff about a testimonial dinner that had been held at the Temple the previous Saturday in honor of Jones and his ministry. There had been hundreds present at the dinner. Others watched on closed-circuit television from other locations. The Temple claimed as many as eight thousand people witnessed the ceremony. The Church had been transformed into a dining hall with white linen tablecloths and potted palms. Willie Brown, then a member of the California State Assembly, presided as master of ceremonies. Phillip and John Burton, both then serving in the U. S. House of Representatives, were there, as well as Mayor George Moscone, attorney Vincent Hallinan, and Lieutenant Governor Mervyn Dymally. Activists Angela Davis and Eldridge Cleaver also attended. State Senator Milton Marks presented Jones with a plaque engraved with a resolution passed by the California State Senate. Describing Peoples Temple, it read, "This is an outstanding institution which has shown that hope and love still reside in this city." San Francisco Supervisor Robert Mendelsohn awarded Jones a Certificate of Honor on behalf of the Board of Supervisors; Reverend Cecil Williams presented a plaque on behalf of Glide Memorial Church. The Fresno Four were present to publicly thank Jones for leading the protests that led to their release, and one of them read part of the group's letter thanking Jones.[3]

Seemingly admired by everyone, Jim Jones was no longer just an unknown minister from Ukiah.

The Radio Show

One week after the field trip to Fresno, Cabral told the students in his Radio Production class about the new school superintendent, Robert Alioto, who had been selected as the best candidate following a nationwide search.

"This is our chance to find out more about Alioto. He's been here about a year now, which should be time enough to get the lay of the land. Let's interview him and find out where he stands. I've called him, and he's agreed to be on our show," Cabral explained.

The kids liked the idea. Manny thought that maybe the new superintendent could help the baseball team get much-needed equipment. With their teacher's help, the kids came up with some good questions to ask the new superintendent.

The radio studio was located on the top floor of John O'Connell Vocational High School on Florida Street, deep in the heart of the Latino-Chicano Mission District; Bebelaar had taken Creative Writing kids there a few times to do poetry radio shows. This part of the Mission District was gritty, full of rundown apartment buildings, single homes converted to duplexes, and small factories and businesses requiring low rents. The school, which looked like an old gray factory building, had been built in the 1920s like almost all the big high schools in San Francisco.

On the day of the show, as Cabral's class headed for his station wagon, they ran into Johnny Cobb, who, along with Tim and Jimmy, had come to visit Ron to discuss starting a baseball team. Johnny agreed to come along when he learned they were going to talk with the superintendent about the team.

At the tiny studio, program manager Ted Samuel greeted the students warmly. A wiry man in his fifties, Samuel vaguely resembled Pete Seeger, but with a graying mustache and beard, and smiling eyes behind wire-rimmed glasses.

"Welcome aboard! You guys ready to set the air on fire again?"

"Well, maybe try to shed a little light on things, Ted," answered Cabral, smiling back. "Is Dr. Alioto here?"

"He just called to say he'd be here shortly. Gives us time to get organized. Looks like we have enough chairs if you kids can share microphones in pairs. Just speak clearly and right into the mesh. And remember, when that sign over the engineer's booth lights up, you are on the air." Just then, the engineer's booth door opened, and Alan Farley, the station engineer, came out. A tall man with a warm smile, he reached out to shake Cabral's hand.

"Hi, Ron, kids. What's the music today?"

Manny handed him two albums. "Track three on this one, and five on the other for the closing."

"Cool. As usual, give me the signal for the fade out." Just after he returned to the engineer's studio, the superintendent entered the room. Robert Alioto was a small, trim man, probably five-foot-two, though a few inches taller with the aid of his obviously expensive black leather boots. His black hair and sideburns were just short of being too long, and he wore a black pinstripe three-piece suit with wide lapels. His tie was bold and bright.

The kids' eyes widened when they saw him. Debbie Liatos turned her head to hide a grin as someone covered a rising chuckle with a cough. Dr. Alioto definitely had

Ron at KALW with Debbie Liatos, Terry Preston

an East Coast take on style. Even on Montgomery Street, the fashionable business district where all the men wore suits, it would have been apparent he was not from San Francisco. Cabral approached Alioto with his hand held out.

"Thanks for making time for us, Dr. Alioto. I know you have a busy schedule, especially with the board meeting tonight."

Alioto shook Cabral's hand. "I'll tell you a secret: this is going to be a lot more fun. Thanks for asking me."

"We're just about ready to start. Ted will give us the signal when we're ready to go."

Ted came out to greet the superintendent. "Nice to see you again, sir. These kids have a good show going here. Glad you're going to be part of it today."

They took their seats and tested their microphones. Manny had made name cards for the other students: Tim, Debbie, and Johnny. They introduced themselves to Dr. Alioto. Samuel held up his finger, and the music for that day's program began. At Manny's signal to Samuel, the music faded out, and Manny began.

MANNY: You are listening to *The Natural High Express* on KALW, 91.7 FM, the school district's radio station, the oldest in the city, founded in 1941. This show is brought to you by the Radio Production class of Opportunity II High, and you just heard music from Stevie Wonder's hit album, *Songs in the Key of Life*. We picked the song "Ngiculela: Es Una Historia" because it's kind of like us: the words are in Zulu, Spanish, and English. That's the kind of school we are—many colors of people working together. And we hope, like Stevie says in the song, that someday "sweet love will reign throughout this world of ours." Today we have a special guest, San Francisco's Superintendent of Schools, Dr. Robert Alioto. We're hoping he'll share with us some of his ideas for San Francisco kids. And now to the show.

DEBBIE: Dr. Alioto, I'm Debbie Liatos. Thank you for granting us this interview. As you are still fairly new to the city, we'd like to welcome you to San Francisco, or as Herb Caen says in the *Chronicle*, to Baghdad by the Bay.

ALIOTO: Thanks, Debbie, it's a pleasure to be here with you young people. I wish I could spend more time in schools and at activities like this. How wonderful that you have your own radio show. From the sound of things, you're doing a very professional job here.

DEBBIE: Thanks, Dr. Alioto. We're starting a brand-new baseball team at Opportunity. We're hoping that even though we're a little school, and we've never fielded a team before, you'll support our efforts. Baseball is the national pastime, after all, and teaches kids about good sportsmanship and working together.

ALIOTO: You're right, and I believe all students should have access to many kinds of activities—sports, dance, field trips to interesting places, and projects like this one. There are more ways to learn than out of a book.

DEBBIE: Right on, sir! But I have a question for you. We read an article in class the other day from *Time*. It talks about "the range of difficulties facing urban school systems today: squeezed budgets, falling student enrollments, rising teacher militancy, and in some areas still-smoldering race problems." It goes on to mention you: "A few harassed superintendents believe that a move can be therapeutic. San Francisco's new school chief, Robert Alioto (no kin to Mayor Joseph Alioto), admits that he was not sorry to leave his old superintendent's job in Yonkers, New York, because there the president of the local teachers' union 'has a strong dislike for me.' Some shell-shocked superintendents maintain that true peace is possible only through retirement." What I wanted to ask is, one: How come the union president disliked you so much; two: Are you facing the same kinds of problems the article talks about in San Francisco; and three: What about that retirement comment?

ALIOTO: You did your homework, didn't you? Well, I really think it was a case of the guy simply not giving me a chance. And I know enough to know you have to get along with the AFT—or, here, it's the California Teachers' Association and the San Francisco Federation of Teachers. As to the other problems, yes our enrollment is falling, and more and more parents are enrolling their kids in private schools, which means a smaller budget for public schools. I want to try to bring some of those students back with good schools, safer schools. In the meantime, budget cuts have to be made, and that's never easy. We've had a few board meetings that turned pretty raucous, but for the most part, things are more laid back here in San Francisco. I think we can work things out with the unions and with balancing the schools racially, at least better than they are now.

DEBBIE: Well, we wish you luck, and hope you don't decide to retire too soon.

ALIOTO (SMILING): Thanks. I'm planning on staying put for a while.

Polished and diplomatic, Debbie would later in life become a politician herself. Next it was Johnny's turn, and he steered the conversation back to baseball.

JOHNNY: What I'd like to know is, who are you for in the World Series? The Reds or the Yankees?

ALIOTO: Well, I'm from Yonkers, so what can I say? How about you, Johnny?

JOHNNY: Me, I'm for the Reds, but we're all split here at Opportunity; I just say may the best team win. It's a great sport. We only hope we get a chance to play the game ourselves as a school district team.

ALIOTO: I'm hearing what you're saying. You keep in touch with me about how things are going, OK, Johnny?

JOHNNY: Yes, sir!

Manny spoke next.

MANNY: Dr. Alioto, I'd like to ask what you think about how our schools are so split, color-wise.

ALIOTO: That is a very astute question, young man. I have a plan to try to make the racial balance in schools more equal. We can't just move everyone around, or young people like you will be riding buses instead of studying for an hour before and after school. But I think we can make a top of, say, 40 to 45 percent of any one race in any one school, and maybe make the populations more balanced. I also think there should be more schools like yours, alternative schools, so kids and their parents have a choice about the kind of education they want, and I think those schools, like yours, will achieve a natural balance.

MANNY: Actually, Dr. Alioto, Opportunity already has a planned balance. We try to make our school represent the percentage of different races and groups in San Francisco. But if someone has a real special problem, like go to school or go to jail, we try to help out, no matter what color they are.

ALIOTO: I'm glad to learn that about your school. It was planned by a group of teachers, right, and Opportunity I as well?

MANNY: Yes, sir, and what's most important, I think, is that we get a lot of choices in classes, more than at regular high schools. For instance, they didn't have a class like this, or Creative Writing, at Washington. We put together our own books, and do a poetry radio show here. Giving kids choices like that is important.

DEBBIE: I agree. Some kids don't like to come to school when they feel they have no choices, and lots of kids, as you must know, aren't coming to school these days. Speaking of choice, we won't have the choice to field a team if we don't even have a place to practice. You know Opportunity is an old office building, with no grounds at all.

ALIOTO: That's one of the problems with finding homes for alternative schools, Debbie. We have to find what the district can afford. Building a brand-new school with a gym and playing field and auditorium is very expensive. At least you've got a kitchen for that cooking class. But I'm sure I can help Mr. Cabral find a field to use on a regular basis. That shouldn't stand in your way, as long as you can get yourselves there.

DEBBIE: We'll get there; don't you worry, supe!

ALIOTO: I like your enthusiasm, young lady!

MANNY: Dr. Alioto, I'd like to know if you support the arts and music in schools, and I'd like to know why we have a top academic school like Lowell, which is mostly white and Chinese, and which has the best of everything in the way of equipment; and a school like Mission, which is mostly Latino and Chicano, or Wilson, which is mostly black—and at both places, the kids have rundown conditions. Is that fair?

ALIOTO: I certainly do support the arts and music, Manny, and I'm fighting to protect those programs from the budget cuts, but it's not easy. You must know there's an admission policy at Lowell. You get good enough grades, and you can apply there. It's a great school, academically. But I agree, those kids at Mission, at Wilson, at Galileo deserve better. We're working on that, applying for grants and using federal money when we can.

After a few more questions, including a few more about the baseball team, the show ended with Manny announcing that the next show would feature the Opportunity baseball team.

MANNY: And the week after that, Bob Morrow will be our featured guest. Bob teaches music and reading at Opportunity, and plays jazz. He's going to play some of his favorites: John Coltrane, Miles Davis, Charlie Mingus, and Charlie Parker. Following that, we'll have the Creative Writing class, including yours truly, reading from our book, *In Small Dreams*. Tune in next Wednesday at three thirty and get a lesson in baseball, the week after for a lesson in cool jazz, and the following Wednesday for some poetry by the people, for the people, and of the people. Until then, we'll leave you with a little message from Aretha.

Manny signaled Alan in the booth, and Aretha's "Respect" closed the thirty-minute show.

When the ON THE AIR sign over the engineer's booth went off, the station engineer and program manager came out. "Great job, as usual, kids," Samuel said, as everyone shook hands. "I look forward to those next three shows."

A ragged and excited chorus of "goodbyes" and "thank yous" echoed in the little room. The kids chattered all the way to the small metal elevator.[4]

On-Air Encore

After the Radio Production class's interview with the superintendent, Cabral made plans for a baseball show. It opened with Calvin Williams—like Johnny, from the Temple—doing his Howard Cosell imitation. He was pretty good, getting Cosell's slow, sonorous cadence, New York vowels, and nasal twang just right: "Good afternoon, sports fans. Today I am in the studio with some high school ball players that you will soon be hearing much more about."

"Hello, Howard, I'm Billy Oliver, catcher for the Cobras, the newest team in San Francisco, and we're Number One!"

Mondo chimed in, mimicking a recent television roast: "And I have the fastest glove in the West—I dare anyone to hit it past me. I am the Muhammad Ali of baseball!" The other kids chuckled in the background.

Tim announced, "Howard, I am the pitcher for the Cobras, and I'm working on my fastball and change-up and hope to have a great season. I also want to thank the Peoples Temple for supporting us—the Temple does good things for seniors, for animals, tries to help everyone it can." Tim probably said that partly for his mother's benefit, as she was proud of her baseball-playing sons, and partly to convince his father that the Cobras could be an asset to the Temple.

Calvin, in Cosell's voice, asked, "So Calvin, how is the team looking so far?"

Then he answered in his own voice, "Well, Howard, with me on third base, I am just hoping everyone on the other teams will hit their balls to me: They will be thrown out for sure!"

As the banter bragged on, Cabral joined in the laughter. The Temple kids seemed to be loosening up a little, getting more comfortable with being a part of Opportunity.

The next show featured Dorothy. She opened with music from the Temple's album, *He's Able:* first "Welcome," sung by children of the Church, then "Walk a Mile in My Shoes," a beautiful gospel piece. Dorothy talked about the good works that the Church did with seniors and drug addicts. Then she spoke about the Fresno Four and how the Church believed in defending free speech. She had a good voice for radio, and the aplomb of someone much older. Her love of Peoples Temple and admiration for Reverend Jones were obviously sincere.

Chapter 5

The Cobras Practice
and the Temple Pays a Visit

Fall 1976

St. Mary's Park

or several weeks Vogel and Cabral played catch in Plum Alley between classes and after school, hoping to attract more players to their newly forming team. Vogel pitched fastballs that popped into Cabral's glove with a *wwwhap!* Cabral had been a catcher in high school, and Vogel had pitched in both Little League and high school.

The San Francisco school district assigned the Opportunity team to St. Mary's Park, an old baseball field located at the south foot of Bernal Heights off Mission Street. A few shaggy Monterey cypress trees and modest beige, pink, or white stucco houses crowded against the thirty-foot cyclone fence that surrounded the scruffy field.

The team's first preseason practice in early October was on a cold, gray day, the air heavy with rain, the ground soggy. It did not go well. First of all, to get to St. Mary's by public transit, most students had to transfer from one bus to another. The closest stop was two miles from the park. Cabral and Vogel had to drive most of the team members to practice. Six players unfolded themselves from Vogel's old Volkswagen bus and six more from Cabral's Buick Estate wagon, only to find the rusty gate locked and the field in great disrepair: The tall grass was speckled with clumps of wild mustard, and the diamond base paths were uneven. It took twenty minutes for the teachers to locate the park director to open the gates. The bathrooms, the boys soon discovered, were either locked or out of service.

Junior, who had taken the bus instead of riding with them, came jogging in to where the group stood near the dugout.

"Man," he said, "I had to wait about half an hour for Muni, and it was a long way from Mission to here. Ron, I'll come with you next time."

"Good plan, Junior," Cabral responded. "We'll all squeeze in. Why don't you guys run out and scrape dirt off the bases. Looks like they've been buried in mud from these rainstorms. And check out the outfield." Cabral had played on this field with the Columbia Park Boys Club team back in the fifties, when it had been in pristine condition. "It sure has degenerated over the years," he said to Vogel, who nodded.

"Surprise, surprise. But man, Ron, this sure is a better group of players than the ones we got before. Thirteen, I count. And most of them look like athletes."

Cabral made a visual survey of the boys. Although most were dressed in jeans and tennis shoes, and only Tim had spikes and a glove, it did look like a promising group.

"OK, guys. Let's warm up: Around the park with Norm." Vogel took off jogging. The team followed, most of them moving like athletes, Cabral noticed, loping smoothly, shoulders and arms natural and easy. Mondo Griffith had a football player's build and a dark, handsome face. He ran beside Calvin Williams, also from the Temple. Calvin could pass for a man in his twenties, especially given the sport coat he always wore. He was over six feet tall, agile and strong. As in the classroom, he was obviously ready to go to work. Any coach in San Francisco, Cabral said, would want Calvin on his team.

Jimmy and Tim Jones—one black, one white—were both tall and strong, though Jimmy was leaner. Stephan hadn't joined his brothers, though he no doubt would have if Opportunity had had a basketball team instead. Jimmy and Tim ran behind Calvin and Mondo, followed by Johnny Cobb and Billy Oliver. The tallest kid in the school, quiet and self-possessed, Billy was always dressed neatly. Today he wore a black sweater vest over a white shirt—not exactly baseball togs. He had a big smile that made you want to smile right back. Johnny too was tall and long-limbed, his hazel eyes serious.

Junior, Manny, and Ricky Johnson jogged behind Billy, punching one another in the shoulder and laughing from time to time. Ricky, like Junior, had a huge Afro, while most of the other Temple kids had neatly cropped hair. He was a happy-go-lucky kid, glad to be with his pals.

Behind Ricky was Teddy McMurry. He was the smallest of the Temple kids, but wiry and athletic. Teddy didn't smile much, and wasn't as easygoing and self-assured as the other Temple boys on the team. Bebelaar worried about her counselee a little, but he came to school every day and had these guys as friends.

Lagging a little behind, but obviously doing his best to catch up, was Mark Sly, the only other white student besides Tim and Junior. Mark was slender, slightly taller than Teddy, a good-looking kid with even features and brownish blond hair cut short. He was serious, and had a narrow, sensitive face and a quiet manner.

Far behind Mark were two other kids, new to Opportunity but not from the Temple, boys with troubled pasts who had been drawn in by watching Vogel and Cabral tossing balls in Plum Alley. Lap after lap, they lagged farther and farther behind. When the kids rounded the field six times, Vogel led the group in doing push-ups and jumping jacks. Most seemed to enjoy the warm-up, but the two new recruits gave up after fifteen push-ups, and sat out the jumping jacks. The next time Vogel turned to look at them, they had disappeared.

Cabral told the boys, "OK. Take a quick break, then take your places. Tim, pitcher's mound; Ted, center field; Junior and Mark, left. Mondo, you take second, and Johnny, shortstop. Ricky, you're on first, Manny and Billy, alternate as catchers, and Calvin, third base." Cabral asked Jimmy to help Vogel keep an eye on the action on the field. Jimmy had natural charisma. All the boys respected him, and knew that he would be fair in his reporting.

"Let's see what kind of arms you boys have," Cabral said. "I'll hit some grounders to see how well you can field a ball and make a throw." He tossed a ball and hit a sharp one out to Calvin on third base, who scooped it up and threw it to Ricky at first.

"Good job, guys." The next ball went to Mark in left field, but a clump of weeds got between him and the ball. He retrieved it and threw it to Mondo, who did a neat twirl on one foot after catching it. This caused Junior to fall down laughing.

"OK guys, let's get serious here. You guys want to play, or play ball?" asked Vogel.

"Sorry," said Mondo, and handed the ball off.

Junior tried to stifle his laughter.

The team practiced for another hour, until it was finally too dark to see the ball. In a cold drizzle, the boys headed toward the cars. Cabral commended them for doing well and said that he hoped they would find at least two or three new players.

The Cobras made the trip to St. Mary's two or three more times; each time, a few kids arrived late, grumbling about the bus or the long walk from Mission. Fearing the players would just give up, Cabral asked the city park and recreation office if there was another field closer to Opportunity. To his surprise, the school district reassigned the Opportunity team to Jackson Park, in the Potrero Hill neighborhood a couple of miles away. After just two practices at their new field, three more players came to try out.

Jackson Park

Wesley Breidenbach, from the Temple, was one of them. Wesley was a favorite among his teachers, as he asked intelligent questions and pulled others into discussions. He was six feet tall and broad-shouldered, with a narrow face and serious brown eyes. He was white but, like Tim, he managed to make his curly brown hair look like an Afro, no doubt with the help of "perms" often administered by a girl.

The Miles brothers, also new to the team, had arrived at Opportunity prior to the Peoples Temple students. John Miles was a year older than his brother Mike. Both were good ball players, definitely strong additions to the team. By late fall, almost everyone was regularly showing up for practice.

Still the Opportunity team was not officially recognized by the school district and had only the bare minimum of equipment. Cabral had hoped to get funding from the SNACK Sunday Concert held the previous spring. Bill Graham, the famous rock promoter in San Francisco, had produced a concert to benefit school district athletic and music programs and had raised $200,000. Marlon Brando presented a check from Graham to a school district administrator. Bob Dylan, Neil Young, Joan Baez, Jefferson Starship, Jerry Garcia, Santana, and the Doobie Brothers had all performed for the Kezar Stadium crowd.

But no one from the district's athletic association answered Cabral's phone calls and letters, either about money or making the Opportunity team official. He was almost ready to try another protest, like one he had organized in 1975, in an effort to get the school's team recognized. Then, he had gathered several students who wanted to play baseball, a boy named Don Jennings being the most enthusiastic. Together Cabral and the boys headed down to the nearby school district offices. Bats on shoulders, smiling and waving at curious bystanders, they marched three blocks from the Opportunity campus up Van Ness Avenue. Their destination: "135," as the administrative offices were known to students and teachers, a fading 1920s adaptation of a Moorish temple with minarets and tile work, just down from the Opera House, the Museum of Modern Art, and City Hall. When they arrived, Don, who had the look of a baseball player, and another student took positions at the building's temple-like entrance while the rest of the boys marched in a circle banging bats on the concrete, chanting loudly: "We want baseball! We want baseball!"

Their ruckus had caused drivers on Van Ness to slow down and honk their horns; soon, the sounds of the traffic jam added to their noise. When a woman asked Cabral what they were protesting, he replied, "We're a little school with a great team, and we're tired of being ignored."

"Well, good for you!" she said, smiling at the boys.

A small crowd of pedestrians stopped to watch. People on the third floor of 135 peered down from their windows. Then two black-and-white police cars, lights flashing, pulled up to the curb. An officer got out of his car and came over, one hand on the butt of his revolver—though there was a smile in his eyes. He asked Cabral in an Irish brogue, "Now what's all this about?"

"Baseball, officer," Cabral explained. "I'm a teacher, sir. The district hasn't answered my letters requesting to be in the league, so we thought this was the only way to get their attention."

Just then a burly, glowering man with close-cropped gray hair came down the marble steps, brushing past Don and the other boy at the doors. He was Armand "Turk" Terzian, the district athletic director who refereed professional football games on the side; he looked as if he could handle any problem on the field. He had previously told Cabral, "There's no chance, not in a million years, that your school of goofballs is going to get a team approved by me."

Both police officers smiled at the director, then one said, "These kids seem to really want to play baseball, Turk." Terzian ignored the comment and parked himself nose-to-nose with Cabral. "So it's you again. Get those kids out of here—now! If necessary, these officers will help you." There was no smile on his face.

Cabral hoped that, with all those people watching, Turk might feel obliged to at least give them a chance. He apologized for the disturbance and said they would leave. As the boys followed him to the corner, a few bystanders clapped. The boys smiled and held their bats high. They crossed the street and headed back to Plum Alley, the kids talking excitedly the whole way. Unfortunately, nothing came of their protest, and the kids, except for Don, eventually stopped showing up for practice.

Opportunity continued to be ignored by the school district.

Meeting with the Principals

Cabral didn't have to plan another march. To his surprise, just when he was losing hope that an Opportunity team would ever be recognized by the district, he got a phone call from Turk Terzian, of all people, who told him to report at the next meeting of high school principals to advocate Opportunity High's admission into the league.

A week later, Cabral entered the meeting room full of gray-haired men in gray suits. He had worn a suit jacket and dress shirt with his jeans. His long hair had been cut as of the previous April; he had said he would do so when the war in Vietnam was truly ended. It had not so much ended, as painfully ground to a halt—beginning in 1973, when the Paris Peace Accords were signed, to 1975, when helicopters dangling with desperate people left Saigon with the last U.S. personnel.

Though the teacher had also taken care to trim his sideburns neatly, he felt the men, most of them older than the Opportunity staff, looking at him somewhat disapprovingly.

When the agenda item for Opportunity High came up, Cabral took a deep breath and stood.

"I'm Ron Cabral, Opportunity II. We've got a group of kids who have been coming to practice, faithfully, believing that you principals will let them become an official team. All these kids want to do is play ball. We have a team and some support. They've been working hard. They deserve the opportunity," he paused, "to show what they can do."

The vote was close but the motion to recognize the team as one sponsored by the school district finally passed. Opportunity was now a member of the JV Division for a one-year trial. All the team needed was equipment and uniforms. At this point, they only had a softball catcher's mask, a few balls and gloves, and some wooden softball bats. The principals said nothing about funds, and Cabral didn't want to push his luck by asking. They would get them somehow. When he got back to his ball players, he told them, "Sometimes you do get what you want."

◈

In Cabral's journalism class, the students decided to hold a contest to name a team mascot, and to choose the colors and a logo. They came up with three possible names: the Saints, the 76ers, and the Cobras. Cabral thought the students would choose the Saints because of all the Temple kids on the team, but Cobras was the winner. The cobra, as a snake and as a symbol, appears several times in the 1973 Bruce Lee movie, *Enter the Dragon*, which was popular with urban kids. They chose red, black, and green as the team colors, the colors of the Pan-African flag: red representing the blood that unites all African people that was shed for freedom, black for the unity of all black Africans, and green for the wealth of natural resources in Africa.

Contest results in hand, Cabral, Vogel, Manny, Tim, and Junior walked to a nearby sporting goods store on Mission Street to order uniforms. The owner offered a discount when Cabral explained who they were. However, since three colors would cost more, the group agreed red and black would do. They pored through catalogues until they found what they wanted.

A week later, Cabral brought brown paper packages up to the classroom and let the boys open them. The red team jerseys had COBRAS spelled out in black on the chest and black numbers on the back. The caps were black with a white O on the front.

Without the funds in hand, Cabral had paid the tab, telling the kids, "I'll figure out some way. We've gotten this far."

Since the Cobras continued to struggle to pay for uniforms and equipment, Cabral decided to appeal to Jones himself who frequently appeared in local articles with his name linked with good causes and important political figures. In mid-October he and Hal Abercrombie, a longtime supporter of the team, wrote a letter asking the Temple for a small donation. They didn't really expect the Church to help—especially knowing Jones's aversion to organized sports—but having dreamed of an Opportunity baseball team for years now, they considered it worth a try. They pointed out that many of the team's best players were teenagers from the Temple.

The Temple Comes for Open House

Simultaneously, the school had just sent out its six-week grades, and the staff was making plans to hold their open house. In the past, Bebelaar and Kollias brought homemade cookies, mixed fruit punch in the kitchen, and brewed an urn of coffee for open house. Sometimes the evening included a talent show or a musical slideshow of student life produced by Liu-Klein and his students. Copies of *The Natural High Express* and *In Small Dreams*, along with other student writing and projects, were displayed on tables and in classrooms.

This year, Golden announced it would be different, thanks to Jones and the Temple. "We are being treated to a delicious dinner with turkey, dressing, and all the fixings. Jones will speak and the Temple singers and dancers will perform. I want you *all* to be there, so make sure your students know they won't want to miss this. Give them extra credit if you like—but get them there!"

On Wednesday evening, October 20, two big Temple buses pulled cautiously into narrow Plum Alley. The principal and a group of teachers went out to greet the visitors. From the first bus came several women bearing pots, boxes, and baskets filled with food, and a large group of smiling and laughing Temple Opportunity students. Some of the kids guided Church elders down the steps. The Temple members seemed to be wearing their Sunday best. There was noisy, happy chatter as they entered the first-floor lobby and assembly room.

Women from the Church laid the tables with paper tablecloths and napkin-wrapped place settings. Two men set to carving two turkeys and a big ham. Young people laid out pans of mashed potatoes and yams, bowls of gravy and stuffing—all steaming hot and smelling wonderful. The staff looked on in amazement as the tables in the front of the room filled with food: dinner rolls, dishes of cranberry sauce, several pies, a big bowl of salad, and a bowl of fruit punch.

The teachers' cookies were added to the array, and Bebelaar and Kollias offered to help the Temple women who were setting tables. A small crew of students helped too—for extra credit. Though the Temple folks had everything under control, they welcomed the school's contributions.

Jones entered the room and Golden went to greet him. He wore a dark blue suit and his trademark sunglasses. She gave him a hug, sat him at the head of the first table, and sat down next to him, talking animatedly. After a tasty feast, with many of the kids going back for seconds and thirds, Golden summoned the assembly to take a seat in the rows of chairs that had been set up.

One older woman caught Bebelaar's eye. She wore what looked like a hand-woven Guatemalan shawl; her dark curly hair, combed back from her face, had a swath of white in the middle, just above her forehead. She wore glasses and had a notebook in her lap, a pencil in her hand, ready to take notes. No one at the school knew the woman, but her name was Edith Roller, and she was Jones's official recorder for Temple meetings and outside events.

Edith Roller

Golden waited for people to get settled before she spoke into the microphone. "I want to introduce a very special person from a special community that ... " Here she paused, then continued. "I am just absolutely, just—I'm overwhelmed with the kind of support that we've had ... Before we bring on some student entertainment, I want this person to say a word. For those of you who don't know him, he is a marvelous person. He's the best thing to ever happen to San Francisco, and I'm not just saying that. I really mean that!"

The visitors burst into long and loud applause as Golden smiled broadly. Some students and teachers were taken aback by the length and volume of the clapping and cheering. Eventually, Golden continued. "He is a minister of a community. He is a community activist. He is a developer and an advocate of people's programs in San Francisco. There's a very nice—he has a very huge, I should say, Temple and congregation here in San Francisco and in L.A., and he puts what everyone else has told me that's supposed to be Christianity, *he* puts it to work. He has ... senior citizen programs. He has a drug treatment program. He has a daycare center program, and he's out in the community, and he's making himself heard and ... known. I'm ... really thrilled—*I'm thrilled*—that we've got such a supporter because, I know, I know, what they will do and not do to you when you have that kind of support."

At this point, her talk turned personal. "I'm a *victim* of what the system has done to you. I was *arrested* in my school and put in jail because I stood up against the Nazi party." To this the Temple crowd applauded wildly again. As the gospel-church-style clapping and shouting rang on and on, Jones beamed at Golden. She continued. "We've asked [this person] to come tonight and say a few words, just a couple of words. We don't want to be too long tonight because we want to allow a lot of time for parents to talk to the ... students' teachers. ... And that person is none other than Reverend Jim Jones."

When the crowd eventually quieted down from its now-predictable roar, Jones announced: "First, I would like to present a check for $200. It was brought to our attention ... for a need for physical educational equipment, and we wish we could do more. We're funding so many things across the entire city in the thousands of dollars, but it's $200, and we'll try to do more."

As the applause began again, Abercrombie looked back at Cabral sitting in the row behind him. Both were shocked, but pleased.

Jones continued: "This is the best lady that ever happened to our students. Although we have dozens of our own members here, we chose this high school. We didn't come because we had to. We chose it because it's got the best coordinator and the best teachers in my book, in the entire district. That's right."

This time the teachers smiled at the applause that followed. "It has flexibility. It exposes students to the broad range of information, experiences, curriculum . . . basic skills, survival courses, things I never learned in high school. Swimming, outdoor educational experiences and physical therapy. . ."

Now the teachers glanced at one another, perplexed. Physical therapy? They had no such class.

Jones continued, "A curriculum that's practical, applied to daily living needs, like filling out application forms, welfare forms, food stamps and job applications, as well as having college [requirement] courses. We certainly need to know how to fill out forms being that we are very much oppressed still in this society. . . . [You] only have to look at Yvonne's experience, how many times she has been attempted to be framed mainly because she speaks out her mind. . . . We want you to know, all of you at Opportunity High, we're behind you 100 percent. The most beautiful thing you do is . . . inspire free thinking, and you've got none of that to speak of in most schools. . . . I'm proud that our students—I speak on behalf of . . . a hundred of our students that are here, and they're all happy as they can be. And *thank* you for the privilege of being here."[1]

He finished his talk to yet another round of loud clapping and affirmations. Golden shook Jones's hand, then gave him another hug. "We have a treat for you all," she announced. "The Temple dancers and some of the Temple singers have come to give you a show in way of thanks." More clapping. The band had quietly set up in a corner of the room: an electric keyboard, drums, guitars, a sax, and a record player.

A woman stood and her powerful voice filled the room with "How I Got Over." Then female voices from around the room joined in the chorus. When the spiritual ended, Ollie Smith, Bebelaar's counselee, sang "Sophisticated Lady," backed up by the Church quintet, with her lovely clear voice. A tall young man from the Temple moved his chair to be closer to the front. Bebelaar noticed that he and Ollie, a beautiful, girl with shining, wide-set dark eyes, smiled at each other.

Next, a group of African dancers in skirts and halter tops shimmied to the steady rhythms from a row of conga drums. They whirled and stomped and brought the house down. Then the Soul Steppers performed Earth, Wind & Fire's "Sing a Song," and got the crowd to join in.[2]

There had never been an Opportunity open house quite like this one.

❧

Most knew that Jones had little regard for organized sports, so his wife Marceline had likely been the one to sway the reverend to let the Temple kids join the Cobras. He definitely wouldn't have donated $200 unless someone convinced him baseball was more than entertainment for capitalists. Cabral sent a note of thanks to Jones with an update:

> *November 21, 1976*
> *Dear Rev. Jones,*
>
> *I want to tell you how much I have enjoyed working with Tim, [Jimmy], John Cobb, and all the rest of the fine people from Peoples Temple.*
>
> *The launching of our '77 AAA baseball team has been made possible by the sincere interest shown in baseball by the over twenty-five [students] who went out for the team. We also appreciate your support and interest in our efforts.*
>
> *This team has unusual talent and will give the AAA a real surprise. Of the nine starters seven are from Peoples Temple—Tim Jones (P), Billy Oliver (C), Amondo Griffith (2B), John Cobb (SS), Calvin Williams (3B), Emmanuel Blackwell (RF), Jimmy Jones (LF/1B).*
>
> *Spring training begins in mid-January with scheduled practice games against John O'Connell. League play begins in late March. As coach, I can say we enter the league with no intentions of losing any games.*
>
> *The boys appeared on our KALW radio show The Natural High Express for thirty minutes of baseball talk—it will be aired Tuesday, December 7, 3–3:30 PM, and Friday, December 10, 3–3:30 PM.*
>
> *Thank God for the Peoples Temple,*
> *Ron Cabral, Baseball Coach*
> *Opportunity II High*[3]

When Cabral read the letter to the kids the next day, Manny said that he was not a Temple member but was "just friends with these guys." In fact, Manny and his mother and sister lived in the Valencia Gardens housing project, an oddly pink block of rundown apartments that was dangerous at night, with frequent arguments over drugs and money that occasionally involved gunshots. But Manny was not into drugs or fighting. All the teachers and students thought highly of him, and only decades later was his real story revealed.

Cabral later considered his letter to Jones naïve, even misguided. But at the time Jones was a front-page hero in San Francisco, sought out and supported by many politicians. Mayor George Moscone had recently appointed Jones to the city's Housing Authority. In a photo on the front page of the latest issue of the Temple newspaper, the *Peoples Forum*, Supervisor Bob Mendelsohn, Sheriff Richard Hongisto, and Governor Jerry Brown stood shoulder to shoulder with the reverend. Another photo showed Jack Anderson, a popular local columnist, shaking hands with Jones, extending his congratulations for the minister's participation in supporting the Fresno Four. Jane Fonda was

Jerry Brown and Jim Jones

one of many celebrities who had attended a service at the Temple. In the same issue of the *Forum*, there was a shot of Jones and Moscone at the San Francisco airport, where they were waiting to meet with vice-presidential candidate Walter Mondale. The preacher wore his new national celebrity attire: leisure suit, black shirt, and his trademark sunglasses.

Linda Mertle

A few days before Thanksgiving, Cabral noticed that Linda Mertle, a Temple girl in his reading class, had bruises on both arms and a blackening eye. Linda, who was white, sported a "'fro" like Tim Jones's, although hers was light brown, with slightly ragged curls framing her open face and square jaw.

Her large dark brown eyes were serious, and the dark circles under them made her look a little sad, belying her usual smile. She lived in San Francisco in Temple housing; her parents lived in Berkeley where they operated a home for the elderly. After class Cabral asked Linda what had happened. She said it was no big deal, just the result of some roughhousing with a friend that got out of hand. "I guess fighting—even in play—isn't really in my nature. Don't think I'll try that again." Though he questioned her further, she didn't want to say more, repeating that she was fine. The bruises looked pretty bad to Cabral.

A 1974 federal law against child abuse mandated that he report any suspicion or signs of abuse to authorities, so Cabral took his concerns to principal Golden who told him that she would check it out with Linda. "You don't need to bother about it, Ron."

When Linda was absent from class for two days after the holiday, he again asked Golden about the girl. "Transferred out," Golden reported. "Her parents moved to Berkeley a while ago. I guess she'll be living with them, going to Berkeley High." She sounded almost angry.

In retrospect, Cabral felt he should have paid more attention to Linda when he had the chance. Later, he learned more about the probable cause of her injuries and the real story behind her departure, that she had neither gone to live with her parents nor attended Berkeley High.

Natural High Express with baseball team 1977

Chapter 6

The Cobras Play

Winter 1976 – Spring 1977

Jackson Park

The Cobras' next practice was held at their new field in nearby Jackson Park. The neighborhood on the bottom slope of Potrero Hill had been home, consecutively, to Portuguese, Irish, Italian, Slovenian, and Russian immigrants, and then African-Americans during World War II. In the 1950s and '60s, writers and artists sought out the affordable yet picturesque Victorians.

The first thing Cabral and Vogel saw as they walked down the path to the field was the wooden sign: TONY LAZZERI FIELD. "Push-'em-Up Tony" Lazzeri, a San Francisco native, was a great New York Yankee, teammate of Babe Ruth and Lou Gehrig. Tony was the first Italian-American to rise to the status of a baseball leg-

Jackson Park

end. He got his nickname from the way he made hitting balls out of the park look easy.

This field, like the one at St. Mary's, was not in great shape; it had bare spots in the outfield, a rough and bumpy infield, and patches of weeds here and there. At least the outfield had just been mowed. The coaches spotted fourteen players waiting in the dugout: ten Temple kids and four others, including Junior, who not only showed up for every practice but was also attending his classes. Tim Jones had told Cabral that he would make sure the team showed up on time; clearly they had obliged. It seemed obvious that they were already viewing Tim as their leader.

Cabral had brought a few extra fielder's gloves and a catcher's mitt donated by friends. With what was left from Jones's $200 donation, he had purchased baseballs and metal bats from the Mission Street sporting goods store, as well as a surprise for the kids.

The team waiting in the dugout all looked like athletes, though not everyone appeared to be ready for official baseball. Several kids wore street shoes; some had no gloves. Cabral handed out mitts as needed and passed out jerseys and caps. He took a picture to commemorate the moment. Especially notable in the group were Vogel with his big beard, his cap sitting atop his wild hair, and Junior with his cap perched several inches above his head of thick curls.

The boys were set to run laps. After completing three or four, Tim, who hadn't even broken a sweat, headed to the mound and called out to Billy Oliver: "Let's throw some balls." They got a good rhythm going—looked almost like pros. Both Tim and Billy were much taller and stronger than most high school kids. In the few practices at St. Mary's, it was obvious that many of the boys had talent, but today was different.

A rumor was flying about among the kids that the Giants wanted Tim as soon as he graduated. When the coaches saw some of the pitches he had been working on—fastball, curve, knuckle ball—they saw real heat behind those throws. No longer running laps, the rest of the boys watched from the third baseline. Tim's brother Jimmy yelled, "Show 'em what you've got, Tim!"

Billy Oliver

Tim, who had been playing since he was a little kid, said later: "You know, I think I was born loving baseball. All of us guys who signed up do. We practice together, play whenever we can, which used to be more often when the church was in Ukiah and we had a field to practice on close by."

When Cabral called out, "Let's play ball!" Calvin headed to third base, Johnny stood at shortstop, and Mondo took his place at second. Mondo had attended Mission High the previous year, and had made quite a name for himself playing for the Bears.

Henry Flood and Kevin Eddy were the only non-Temple kids on the team, besides Junior and Manny; Henry was black and Kevin, white. Henry, who was also in the Creative Writing class, was related to Curt Flood, the famous player for Cincinnati and St. Louis who had challenged the reserve clause and helped initiate free agency. Henry believed that baseball was "in his blood" because of Curt, and had promised Cabral that he would never miss a practice.

As much as he loved baseball, however, Henry's main interest at school was Debbie Liatos, the student who had done such a great job interviewing Superintendent Alioto. Now and then the pair were spotted snuggling on the couch in the lobby, or nuzzling in Plum Alley after classes. One of Henry's poems, "Paint Me Like I Am," refers proudly to his color. "Paint me in my native land / Paint me as dark as the earth." They were a brave and beautiful seventies couple, Henry dark and muscular, Debbie blonde and lithe. The couple was representative of the fact that biracial dating was becoming more common in the Bay Area and elsewhere. At Berkeley High, students had recently staged a production of Shakespeare's *Romeo and Juliet*, cast with a white Romeo and black Juliet.

Debbie Liatos

Kevin Eddy, Wesley Breidenbach, Mark Sly, and Tim were the only white students on the team, Junior the only Samoan. Cabral remarked at a teachers' meeting that he didn't think "the boys really noticed colors. The Temple guys sort of set the tone for the team, and it's not an issue."

Kevin seemed to be a pleasant kid, quiet, like Teddy, but obviously glad to be on the team. He didn't seem like a troubled student; he just wasn't much interested in school. Vogel had gone for a couple of runs with Kevin after school, and noted that the kid was fast. He asked Kevin to come to a practice.

By then Wesley was also coming. Abercrombie thought highly of Wesley: "He's really a thinker, likes to read, very politically aware." Cabral noted that Wesley was a good hitter and could pitch, too, adding, "You know, I think we really have a chance; most of these guys are naturals, and the ones that aren't are willing to work. It's a dream come true for me. They all love the game as much as I do."

Mark and Michelle

The team's youngest player, Mark, seemed unsure of himself, so the teachers spent extra time to nurture his strong desire to play. Like Henry, Mark had another interest besides baseball. Anna Wong, the art teacher, had mentioned to a group of teachers that Mark and Michelle DiQuattro, a non-Temple girl, sat across from one another in her class every day, talking quietly or just exchanging smiles. Wong was glad that Mark seemed to have found a girl-friend, and that he had joined the baseball team. It was no wonder that Mark and Michelle were attracted to each other: both were especially sensitive, a characteristic demonstrated in their artwork. Mark loved to draw detailed landscapes. He seemed lonely, but perhaps it was the introspective artist in him and he was just lost in his imagination. He was taking a risk by having a girlfriend who was not a Peoples Temple member. Although it was not known by the teachers at this time, the Temple rules forbade that their kids be in relationships with non-members.

Michelle's dad was a fairly well-known Bay Area musician, a pianist in a popular band, Azteca, with several albums to its name. Michelle lived with her grandmother in North Beach and had previously attended a Catholic school. Her "old country" grandmother was strict, so Michelle started run-ning away in middle school. Even on the run, she went to school whenever she could. Eventually she moved in with her dad and attended Jefferson High in Daly City, until someone suggested Opportunity.

A Change on the Team

Toward the end of practice, Jimmy hit a ball over the center-field fence that would have been a home run in any major league park. Cabral watched the ball sail up and away, thinking that maybe little Opportunity *could* take on some of the big high schools, despite their thousands of kids and fifty-year baseball traditions.

After a last lap around the field, with the other boys putting on their street shoes, Jimmy caught up with Cabral as he headed back to his car. His teacher noticed a kind of sad, reluctant look on Jimmy's face.

"Hey, coach," Jimmy began, "I'm really sorry, but I won't be here at the next practice. I . . . I can't really be on the team. I'm needed at the Church." Though Cabral tried to hide his disappointment, he kept seeing that ball soaring out of the park. Jimmy promised to attend as many games as he could, and that he would talk to some of the other kids who could play ball. When he repeated how sorry he was, Jimmy looked his teacher right in the eyes, looking about as sad as Cabral felt.

Later, Cabral told Abercrombie: "He's such a good kid, you know? Obviously he felt bad about letting the team down. So I just told him, 'That's okay, man. You gotta do what you gotta do. We'll miss you. Maybe things will ease up later.' Told him he could come back any time. He thanked me and headed out after the group on the way to the bus stop. Must be hard sometimes to be a preacher's son."

Jimmy could preach too, some of the teachers had heard. He was smart, eloquent, and seemed dedicated to his adoptive parents, Jim and Marceline Jones. Without them, he might have grown up in the orphanage where they had found him. Nevertheless, it must have been a hard choice to quit the team—if it had been a choice.

Lefty O'Doul, Country Joe, and Vietnam

Jimmy's leaving the Cobras was a blow, but even without him the team had a good chance to play well. The day after that first practice at Jackson Park, all thirteen players showed up after school for a team meeting, along with the two newest players, the Miles brothers. Kids sat on desks scattered around Cabral's room or perched on the window ledges. Cabral congratulated the team on a good practice, and told the kids they were going to have to work hard if they wanted a chance against the other schools. From then on, practice would be every day except game days, which would be twice a week once the season started.

"You guys have talent. You show up. And you listen. That's all we need to put Opportunity on the sports map. You know as well as I do that no one believes we can field a decent team. But we're going to show 'em." The boys' heads nodded to a rumbling chorus of assent. They were ready.

Cabral related a little of his own baseball history, telling them how he had gone to games played by the San Francisco Seals as a kid and waited outside the dressing rooms to ask for autographs from players: Chuck Connor, Lefty O'Doul, Reno Cheso. Ty Cobb, an old man then, had signed Ron's book at a youth baseball clinic in the 1950s. Ron passed around his autograph books along with letters he had received from Jackie Robinson, Ted Williams, and others. The kids handled the relics like the precious documents they were.

Cabral had been on Polytechnic High's baseball team, and had coached for his son's and daughters' Little League teams. When he joined the Navy in 1959, he met former Hollywood Stars player Mike Solomko in Japan. Solomko had been drafted and was playing for the U.S. Army team at Camp Zama, Japan. He later went on to play several years in the Japanese major leagues.

Wesley asked, "So what was it like to be in the Navy, Mr. Cabral? Did you sign up right after high school?" Cabral said he had, explaining that he had been having problems at home, thought it would help to get away, be on his own. "I'd seen those posters, guys looking cool in their uniforms on ships out at sea—sounded like adventure to me."

Natural High Express — Cobras 1977

"But weren't you against the war?" Mondo wondered aloud. Cabral explained that in 1961 he didn't know much about the war in Vietnam; no one did. "There were advisors there from our military, but I didn't know anything other than that Saigon sounded like a faraway, exotic place."

"Yeah," said Manny, from the couch in the corner of the room, paraphrasing a popular poster. "'Join the Army—or make that Navy—go to faraway exotic lands, meet interesting people—and kill them.'" Some of the kids laughed; some looked concerned.

Cabral told them about how he had met Country Joe McDonald, lead singer of the San Francisco band Country Joe and the Fish, who had played at Woodstock. Ron and Joe came to be buddies in the service.

Wesley asked, "Didn't he write that song, 'Well, it's one, two, three, what're we . . .'" Henry and Manny joined in, "'fightin' for. Don't ask me, I don't give a damn, next stop is Vee-et-nam.'" By that time, everyone was laughing.

At the end of the meeting, Cabral told the team he had uniforms and equipment covered, but that they would have to find a way to get their own cleats. Mark said that might give him some trouble. Could Cabral talk to his father? He told Mark not to worry about the cleats, that he would get some for him.

The next day, Mark told Cabral that his father wouldn't let him play at all. Cabral told Bebelaar about this when they were en route to their classrooms that afternoon. "Because he was needed by the Church, like Jimmy?" Bebelaar wondered.

"No," Cabral responded. "It seems his father is very strict with him, and money is an issue for the family."

The following day Cabral told Bebelaar with a smile, "I talked with Mark's dad and he changed his mind! He said Mark could play after all."

"What was it that changed his mind, do you think?"

"I don't know—maybe it was what I said about college scholarships and athletics that convinced him."

"I hope he does get the chance to go to college. Anna is trying to convince him to major in art. She thinks he's got real talent."

The conversation turned to Stephan, how they wished they could engage him more, have him join the team, sign up for Creative Writing. "He's going to his classes," Bebelaar said, "doing okay. But he looks kind of distracted. I wish I could get him to talk to me. He kind of has his guard up. And he always leaves right after school."

A New Kid on the Team

Word about the team spread rapidly around school, and several other kids got the bug to play, including senior Debbie Liatos, Henry Flood's girlfriend. She came into Cabral's classroom one day after class. Her hazel eyes held fire, and she spoke with determination:

"I know what you're going to say about a girl on the team. But let's face facts. You're lucky to have got a *guys'* team together. There will *never* be an Opportunity girls' team. I've played lots of softball and I'm really good, and I think it's about time a girl should get a chance to play baseball."

She went on, barely taking a breath, "I've dreamed about this since I was twelve. I have my own mitt and my own spikes, and I will make every practice and every game—cross my heart. Plus, you know I'm dependable. Don't I always come to class on time, with my homework ready? So, yes or no: Can I come out for practice?"

Speechless, Cabral paused for a minute, then admitted, "To tell you the truth, I never even considered having a girl on the team. You know the rest of the district already thinks we're . . . a little out of the ordinary—to say the least. Let me think about it, okay? I'll talk to you tomorrow."

Debbie looked disappointed. "I thought the teachers here were hip, that you guys don't believe in doing things the way they've always been done just because they've always been done that way. That's why I transferred here from Lowell. Way too status quo for me. And there, I wouldn't even *think* of asking if I could be on the guys' team. C'mon, Ron. Give me a chance."

Cabral said, "I promise you, I'll think about it carefully. I just have to have a little time, maybe talk to my wife about it."

Debbie smiled at that. "OK, coach. You ask her what she thinks!"

❧

There were no smiling faces when Cabral presented the team with the idea at the next practice.

"Coach, you are not serious are you?" Tim asked. From the looks on the boys' faces, he spoke for most of the team. Someone else added, "You know, a lot of people think it's bad luck to have a girl on the team." Cabral countered their worries as best he could. "You guys aren't superstitious, are you? You know what Stevie Wonder has to say about that."

Chagrined, Tim said, "Of course not. But other guys are. Might mess up their game." Another added, "And besides, she probably just wants attention or something. *We're* really serious."

Cabral, of course, knew Debbie was serious too, but said that, like all of them, she would have to prove herself.

He asked other teachers what they thought. Abercrombie laughed and said, "Hey, why not? Go ahead, let her try out and see what happens. She's in my karate class, handles herself very well."

It was the response of Cabral's wife, Rita, that decided it for him. "Of course she should be given a chance. Don't you want your daughters to have the same chances guys have been getting?"

The next day Cabral gave Debbie the green light to come out for practice. "What difference would it make at this point?" he said to Vogel, who seemed to enjoy the idea of a girl on the team. "We can always wait and see how she does. Who knows, this might prove interesting. Might make a statement. I'm sure Yvonne will be behind it. And don't forget that stuff Jones himself said to everyone about Eve not having been given a fair break in the Bible."

Vogel responded, "What the hell, maybe she'll make history as the first girl to play on a triple A baseball team in San Francisco. She has my vote."

On Thursday, Debbie showed up at Jackson Park with Henry. She got a few polite nods from the Temple kids, but no one except Junior, Manny, and Mark actually said hello. Debbie didn't appear to notice. She was smiling, and her long ponytail, hanging out from the back of her baseball cap, swung jauntily as she moved. Her shoulders were back; she looked ready to play with the guys.

Cabral asked her to take some fly balls in right field. Vogel hit a few long ones that she had no trouble catching—in fact, she made it look easy, which impressed the other players. However, even though there were smiles on the faces of Manny, Ricky, Wesley, Junior, Mark—and Henry, of course—but the rest of the guys looked glum.

When the practice got around to batting, Debbie proved she had a good eye too.

Wesley, who was pitching, was obviously unsettled. At first, he lobbed some balls over the plate that Debbie hit easily. Then he fired one across the plate. Debbie didn't swing, but she didn't flinch either. At the next pitch, just as hard, she took a good cut, and hit a line drive into the outfield that would have been a single. She repeated this feat again, and then again. On her tenth swing the looks of surprise from the boys on the bench only got wider.

"Nice going, Deb," said Henry as he came up to bat behind her. Tim and Johnny said nothing, their arms still folded across their chests. The dour looks had definitely softened though, and some eyes sparked interest.

After everyone had a couple of chances at bat, Ron sent Teddy and Manny to center field, Junior and Mark to left field, and Debbie and Mike to right. Vogel hit a towering fly to Mark, who caught it and threw it to the cutoff man in the infield, Johnny Cobb. Then Vogel hit one to Debbie. She got right under the ball and caught it easily, then threw it in. After practice, Cabral thought he heard Tim say to Johnny, "Man, she's a player." Johnny nodded, looking a little nonplussed. The growing feeling of grudging acceptance was palpable.

Cabral added Debbie to the roster as a position player. A girl had made the Cobra team! Opportunity was living up to its name.

Interviewing Giants' Catcher Mike Sadek

The baseball team's next piece of good news came when Mike Sadek—a catcher for the San Francisco Giants, with 14 runs and 9 RBIs in his previous season—agreed to be interviewed for the kids' radio show. Manny opened the program with a song that was unusual for him: Tony Bennett's "I Left My Heart in San Francisco." When he gave the signal, the music faded.

Mike Sadek

MANNY: We have a very special guest today, ladies and gentlemen. And we chose our lead-in music today to give tribute to our guest's team, the San Francisco Giants. The Cobras want to thank you, Mike Sadek, for honoring us with an interview.

Debbie began to applaud loudly and the others joined in, smiling at Mike, who grinned back at them.

MIKE: Manny, it's my pleasure.

MANNY: Let's get started then. I thought I'd begin with letting our radio audience know a little about you. Mike, known as "the Sheik" by his teammates and fans, has been with the Giants since '73, when he was drafted, a very good choice on their part. Last season he averaged .204, and in '74, .236, not bad for a catcher.

MIKE: And it's going to be a lot better this season, I can assure you, Manny!

MANNY: What kind of advice can you offer a new team, the first our small school has ever fielded?

MIKE: Play your hearts out, kids. And have a good time. It's all about love of the game.

TIM: We've got that part down, Mr. Sadek. And as I'm pitching for the Cobras, I'd like to know if you have any good words for me, like how I can tune in to the catcher better.

MIKE: Just stay focused, man, and keep your eyes on the signals and the ball. It's one of those simple things that takes years to learn so that it's just there in your eyes and your body.

DEBBIE: Hi. That was Tim Jones, our fantastic pitcher. And I'm Debbie Liatos. If it's not too personal, sir, could I ask where you went to college, and your sign?

MIKE: Not at all, young lady: University of Minnesota and Gemini. And I understand you're on the team too.

DEBBIE: Yes, sir. First girl in San Francisco on an official school district team, even though they made us start as JVs.

MIKE: I have to admit, when I first heard about it, you being on the team, I was a little shocked. But you know, after I thought about it, I said hey. If someone can play well and tries hard not to let their teammates down, why not? So I wish you luck, Debbie.

The boys exchanged glances. If Mike Sadek thought it was OK, maybe having Debbie on the team wasn't so weird after all.

MANNY: Mike, how much longer do you hope to play for the Giants?

MIKE: As long as I can be of value to them . . . and three years more.

The kids laughed.

At the end of the interview, Mike generously agreed to do another the following week.

❧

Bebelaar congratulated Cabral on the show the next day. He flashed a Sadek baseball card, which showed a good-looking guy, with shoulder-length dark brown hair, high cheekbones, and a narrow face framed by sideburns. "I really liked his way with the kids," Cabral said. "Treated them like adults."

Stephan Leaves

In late February, Golden appeared at the open door of Bebelaar's room, something she rarely did, and made a startling announcement. "Judy, I'm taking Stephan as my counselee. I'll need his transcript."

"Why? Is there something wrong? Is Stephan upset about something? He could be doing better, but his grades are good, and he has all the classes he needs toward graduation."

"It's a matter between me and his dad. Reverend Jones wants me to be Stephan's counselor."

Bebelaar searched for something that might have triggered this abrupt change. She felt fired. But Stephan was as friendly and polite as ever toward her, even though he still didn't seem to want to open up much. He was not in any of her classes, which would have made it easier to get to know him. She had always sensed that something was troubling Stephan. But maybe, she thought, he was just one of those sensitive kids for whom all of adolescence was agony.

Bebelaar went to her file cabinet and handed Golden Stephan's transcript, trying to point out his spring class schedule. "As you can see—"

"Never mind. I know what he needs." Golden, taking the papers from Bebelaar's hand, turned abruptly and left.

The next week, Stephan was gone. "He's gone to join his father on that Church project in South America," Golden explained when Bebelaar asked why she hadn't seen him.

"Will he be back soon, so he can finish his classes?"

"I've taken care of all that. He may be there for a while."

Big Wins

The Cobras began preseason games at the end of February. Tim as starting pitcher, had been had elected team captain. He seemed quietly pleased. "He's not at all conceited, just kind of modest about how the other kids admire him," Cabral said to Bebelaar who agreed: "Tim's like that in Creative Writing too, sure of himself, but modest."

Tim's extraordinary pitching skills would make him the most valuable player for nearly every preseason game. He had a strong fastball, and wicked curve and could strike out almost everyone he faced. But he wasn't the lone team hero: he got good support at bat from Calvin, Mondo, Junior, and Teddy.

The team won their first preseason game against O'Connell High. The following week, they beat Mission, 7–1; Tim struck out twelve batters, and at bat, drove in five runs. Then the Cobras won the Wilson game, 12–3: Tim struck out ten batters, hit a home run, and picked off three players trying to steal a base.

At the Washington game, the team had a surprise. During the second inning, three shiny black Chevy Impalas pulled up just outside the fence on the left of the field. Three men wearing dark suits and sunglasses got out of one car and came over to watch the game for a while. Tim was pitching a good game and had struck out the last batter. One of the figures, hands grasping the fence wires, yelled out, "Come on, Cobras! Show 'em what you've got!"

Smiling, Tim glanced over, and Cabral realized that had been Jimmy's voice. Was the tall one Jim Jones? And was Stephan standing behind him? They were too far away to tell for sure. After about twenty minutes, the men got back into their car, and all three sedans, in a kind of military precision, pulled out from the curb and disappeared down the street.

The Cobras won that game too, 4–3. The next day Cabral asked Tim to stay for a minute after class. He told Tim he had helped to put Opportunity on the map and that his skill encouraged the other guys to aim for their best, that the Cobras never would have won all those games without him. He looked good enough to draw some interest from colleges like the University of San Francisco or even U.C. Berkeley. Both schools had strong baseball programs. Cabral wanted to write a letter to Jackie Jensen, a U.C. coach and former All-American football player at Cal, as well as a major league player for the New York Yankees, the Washington Senators, and the Boston Red Sox.

Tim said that he would love to play ball for Jackie Jensen. "Please," he said, "write him a letter like the one you wrote my dad."

The next match was against Lowell at Jackson Park, and it was another exciting game. By the third inning the Cobras were leading, 4–1. In the fourth inning, though, Tim made a sudden throw to third, trying to pick off a runner inching toward home. Instead, he hit the Lowell third-base coach in the chest with an 80 mile-per-hour fastball. The coach, a fiftyish man with graying hair, went down with a thud.

Tim, his face stricken, ran over and knelt down beside the man. Cabral and Vogel joined them. It seemed many long minutes before the coach began to get up, holding his chest.

"I'm okay, it's okay, man," he said as Tim helped him to his feet, "but watch where you aim."

The game resumed and, once again, the Cobras won: 8–1. The victory was especially sweet for Debbie, as there were Lowell kids in the stands who knew her.

The Cobras won their sixth practice game, at Mission, in late March. The seventh and last preseason game, against Galileo, ended in a 15–15 tie. Not bad; Galileo had a good team, a good pitcher. The opposition coaches seemed stunned by the new team's successes. Some grumbled that the Cobras were fielding juniors and seniors, whereas sophomores made up most other JV teams. This was how the athletic league had allowed the team their chance, so there was nothing to be done about it. The Cobras, of course, counted on being a varsity team the following year. Later, when Cabral, Liu-Klein, and Bebelaar talked about the Cobras' wins, Bebelaar said, "Do you realize there are four poets on that team: Tim, Manny, Henry, and Mondo?"

"Right. I'm *sure* that's why they won, Jude," Liu-Klein said with dry humor.

Making News

In the lobby after school on March 23, Cabral read from the *San Francisco Progress* to several Cobras: "Opportunity Knocks, AAA Officials Listen: So beware AAA Varsity coaches of years to come. If the Cobras continue to perform as they have, a new contender could be waiting in 1978. . . . It seems that Cabral and company have surprised everyone, including themselves.'"

Cabral interjected, "I think Leo Pierini got that one right, didn't he? Then he talks about our winning six preseason games, tying the last, and goes on to our newest player."

Henry gave Debbie a mock trumpet introduction, bowing in her direction.

"*Henry!*" she protested.

Cabral continued reading: "The Cobras bring another unusual twist to the grand old game in the form of outfielder Debbie Liatos, a transfer from Lowell. She's the first female to ever play AAA baseball. 'We intend to use her as much as we can this coming year,' pointed out coach Ron Cabral. 'I can't say she's done anything spectacular so far, but she hasn't done anything wrong either.' Cabral believes Liatos will be a psychological plus for his club."[1]

Cabral said gleefully, "Did you guys see the way the Mission pitcher kind of lobbed the ball to Deb? They didn't know what to make of a female player."

"Hey, Ron!" Debbie bristled. "I don't want to be seen as just a kind of curve ball thrown at the other team! I know my hitting is not going well, but I'll do better next game. I was just a little nervous." She turned to the boys behind her. "You guys would be too, if you were the only male on an all girls' team!"

Tim and Johnny laughed. Mondo gave a low whistle as if imagining himself on such a team.

"Right on, Deb," Manny said. "You were solid. Maybe you didn't make a run, but you were no slouch either. None of us except Tim, Teddy, and Johnny can really brag about how we did at the Lincoln game. But did you see the looks on those guys' faces as we walked off the field? They didn't expect we'd give them a run for their money."

"Yeah!" they chorused and high-fived. Debbie smiled broadly at Manny. Henry lifted her ponytail and gave her a hug and a kiss on the back of her neck.

"And Manny's right, Teddy," Cabral said, "you were looking good out in center field." Teddy looked pleased, but didn't say a word. "Johnny, I was proud of you. And Tim, your curve ball is absolutely wicked. I didn't think it was possible, but you're getting even better. I think we're ready for the real thing."

The Cobras Lose Their Winning Streak

The Cobras won all their preseason games except the tied game with Galileo. The Lincoln game had been the first game of the real season, and counted toward their standing in the league. Lincoln played at Sunset Park, out near the ocean. It was almost always windy there, especially in the spring. The day of the game, the sky was blue and the Cobras felt good. They were first at bat and even had a little cheering section.

Debbie came up to bat, but struck out. Next, Mondo hit a double, sending Teddy all the way from first to home plate. Then Tim hit a long fly ball over the center fielder's head and slid into third with a triple, driving Mondo ahead of him. The Lincoln pitcher tried to pick off Tim at third three times.

There was a certain magic with Tim on the mound, but Cabral thought he looked tired in the sixth inning, and decided to bring Wesley in as relief. Tim didn't look happy when Cabral walked out to tell him, but gave his coach the ball without a word. And Wesley did strike out the next three batters.

Finally, it was down to the last batter in the Cobras' lineup: Mark. After swinging at the first two pitches he was hit on the right arm, which gave him a pass to first. The bases were loaded for Teddy, who had gotten a hit—and a cheer—every time he was up at bat. Abercrombie yelled: "Way to go, Ted!" Teddy had the biggest smile Cabral had ever seen.

It was now windy and the fog had started to roll in. The first two pitches were balls. All the guys on the bench and the crowd in the stands were yelling: "C'mon, Teddy! You can do it Ted! Hit one home!"

Teddy hit a hard liner down the third base line that was foul by inches. After one ball and four fouls, the Lincoln pitcher leaned back and came at Teddy with a furious fastball right down the middle. Teddy swung—and missed.

His smile was gone. The game was over: Cobras 7, Lincoln 10.

Cabral told Bebelaar and Kollias later in the cooking room: "We were all disappointed, but it was a hard-fought game, and Lincoln knew it. We've already proved we can play well. Still, it was rough on the kids. Norm and I did our best to talk up the successes of the game on the drive home. I told Teddy he was going to make a record for bases stolen. But when I reached back to pat him on the shoulder, he just nodded, looking glum. And I told Tim what a fantastic job he'd done, and Wes as relief. And Norm added his two bits. But both kids were kind of quiet. Tim seemed preoccupied."

They grew quiet.

As she looked out the window at the original Mel's Drive-In, closed and soon to be torn down, Bebelaar said, "Every time I look out there I think of *American Graffiti.*

"That was a great movie," Kollias said. "Not much like the teenage situation here in the City, though."

Bebelaar nodded. "It's so much harsher now, for city kids. Drugs and guns. And none of our kids have cars—except perhaps ones they've stolen for a weekend joyride. The teenagers in the movie seem like such innocents compared to ours. Though the Temple kids have a touch of that quality—naïve, maybe, but not in a childish way. I guess growing up in Indiana or Ukiah was something like growing up in Martinez thirty years ago."

Cabral offered, "One reason Rita and I bought a house in Concord is that it's a quieter world out there. And, of course, the fact that we could find something we could afford."

Bebelaar added, "John and I bought in Berkeley mostly because he was teaching in Richmond, and Berkeley was sort of halfway between his job and mine, but now we're glad Kristy's growing up in Berkeley instead of here. Every once in a while, just walking down the street, I'm aware that most city people wear a kind of psychological armor, especially in the neighborhoods where most of our kids live."

Then the bell started ringing, and the three headed off to class.

Chapter 7

More Departures

Spring 1977

A Visit from the Minister's Wife

On the morning of March 27, Cabral was called to Golden's office, where he found Tim and the principal sitting with Marceline Jones. Tim looked uncomfortable as he glanced at Cabral with an attempt at a smile. When Golden asked Cabral to sit down, Tim looked at the floor, which was not like him at all.

Mrs. Jones spoke quietly, "Mr. Cabral, we have decided to take Tim out of school as his dad needs him in South America at our agricultural mission there."

Cabral thought this must be some kind of error. She just didn't understand—Tim was the team captain, the starting pitcher, and potentially the best hitter. Trying to recover from his surprise, Cabral told her how talented Tim was, a real leader, and that he had even written to a coach at U.C. Berkeley about him. He asked if perhaps they could wait until after the season ended in May.

She replied politely but firmly, "No, I'm sorry, Mr. Cabral, his dad needs Tim now, and you must realize that the work of the Church is much more important than baseball, although his father and I certainly appreciate what you here at Opportunity have done for our boys. That's why I'm here, since we've already called Jimmy away, and now we have to take your star pitcher."

Golden said, "Of course we understand, Mrs. Jones." Cabral repeated, "Of course," though his heart wasn't in it. He turned to Tim. "We'll miss you." The two shook hands. Again, Tim forced a smile.

Two days later, U.C. coach Jackie Jensen, wrote that he'd be happy to follow up on Tim and suggested that Cabral stay in touch.

It wasn't certain if Tim would be going to *any* college, let alone U.C. Berkeley.

Without Tim

The Cobras' next game was with Lowell again, on April 1. As Cabral and Vogel waited for the boys in Plum Alley, Vogel said, "Guess it's April Fool's on us, thanks to the reverend. Maybe Bob and I shouldn't have gone on that bus trip. Maybe we didn't march hard enough to suit him."

April Fool's it was: The Cobras lost the Lowell game, 9–4. Their next game, with Wilson, had an even worse score: 16–2.

The Cobras played the fourth league game against Balboa on their home field at Jackson Park. April 14 was warm and breezy, the sky an intense San Francisco blue. Since Tim's departure, the pitchers had been Wesley and Mike and John Miles. Cabral decided to take some of the pressure off Wesley, who'd been nervous and worried since Tim's departure, so John Miles was the starting pitcher, with Wesley playing first base. The rest of the line-up remained the same with the exception of Debbie, who played right field—her first starting assignment. Manny was catcher, his first time. Billy sat out this game nursing a hand injury.

Balboa's first three batters walked. Then they got a home run, then two more runs. By the first inning the Cobras trailed Balboa 0–6—nothing new to them by this point—so Vogel suggested bringing Wesley back as pitcher.

Looking relaxed and in control, Wesley took the mound to start the second inning. One Balboa hitter sent a long drive into right field, and Debbie made catching the ball look easy. By now Debbie's hair had fallen out from under her Cobras cap, as it usually did by the second inning, and the Balboa players started to notice. The hoots and falsetto insults began.

By then the team had learned to act pretty cool, maybe even became more focused because of learning to ignore the predictable reaction to Debbie. But the Cobras didn't get a single player on base the second inning. Nobody from Opportunity had come to watch the game. Cabral was beginning to think it was just as well.

In the third inning, Wesley changed. He stood up tall; he looked determined. And he struck out the first two batters. But though the Cobras fought hard, the game ended in a tie, 12–12.

The Balboa coach came over after the game: "Good game, Ron. Your team looked like fighters." The players were glad to hear this, and hoped they could still turn their team around.

But then the Cobras lost their next game against Galileo.

Wesley and the Balks

It was a chilly April day at Funston Park in the Marina where the Cobras faced the Galileo Lions. Wesley had tried earnestly to take over the leadership that Tim had established, but he did not command the same respect, and walked as many batters as he struck out. Still, he was a good pitcher, and yielded a heavy bat, hitting over .300 for most of the season. He was easy to work with but tended to argue with coaches, sometimes the umpires too, when his sense of injustice was roused.

A "balk" is an illegal move a pitcher makes when he acts as if he is about to throw a pitch but never intends to. An umpire is likely to call a balk when the pitcher's foot leaves the rubber and there are runners on first and third. A called balk allows runners to advance one base. Ordinarily there are no more than one or two balks called against a pitcher in a game. The umpire at the Galileo game had called three against Wesley by the fourth inning.

Cabral was getting angry: it didn't seem to him that Wesley had balked except perhaps the first two times. Then the ump called another. This umpire was a big, heavy-set guy, and he had an ugly look on his face as he walked up to Wes and said, "Kid, that's illegal. And that's the fourth time. Cut the crap."

Wesley stiffened and said, loudly enough for the others to hear, "Ump, you're just trying to show you're in charge. My foot never left the rubber. You know it didn't. What is it that you don't like? My long hair? The fact that we have a girl on the team?"

Cabral heard the umpire growl, his face inches from Wesley's. "Just cut the crap, kid."

When the umpire called a fifth balk, Cabral ran out onto the field and said, as politely as he could manage, "Excuse me, sir, but I didn't see anything like a balk."

The umpire growled at Cabral too. "Listen. I've been in this game for thirty years. I know what I see and I call what I see, and if you don't get back to your bench right now, I'll throw *you* out of the game."

Cabral could do nothing but walk off the field. Wesley looked rattled, his face red.

After Debbie braved catcalls when she was struck out, Mondo came to bat with two men on base and hit a home run. The Opportunity crowd stood, cheering as Mondo roared around the bases. As he got near third, Wesley ran full speed out to congratulate him—but he was directly in Mondo's path and the two collided before Mondo reached home.

"You're out!" the ump screamed. "Interference!"

Wesley shouted back at him. "That's not right! That was a home run, fair and square. You can't do that to Mondo!"

It was clear by now that the ump had no love for any of the Cobras. The whole fiasco made Cabral wonder if there was some kind of league conspiracy to keep Opportunity out of contention. He walked over to Wesley, put a hand on his shoulder, and said, "Back to the bench, Wes." Cabral held out his hand out to Mondo, who was still on the ground, a look of stunned disappointment on his face.

When play resumed, the ump called Wesley on four more balks for a total of nine, which advanced quite a few Galileo runners. All in all, from having led the Lions 13–4 earlier in the game, the Cobras finished one run short, 16–15.

They lost the next two games: O'Connell, 6–2, and Mission, 7–1, though Debbie almost scored a run. Teddy, Manny, Calvin, Junior, and Johnny were solid players, but they were no match for the other schools' best players. The heart of the team had left with Tim. But even through the humiliation, the Cobras kept showing up. And Debbie kept trying, getting walked quite a few times and even making it home once. She and Henry had taken to curling up like two puppies in the dugout. The rest of the team ignored them.

The final league game was against McAteer on May 6. Another loss: 5–4. The season was over without one win.

And then, without notice—as with Stephan and Tim—Wesley, Calvin, and Johnny all left to help with the Temple's Guyana plans.

Mark Sly

Mark played hard for the Cobras. He had walked a few times and managed to steal bases and score some runs. Cabral thought it must have been rough for him when he was replaced in right field by Debbie. The other players had ribbed him about it, but he wasn't easily riled. He was also the editor for the Opportunity paper, and a good student. Anna Wong, the art teacher, talked to Bebelaar about him after school one day.

"You know, Judy, I think he has no idea how good he is. I told him his work reminded me of Escher's, very detailed, realistic, but surrealistic too—we've talked about surrealism in class. I told him I'd bring him an Escher book and suggested that he think about going to college to major in art. Cal has a great art department, though City College has a pretty good one too, since I know his parents don't have a lot of money.

"He said to me, 'Thanks, Miss Wong. I love drawing, especially drawings like this. But I don't think my dad has my going to art school in mind.' He said he likes more practical stuff—his dad is the mechanic for all the Temple buses. It's kind of sad. He's got such talent, and his dad doesn't seem to understand. I want to talk to Mr. Sly, to tell him just what kind of son he's got."

Bebelaar encouraged Wong, pointing out that Cabral had talked his dad into letting him play baseball. "So at least we know he's open to options."

Mark arranged for Cabral and Debbie, who also worked on the paper, to visit the head printer at the Temple to discuss their producing a special edition of *The Natural High Express*—its first non-mimeographed, real printing press edition. When the two arrived at the Temple, to their surprise two tall, burly men searched them before they were allowed to enter. As they walked through the door, Debbie turned to her teacher and asked, "What are they so afraid of?"

In mid-May, Mark came into Cabral's room after school wearing his trademark blue fisherman's cap with a red star. He joined Cabral on the small adjoining balcony overlooking Plum Alley.

"Here's the final layout for the *Express*," Mark said, handing his teacher a large envelope. "Well, almost all of it. I have a couple of questions about two of the stories and where they should go."

"Great, Mark. Thanks for all your work."

"And there's something else." Mark's tone changed. "You know, my parents have been Temple members for a long time. My dad wants me to go to Guyana. He said it would be a great experience for me. Toughen me up. Man, I really don't want to go. I want to stay here, play ball, work on the paper, draw. Miss Wong says I have talent. But Dad said he wants me to go there, this summer, for who knows how long."

"Is there any way you can get out of it," Cabral asked, "anyone you can stay with?"

"No, the only way I could get out of it would be to run away." He took off his cap and turned it around in his hands. "I pretty much have to do what my dad says."

Cabral thought back on the few times he'd spoken with Mark's father when he'd come to pick up kids after school. Don Sly seemed like a man who cared about his son, gentle and serious like Mark.

Cabral said to Mark, "Well, I joined the Navy because I had different ideas from my parents', but I don't think I should advise you to do that. It won't be long until you're old enough to make up your own mind, do your own thing. You're smart, Mark, and you know how to get along with people and how to get jobs done. You probably have to do this. But maybe put your mind on a couple of years from now—think about college, or a job you'd like."

"I guess you're right," Mark said. "You know, I'll miss this school. I really love some of the classes, especially art. And some of the kids . . ." he paused, looking a little stricken, "and the staff here, you guys really care about us—you're friendly and easy to talk to, different from some teachers I remember at other schools."

"I enjoyed getting to know you too, Mark. Sorry you'll be leaving. Keep in touch, okay?" They stepped back into the room, and Cabral watched as Mark walked to the door, stopped, and turned back. "See you, Ron," he said.

Cindy Explains the Temple

A couple of weeks later, a Temple truck delivered the special spring edition: four neatly tied bundles stacked just inside the front entrance of the school. Cabral, Liu-Klein, and Bebelaar were the first to see it. Raymond Berrios, her Creative Writing class aide, joined them.

Cindy Cordell

"Wow, Ron, is that *The Natural High Express*? It looks like a real paper! Very cool."

Cabral handed him a copy. "Look at this article Cindy wrote." Raymond and Bebelaar spread out the paper on a nearby table.

WHAT IS PEOPLES TEMPLE?
— *Cindy Cordell, a member of Peoples Temple*

Peoples Temple Christian Church, of the nationwide Disciples of Christ denomination of the two million members, is an organization many of us have heard a lot about lately. So surely many of us want to know exactly, "What is the Peoples Temple?"

Peoples Temple is many things to many people.

Its demonstration in September of 1976 on behalf of four jailed Fresno Bee newsmen is emblematic of its active role in society. The church based in the Bay Area, provides housing and care for the elderly and orphans, and dormitories for college students.

Its youth carry on many responsibilities rarely seen elsewhere. The youth take pride in helping seniors along their way, in tutoring other students wherever they can in schoolwork and simple trades.

Some of these youths' activities are volunteering services in passing out the church's newspaper, providing entertainment for community programs, setting up bake sales to raise money for the church's many services, and setting up field trips to places of interest where they may learn, such as a trip recently taken to Alcatraz. The youth of the Peoples Temple go to visit the sick and lonely in homes and hospitals, go to the church and volunteer to clean up and help in the church kitchen. They clean the church's eleven busses spotless without supervision. The youth of Peoples Temple also stay away from any unnecessary drugs and completely away from smoking and alcoholic beverages.

Peoples Temple operates a farm mission in South America to produce food for the underprivileged while teaching the nationals self-sufficiency and attempting to dispel a bad image of the United States.

It offers legal services and health care.

The Temple has a boat, which provides medical and agricultural assistance.

Each year it channels thousands of dollars to many charities.

In the last year the congregation's donations have:

- *Helped keep open a medical clinic in San Francisco.*
- *Provided emergency cash to distressed families, particularly those of slain law enforcement officers.*
- *Benefited research in the medical field of cancer, heart disease, and sickle-cell anemia.*
- *Supported educational broadcasting such as KQED.*
- *Boosted the treasuries of groups fighting hunger, building schools, developing hospitals, opening church programs, or working with Indians.*
- *Aided civil rights causes, both financially and through demonstrations, including those involving discrimination and jailing of the Bee newsmen and the L.A. reporter William Farr.*

Peoples Temple was described by one religious writer as the "most multiracial congregation ever seen."

"We go out of our way to break down all the barriers between socio-economic and ethnic classes," said Rev. Jones in one interview. "We find a very wholesome unison between all those people.

"We think there is something important in the Kerner Commission Report which said that we are heading towards two societies—separate but equal, one black and one white. One of the sharpest messages of the scriptures is that God does not see a difference in people."

One of the challenges of this church is that there are no barriers between young and old.

It is a church without permanent pews so that the facility can be transformed into a community center.

From there, area residents are offered free medical care provided by volunteer nurses and doctors, and free legal services provided by volunteer attorneys.

Additionally, there are geriatric facilities for the elderly, a drug rehabilitation program which has helped 125 persons kick the habit, and a food commissary.

However, unlike rescue missions, Jones said Peoples Temple does not require any kind of religious indoctrination of hungry persons before giving them food.

Rev. Jones said the money for all the Church's activities comes from members "and others just willing to help."

"We have no demand on tithing," said Pastor Jones. "When the congregation sees things happening they tend to respond. Some cases just stir people so that they put on rummage sales. That helps raise money."

Rev. Jones said the motivating force for many involved is the work or the cause.

"Freedom should be a concern for everyone," says Pastor Jones.

Raymond said, "I didn't know the Church did all that good stuff, did you, Ms. B?"

"I had some idea, from the articles I'd seen before, but this really gives details," Bebelaar said.

A Message from Dorothy

Dorothy came through the front door and walked toward Bebelaar and Raymond, a smile shining from her large dark eyes.

"Hi, Raymond. Hi, Miss B. Have you seen my article in the paper?" A flash of worry crossed her face.

Dorothy was in the Creative Writing class and served as Opportunity's Student Coordinator, a job she took seriously. The position had in the past been filled by a student chosen in the spring semester by the Teacher Coordinator, with input from staff and students. This year, Golden, as the principal, chose Dorothy, and it was probably Jones whose opinion she kept in mind.

She had told Bebelaar about the article in class. "I haven't, Dorothy. What page is it on?" She pointed to the article, to the left of the editorial column and just below a hand-drawn ad for Books Plus. The three of them bent over the table to read it together.

MESSAGE FROM DOROTHY
— *Dorothy Buckley, Student Coordinator*

As student body president, I would like to discuss a problem we're having: some feel there is a division between students in this school. I feel there is no room for divisions. We're all victims of this society; whether we are black, white, brown, purple, or green—we all have to sell ourselves in order to survive. It's my opinion that we should not think of ourselves as members of any group. We are all a part of this society based on profit.

We have to stop worrying about which person doesn't speak to you or doesn't respond just the way you want to. I'm saying that we all have a responsibility not to lose our perspective because someone has hurt our feelings. There is no time for these petty differences.

It's time for all of us youth to understand this society and grasp that little education that we can in order to survive. There is something more important than our individual selves—we can be an effective force for change if we are together. The people have done it (made revolutionary change) in Angola and Vietnam. They will soon do it in South Africa. If we wish to have definite change, we must stand together. We have done it for almost a year at Opportunity. Let's keep on doing it while we have the chance.

Bebelaar congratulated her. "Maybe this will help kids be more open to you Temple kids, and encourage the Temple kids to do the same. I know some of them feel you kind of keep to yourselves. Not you, of course. You're friendly to everyone."

Later, Bebelaar would come across a photograph of Dorothy with Jim Jones, taken in Ukiah when Dorothy was about ten, that seems to indicate a special bond between the two of them. There are ten children in the photo, but Jones's attention is on Dorothy, his left arm around her, gazing intently at her. A curious white light—likely caused by some wrinkle in the negative—appears to radiate from Jones's heart to Dorothy's. Jones dubbed this picture "The Shekhinah Glory": In Christianity the shekhinah light symbolizes "the presence and the glory of the Lord." No doubt being singled out by Jones at a young age had had a powerful effect on Dorothy and made her especially committed to the Church.

"Well, you've got me convinced, anyway!" Raymond said to Dorothy. Just then Golden came out of her office ringing the bell for class, and the three headed up the stairs following Cabral and Junior, who was helping Cabral with the bundles of newspapers.

End of the School Year

When Junior resumed his pattern of spotty attendance after baseball season was over, Bebelaar, as his counselor, made the familiar call home. Junior's mother promised that he would be at school the next day but his absence continued.

After calling to arrange a home visit, Bebelaar was greeted at the door by Junior's mother who presented her with a necklace of cowry shells and invited her into the kitchen to share some fresh crab her husband had caught. Bebelaar had been treated very politely at all the homes she had visited, but she had never had this kind of royal reception.

She explained that Junior had been doing well lately, but was missing school again. "You know, Junior could become a real leader in the school, as well-liked and respected as he is. And the baseball team may be a real varsity team next year. But Junior has to come to school, keep his grades up, if he wants to keep playing."

"We'll talk to him," promised Mrs. Siufanua. "Don't you worry, Ms. Bebelaar. He won't miss one more day. And he'll do his work." She and her husband, two tall, handsome people, serious and smiling at the same time, stood side by side as Bebelaar left.

Junior started coming nearly every day, until the last few weeks of school when he began missing again. Then he came in with a note from his mother, which he gave to Bebelaar without his usual big smile:

Dear Ms. B,
Junior was absent from school for two weeks because of an injury, which was one missing tooth, a stab in the back, deep cut in hand, and split lip.

Mareta Siufanua[1]

"Well, that's pretty convincing, Junior!" It would join her collection of the more interesting notes from parents and students. "Can you bring some work, stay after school, and make up some of your missed time? I'm glad you're OK. That sounds pretty bad. A fight?"

"Yeah, I'll stay after school, but on Tuesdays and Thursdays I have to go to St. Anthony's. You know, serve food to street people. My P.O. wants me to. I guess he thinks it will wise me up." He grinned ruefully. But after a week, he missed school again.

His parole officer called, asking Bebelaar to come to a court hearing: Junior was being sent to Log Cabin, a juvenile detention center in the hills above the South Bay wetlands, far from the city streets. The officer thought a teacher's testimony about Junior's school work and the baseball team might help lessen the sentence.

Junior's parents came to the hearing too, and thanked Bebelaar for coming. But her enthusiastic testimony didn't help—he was going to Log Cabin.

And then school was over. Junior wouldn't return for school the following September.

So in addition to the Temple players Jimmy, Tim, Calvin, Johnny, Wesley and Mark, the Cobras lost Junior too. As it would turn out, almost all of the Temple kids would not be back at school in September. Along with Stephan and his brothers, most of the students the Opportunity teachers had grown so fond of would be gone.

Opportunity High staff circa 1975, photo by John Liu–Klein

Chapter 8

Temblors

June 1977 through September 1978

School's Out

O
n the last day of school the teachers gathered to celebrate at North Beach Italian eateries like the U.S. Restaurant for big plates of spaghetti and ravioli, bowls of salad, carafes of wine, and lots of laughter. In June 1977, however, there was no party. No one was in the mood. Opportunity just wasn't the same. On top of that, the district was selling the Plum Alley site; the school was moving again.

Instead of holding their usual party, the teachers toured the new school site. Frederick Burke, a one-story brick-and-redwood building, was the old demonstration elementary school of San Francisco State University's education department. Located on Font Boulevard, it sat across from an apartment complex called Park Merced, far from the city center—and from field trip destinations like museums and movie theaters. On the other hand, the new site had compensations. What soon became known as "Freddie Burke" was the most attractive and suitable building of the sites Opportunity had ever had. Each room had floor-to-ceiling classroom windows that looked out on small patios, trees, and grass. The rooms were large and airy, with cedar paneling; myriad cupboards and drawers of all shapes and sizes; attractive bulletin boards and new chalkboards—not old-fashioned black, but modern green—as well as sturdy desks, tables, and movable chairs that hadn't (yet) been defaced. One of the rooms had a small stage that could be used for events or meetings, and the kitchen was large enough for a cooking class. A good-sized office branched out from the main entryway. The university library was nearby, and on warm days students could eat lunch on the wide, tree-dappled lawns. The few physical problems were small, literally: the low toilets, sinks, and water fountains, all designed for little children.

The teachers followed Golden as she led them around the building, which spread out like a ranch house in the suburbs. They quickly laid claim to favorite rooms. Maybe it wouldn't be so bad after all. Many students, though, would have long bus rides, with more than one transfer, as few if any lived in the nearby middle class "Avenues," the neighborhood that flanked Golden Gate Park and spread west to the ocean. How would those with attendance problems ever make it out here? Still, most of the books and equipment were packed and ready to be delivered by district movers. And most of the teachers still harbored lingering idealism.

But for now, it was summer, with no homework to grade, no lesson plans, no phone calls to parents, no administrative paperwork, and no principal. Many Opportunity teachers taught summer school or held other jobs to make ends meet, but all the same, as with all teachers, summer was their time to relax and recharge their batteries, a respite especially appreciated by those working with troubled teenagers. And up until the arrival of the courteous, well-behaved Temple kids, most of Opportunity's students had required large amounts of patience, attention, and extra care.

Junior at Log Cabin

Junior was one of those troubled kids, but one who rarely *gave* trouble. What he did outside school was the problem. In mid-June, Bebelaar received a carefully scrawled letter from him, dated June 14.

Here I am back at Log Cabin. I will be here all summer and going to school, and improving my reading and everything else. Sure wish we could go for a ride, instead of me being here. Maybe we can on a home pass or when I get out.

I hope I can return to Opportunity when I get out. Perhaps you can change my 3rd and 4th periods, even though I know I need them. What are you going to do this summer? Hope you enjoy your summer and have a good time. Summer school at Log Cabin is easier because the regular teachers are not here, so we don't work as hard as we have to do during the school year. Please say hi to Yvonne, Ron, Tina, and Cubby. Tell Ron I will practice my baseball. That's all for now Judy. If you like "please write Back."

P.S. Thank you for coming to my court hearing "AGAIN."[1]

Bebelaar, touched that he would write to her, hoped Junior might be able to make it back to Opportunity sometime in the fall. There was still a chance he would be able to graduate. And the Cobras would need Junior more than ever, now that Debbie had graduated and Tim, Jimmy, and Mark—and so many others, as all the teachers would soon discover—were in Guyana.

A few days later, on June 18, the *Chronicle* reported a "strange" break-in at the offices of *New West Magazine*, a liberal, muckraking journal that was planning an article about Peoples Temple. At the time Bebelaar didn't think much of it.[2]

Living in Earthquake Country

Then on Sunday morning, July 17, Bebelaar sat at her kitchen table reading an article in the *San Francisco Sunday Examiner-Chronicle Magazine,* "Magazine attacks Peoples Temple," by Raul Ramirez. The story reported that the Temple exposé *New West* was about to publish for its August issue would detail how several Church members had left the Temple in protest. It would further allege that "church leaders staged phony cancer cures, lied to their congregation about contributions collected at services, routinely 'paddled' members for minor infractions and pressured members to turn over their property, money and homes to the church."[3]

Probably, Bebelaar thought, because Jones is a declared socialist there are plenty who would love to find fault with his Church. Though many liberal politicians championed Jones, it was still the height of the Cold War and most Americans on the right distrusted socialists as well as communists.

The article called the Church defectors "disgruntled," and quoted a Temple spokesperson who denounced the upcoming story as "massive distortion, exaggeration, lopsided characterization and outright lies, which together amount to a travesty of truth."[4]

The first big shock came with the publication of the *New West* article, "Inside Peoples Temple," by Marshall Kilduff and Phil Tracy. It began: "Jim Jones is one of the state's most politically potent leaders. But who is he? And what's going on behind the church's locked doors?"

New West *article*

The article described Rosalynn Carter's visit to a San Francisco rally to support her husband Jimmy Carter's candidacy. The event was held at the new Democratic campaign headquarters downtown. Apparently, the Temple had supplied most of the crowd. "Some 600 of the 750 listeners were delivered in Temple buses an hour and a half before the rally. . . . 'You should have seen it—old ladies on crutches, whole families, little kids, blacks, whites. Made to order,'" as a rally organizer said. Another organizer reported that it was awkward when Jones received longer and louder cheers—a "wall-pounding outpour" that lasted a minute and a half—more than there had been for any of the other dignitaries, including Rosalynn. Bebelaar remembered feeling a similar consternation when Jones came to speak at the school. Now, as she looked back on it, the exaggerated applause seemed to have had ominous overtones.

> Jones, who has several adopted children of differing racial backgrounds, is more than a political force. He and his church are noted for social and medical programs, which are centered in his three-story structure on Geary Street. Temple members support and staff a free diagnostic and outpatient clinic, a physical therapy facility, a drug program that claims to have rehabilitated some 300 addicts and a legal aid program for about 200 people a month. In addition, the temple's free dining hall is said to feed more indigents than the city's venerable St. Anthony's dining room. And temple spokesmen say that these services to the needy are financed internally, without a cent of government or foundation money.

This sounded more like the Temple the teachers at Opportunity knew. The article also cited Jones's stand supporting the Fresno Four, as well as contributions to twelve newspapers in California "in the defense of a free press," in the amount of $4,400.

> In addition, at Jones's direction the temple makes regular contributions to several community groups, including the Telegraph Hill Neighborhood Center and Health Clinic, the NAACP, the ACLU and the farmworkers' union. When a local pet clinic was in trouble, Peoples Temple provided the money needed to keep it open. The temple has also set up a fund for the widows of slain policemen, and the congregation runs an escort service for senior citizens.
>
> To many, the Reverend Jim Jones is the epitome of a selfless Christian.

The article also noted that the original temple in downtown Indianapolis—at one time the Ku Klux Klan's national office—had integrated long "before Martin Luther King became a national figure," and that the San Francisco congregation was racially mixed, though "80 to 90 percent black."

That percentage was similar to the Opportunity population now that the Temple students had arrived en masse. Neither the Temple congregation nor Opportunity's new student body accurately reflected the city's multicultural population.

The article went on to detail some disturbing policies of the Temple. Guards watched over Temple services. Two locked entrances were installed at the San Francisco building. No one was allowed to visit Church services without making prior arrangements. Even more outlandish was Jones's prediction of Nazis eventually overthrowing the government.

> *How does Jones manage to appeal to so many kinds of people? Where does he get the money to operate his church's programs, or maintain his fleet of buses, or support his agricultural outpost in Guyana? Why does he surround himself with bodyguards—as many as fifteen at a time? And above all, what is going on behind the locked and guarded doors of Peoples Temple?*[5]

Bebelaar recalled the story of the mysterious break-in at the *New West* offices, and remembered the guards who had searched Cabral and Debbie when they went to the Temple to consult about their special edition—and the men who questioned Morrow and Vogel when they arrived for the Fresno Four protest. These events started to take on a more sinister cast as she read through the *New West* article.

Prior to the article's publication, the Temple apparently had initiated a campaign, of up to fifty phone calls and seventy letters a day, asking *New West* not to attack "a good man" who was "doing good work."

The magazine got other calls too, about "cruelty" to Church members; the reporters didn't put much stock in what seemed to be nothing more than rumors. But it was a different matter when ten Temple members who had defected from the Church—including Al and Jeannie Mills, Opportunity student Linda Mertle's parents—all agreed to give their names and have their pictures taken.

> *Based on what these people told us, life inside Peoples Temple was a mixture of spartan regimentation, fear and self-imposed humiliation. . . . the Sunday services to which dignitaries were invited were orchestrated events. Actually, members were expected to attend services two, three, even four nights a week—with some sessions lasting until daybreak.*[6]

Bebelaar reflected on how tired the Temple students sometimes looked. But surely, she argued with herself rather feebly, they wouldn't keep the kids up too, would they?

When the article went on to speak of "catharsis sessions" at the Church, it didn't sound altogether strange to Bebelaar. *Catharsis* had become part of the seventies vocabulary, especially in the San Francisco Bay Area. Delancey Street, a San Francisco group home that rehabilitated ex-convicts and substance abusers, grew out of Synanon, which worked with drug addicts. Both were well-known organizations that used catharsis sessions as part of their healing process.

The worst of the defectors' tales related physical abuse, including the brutal paddling of Linda Mertle as punishment for hugging and kissing her female friend (who was thought to be a lesbian) in greeting after a long absence. "She was beaten so severely," her father reported, "that the kids said her butt looked like hamburger." The paddling had purportedly occurred in Ukiah, before Linda came to Opportunity, but Bebelaar couldn't help thinking of Linda and those bruises the girl didn't want Cabral to worry about—and the strange manner of her abrupt departure. Bebelaar read on, her heart sinking, about "phony" cancer healings, lies Jones told to the congregation concerning contributions collected at services, and members pressured to sign over to the Church social security checks and even rights to property.

A group of young people in the church had been among the first to rebel. Mickey Touchette and Jim Cobb, Opportunity student Johnny Cobb's older brother, along with five other young adults, had left the church in 1973 without telling friends or relatives.

The interviewees, Linda Mertle's parents and others who had defected from the Temple, hoped the revelations would spur an investigation that would force Jones to leave the Church, or at least retreat to Guyana with his most loyal members. A sinking feeling now in her stomach, Bebelaar thought again about how Mark hadn't wanted to go. She put the magazine down, then picked it up again.

The article quoted Laura Cornelious, a defector who'd been "one of the privates in the Peoples Temple's army," who was disturbed about the "constant requests for money. . . . The money was needed, she was told, 'to build up this other place [Guyana—the "promised land"], so we would have someplace to go whenever they [the fascists in this country] were going to destroy us like they did the Jews. [Jones said] that they would put [black people] in concentration camps, and that they would do us like the Jews, in the gas ovens.'"

Grace Stoen, another defector, had left without telling her husband, fearing he would report her and she'd be pulled back in. Their five-year-old boy was reputedly now in Guyana; Grace was taking legal action to get custody of her son. She told of exhausting work schedules, long bus trips, increasing pressure to raise money.

Some of the defectors, the article stated, held the belief that Jones and "a few hundred of his closest followers may be planning to leave for Guyana no later than September."[7]

If this were true, Bebelaar wondered, stunned, would more students leave? Would there be an investigation, as the article concluded there should be? Would there be answers to the questions the politicians didn't ask because they didn't want to know? She couldn't help thinking she and the other teachers should have asked more questions.

The next week, on July 27, *Chronicle* headlines announced "Mayor Won't Investigate Rev. Jones," a response to repeated exhortations put forth in the *New West* story.[8] Around the same time, columnist Herb Caen, occasionally called "the Pope of San Francisco," reported that Jones had hired well-known liberal attorney Charles Garry to pursue a possible libel suit.[9]

Most at Opportunity trusted the mayor, considering him a good, honest man. Many of those on the left found it difficult to believe a fellow traveler on the road to a better world could be suspect. Many, including Opportunity teachers, remembered the Red Scare and its inequities, so they required a heavy dose of corroborated, damning evidence before being willing to reconsider someone whose intentions they trusted.

Shortly after the *New West* article came out, Cabral received a call one sleepy August afternoon. It was E. Cahill Maloney, a reporter for the *San Francisco Progress*. She said she had a few questions about Opportunity. As coach, Cabral was used to reporters calling about the Cobras, so he agreed to speak with her.

"Is it true that many of your students belong to the Peoples Temple?" she began.

"Quite a few; and about 85 percent of the baseball team are Temple members."

"How many Temple students are enrolled altogether?"

"I believe about a hundred. They came in a block enrollment last September."

"Isn't that unusual? So many at once?"

"Yeah, kids coming in as a large group isn't our usual admission pattern. Our principal, Yvonne Golden, worked it all out, and the Temple students turned out to be such great kids that none of the teachers made too much of it."

After answering a few more questions, Cabral told the reporter he was concerned about a recent statement in the *Progress* that some of the communes where Temple kids apparently lived were now empty, and asked if she had any proof that Jones was taking more people to Guyana.

Maloney said that was being looked into.

After he hung up, Cabral sat at the table for a long time, wondering. He could understand the Jones boys going. Their dad was the preacher. But maybe it was a bigger deal than any of the teachers at Opportunity thought, this mission in Guyana.

ーゆー

When the *Progress* article came out on August 3, Cabral read some of the Maloney piece to his wife.

"This is not exactly what I said, Rita, but I guess it's right. Says here, 'Opportunity II was used as an educational base for Temple affiliated young people during the 1976–77 school year. Although the alternative high school has a long waiting list, more than 130 Temple teenagers were enrolled at the school at one time last September.'

"I don't think the waiting list was very long, Rita, and I wonder, was it really a hundred and thirty kids? They got this right, though: 'Some sort of deal was arranged between school coordinator Yvonne Golden and the Rev. Jones.'

"And this is going to get Yvonne's dander up for sure: 'The San Francisco Unified School District provided the Rev. Jim Jones's Peoples Temple with what amounted to its own Temple high school.' It says Golden wouldn't tell them much, said they should talk to downtown." He read on. "'Cabral identified Temple member Tim Carter as the contact for any problems that arose in connection with students.' And they quote me again, about the Temple counselors, that I 'did not know the exact nature of the counseling arrangement,' and that I said Yvonne 'sort of wanted to take care of everything to do with the Temple.' And they talk about Tim Jones, how hard it was for the Cobras when he left just as the season began. September is going to be interesting, to say the least."[10]

"Ron," Rita replied, "I'm sure Yvonne will be upset with what you said, but I'm glad you were honest. It's sounding pretty bad. I hope some of the kids will write and let you know how they are down there."

No letters came.

A few days later Cabral received another unexpected phone call, this one from Dr. John Cleveland, the school district deputy superintendent, summoning him to the downtown district offices. When Cabral arrived that afternoon, hot and a little nervous, the administrator was sitting at his desk.

Cleveland pushed a copy of the *Progress* toward Cabral—Maloney's article was on the front page—and asked him to sit down. The man didn't look happy and asked Cabral to explain. Cabral responded that "never in a million years" did he think the reporter's questions would become the source of a front-page article. He added that he didn't think the article included anything he shouldn't talk about. Cleveland shot back, "What makes you think you can speak for the district?"

Cabral replied he was only speaking as a teacher at Opportunity High and telling the truth as he knew it, all of it public knowledge. Cleveland repeated that Cabral had no authority to speak for the district.

"But, sir, I *am* part of the district. The reporter was asking about my school, my students. I've talked with reporters before, many times, about the Cobras. No one has ever objected."

Then Cleveland asked if Cabral was aware that Yvonne Golden was a "professed socialist." Cabral told him, "She calls herself that. But I didn't say anything about that to the reporter, if that's what you're worried about."

Cleveland said he wasn't worried, just curious, and told Cabral he could go but that he might need to call him later, and that Cabral should keep him informed about any further interviews.

Long Shadows

In August, John and Judy Bebelaar and their daughter Kristy went to Laguna Beach to visit John's parents. One lazy day Bebelaar and her daughter lay side by side on beach towels. Surfers called this beach Trestles, as it was just below the train trestle at San Onofre State Beach. Bebelaar glanced up from time to time to see if she could spot John catching a wave. It was easy for her to tell him from the other surfers, even if they were far out, as he was the only knee boarder. When he paddled out, she could see the foam from his swim fins; coming in, he was on his knees, one arm out like a wing, the other holding the board.

For beach reading, Bebelaar had brought the August 4 issue of the *Chronicle* she had bought at a newsstand in Laguna. Marshall Kilduff, one of the authors of the shocking *New West* article, had followed that with another article. "A Peoples Temple 'Bloc' at S.F. School" was on page one, next to a story about President Carter pardoning Vietnam War draft evaders. The sinking feeling she had experienced when reading the *New West* article returned. The story quoted Cabral on the influx of students from the Temple, and also Golden, who had refused to comment on whether it was unusual for a third of a school's students to stem from a single source. "I regard such speculation as confidential," she'd said.

There must be something wrong, Bebelaar thought, if shoot-from-the-hip Golden was being so closed-mouthed. The staff had always been somewhat protective of Golden regarding criticism from outside the school. Even though she and some of the others often disagreed with the principal's methods and the way she justified bending the rules, they felt Golden was attacked for the wrong reasons—because she was an outspoken black woman and a declared socialist.

The article also reported that thirteen Temple students—including Stephan, Tim, and Jimmy—had been enrolled in Drew Preparatory, a private San Francisco school, before leaving at the end of December to attend Washington High. The Temple had apparently reneged on tuition-related penalty fees of $4,269, which it had agreed beforehand would be levied should the thirteen students withdraw from Drew before the end of the year. According to the article, the Temple had pressured the headmaster to drop the fees owed, and five or six members made threatening calls to the man's home.[11]

Bebelaar thought again of Joyce's poem about the jungle paradise:

As the rain tingles on the roof of the tropic island
Birds fly to the nest in the tropic trees,
Little creatures hiding from
The small rain.

What was it really like in Guyana?

The emerging Peoples Temple story cast a shadow even in sunny Southern California. Bebelaar remembered she had seen a *San Francisco Examiner* at the Laguna newsstand, and decided to go back to buy it in case there was more about the Temple. Sure enough: In an *Examiner* article she learned Jones had resigned as head of the San Francisco Housing Authority, saying "responsibilities to the mission left him with a 'lack of time' for other work." Even more significant, despite Mayor Moscone's previous statements, the article indicated the district attorney's office had decided to begin "investigating the temple and was interviewing former temple members."[12]

Maybe the newspapers weren't merely hounding Jones—maybe the charges were true? Had other kids, besides Linda, been abused?

Then Bebelaar remembered the day one of the Temple girls she didn't know well had asked her for help getting an abortion. When Bebelaar suggested she talk to the woman counselor from the Temple, a strange look had crossed the girl's face. Fear? Something more? At any rate, she seemed desperate enough that Bebelaar gave her the address of the closest Planned Parenthood, on Eddy Street.

The sinking feeling had morphed into a rock in the pit of her stomach.

The News Gets Worse

On August 7, another worrisome *Examiner* story appeared. The Church was deeply involved in politics—not only by sending protesters out on buses, it turned out. Apparently every member of the church was required to write letters on political topics, sometimes more than one hundred a week, using fake names and varying the handwriting, paper, envelopes, and color of ink they used. The letters were carefully screened by Temple personnel, then mailed from different cities. And Jones had chosen solid, respected politicians to support: Mayor Moscone in San Francisco and Mayor Tom Bradley in Los Angeles, city councilmen, and state senators such as Milton Marks.[13]

On August 11 came yet another jolt. In at least three instances, "families complained their children had traveled to Guyana without permission," according to Kilduff's story, "Peoples Temple—Families Complain," which ran in the *San Francisco Chronicle*. That article also mentioned Mark Sly and Al and Jeannie Mills:

> *Neva Sly, who left the church within the past week . . . now charges that her son Mark, 16, may have been sent to Guyana against his will.*
>
> *She said that she and her husband Donald were required to live apart in communes run by the church, and were asked to sign over guardianship of their son to another temple family. . . .*

> *[Another] incident involves two small children, Patricia and Paul Petitt, aged 5 and 7 years, whose guardians are Jeannie and Al Mills, two former leaders in the church who left it in 1975.*
>
> *The Mills said yesterday they had obtained custody of the two youngsters when the natural mother was in legal trouble over a child abuse charge. Now, the Mills charge that temple spokesmen have refused to divulge the location of the two children or acknowledge the Mills' guardianship rights.*
>
> *Charles Garry, who is the attorney for the Temple, said that church leaders have told him the Petitt children are living with their natural mother in the Mission district.[14]*

Would this mean Mark could come back? If people had left the church, something must be wrong. Or was it just some kind of internal power struggle? But in this case, it sounded as though Jones had all the power. Had people escaped to the "promised land," or was the jungle settlement as troubled a place as the Church seemed to be?

It was all confusing, and strange, but in a world where anything could happen, the unthinkable could always be true. If Martin Luther King, Jack Kennedy, and Bobby Kennedy could all be shot and killed, what *couldn't* happen?

Bebelaar sadly realized she would just have to wait and see what more could be learned, and hope that further news would refute these awful stories. Maybe a reassuring letter would come from a student in Guyana. Then again, given what was being reported about the Church, could anyone believe such a letter?

Her thoughts returned to Mark. Had he told Cabral something he wasn't supposed to? Had the teachers failed him? Could they have prevented his going? If all these stories were true, wouldn't they have received some kind of message from Temple kids? The only one who had turned to Bebelaar for help was the Temple girl seeking an abortion. But had Bebelaar really helped? Would the girl be back in September? Or, if she had just decided to face the consequences, what would those be?

≈

On August 12 came the largest shock so far. Marshall Kilduff reported in the *Chronicle* that the rumors about an "exodus" were true. "More than 100 members of the controversial Peoples Temple have reportedly left San Francisco in what may be the start of a mass exodus of the secretive church to its remote outpost in . . . Guyana." There was more evidence of the departures.

In addition, Temple officials have attempted to arrange to have pension checks of elderly church members forwarded to Guyana. . . . Jones reportedly has an agreement with the Country's government to settle some 27,000 acres near the village of Port Kaituma along the northern border with Venezuela. . . . As recently as a month ago there were only about 130 people at the mission, according to reports issued by the church.

How many were in Guyana now, Bebelaar wondered, and how many of them were kids from Opportunity?

In the past few months, the church has asked several hundred followers to sell off their homes and possessions and move into temple communes which for the most part are apartments in the Fillmore district.

A tour of ten such locations identified by former temple member Linda Mertle showed three were empty but the others were occupied.

"My friends in the church are telling me that they are all supposed to get ready to leave just as soon as they get the call," said Jesse Boyd, an elderly black woman who left the church in January.[15]

Bebelaar put the paper down. This did not sound like a paradise, socialist or otherwise.

🍌

"The temple—a nightmare world," screamed the front-page *Examiner* headline on August 14. Bebelaar didn't want to believe what she read, but it was becoming more and more clear. The articles were not merely smear stories. The ugliness beneath the surface was undeniable.

Like the first exposé, this *Examiner* piece told of members giving up their incomes and property to the Church. In addition, it described Temple life as "an endless boot camp," where members were told not to associate with friends and family who weren't part of the Church, were allowed little sleep—two to five hours each night—and were even made to sign "confessions" of serious crimes they had not committed. "Former members told [the *Examiner*] of their willingness to forfeit their lives for one man, who proclaimed himself Jesus Christ reincarnated to his religious followers and Lenin reborn to his political devotees."

Another anecdote struck home. "Neva Sly, a nine-year church member, said she gave the church her $1,000-a-month salary from a local radio station and in return got her allowance, meals, a room and a Muni fast pass."[16]

By now the story was no longer just crazy "Left Coast" news. On August 15, *Newsweek* carried a full-page article about the Temple, linking Jones to several liberal politicians—both locally elected officials and those on the national scene—none of whom had spoken out against him.[17] Offering the other side of the coin, columnist Herb Caen quoted Temple spokesman Mike Prokes: "Whereas People's Temple is 80 percent black, 90 percent of those making the wild charges are white."[18]

End of Summer

On August 28, just before the next school year began, Bebelaar turned to a feature she had come across in the *Chronicle-Examiner* Sunday magazine. The story, "Jones and Temple Under Investigation," listed in detail a number of charges and allegations. Followers were expected to donate as much as 40 percent of their income, and to otherwise raise money through "street corner soliciting, mail[ing] contribution requests, and [organizing] bake sales." The value of real estate holdings granted by followers amounted to almost $5 million. "Five former members reported that due to Jones's increased interest in the Guyana mission, Temple leaders had been dispatched with … as much as $50,000 apiece which they carried from the U.S. to banks in Guyana."[19]

On August 30, Jeannie and Al Mills filed a $1.1 million lawsuit against Jones, seeking damages for property illegally taken from them by the Church and for compensation for their and their daughter Linda's "mental anguish" after she endured beatings at the hands of Temple members. [20]

By this time, Jones had nearly completed the exodus of the Church from San Francisco. More than 600 people, two-thirds of the congregation, had moved stealthily to the new settlement in Guyana, what was soon learned they called Jonestown.[21] Newspapers gave no lists of names, making it impossible to identify which Opportunity students were among them.

Bebelaar tried the phone numbers that were on her pink school record cards, but they had been disconnected.

Aftershocks

A pall hung over the opening of school at Opportunity in the fall of 1977. Knots of teachers huddled in hallways or classrooms, talking quietly of the disturbing articles about the Temple that had come out over the summer. Some still refused to believe the allegations about Jones and clung to the idea that people just disliked the man's radical politics.

One day Cabral brought in a pile of issues of the *Progress* with a few articles about Jones and the Temple for his students to read and discuss, but before class started Golden appeared at his door. Behind her stood a white middle-aged man in dress shirt and tie, arms crossed. Neither was smiling. The man declared: "The Temple demands that you remove these materials from the classroom. They are full of false allegations about the Church and Reverend Jones." Cabral told them he planned to go ahead with his lesson, citing freedom of speech; he then excused himself and closed the door on them.

Not long after, Golden called Cabral into her office. Between the summer newspaper articles Ron had been quoted in and now his refusal to throw out the newspapers with articles about the Temple, the principal was fuming. Ron excused himself as soon as he could, saying he had a meeting with a union rep.

This was the point at which Cabral, like many others, began to think of leaving Opportunity. "You know," Cabral told Bebelaar, "it wouldn't be hard, leaving here, except for the Cobras. Guess I'll stick around for a while." With the help of Manny Blackwell, the only remaining team member from the previous year, Cabral worked to reconstitute the Cobras. Instead of being in the JV league as before, they'd play the varsity teams this year, which would be rough without nine of the players they'd had the previous year: Tim, Johnny, Wes, Billy, Ricky, Mark, Mondo, Calvin, Teddy and Junior.

Some time later, Cabral heard that Golden had been talking to Jones, who by this time was in Guyana, over the short wave radio at the Temple in San Francisco. Indeed, it would be learned later that Golden had been given three different code names in Temple communications: Amelia, Mrs. Thornton, and Mrs. Tydeman[22], suggesting that Golden and Jones spoke often. But Golden had told the staff nothing about their students in Guyana.

❧

Bebelaar walked down the hall at the new school, unable to stop her thoughts rolling in like the regular fog at the new campus near the ocean. She was still reeling from the way the Temple kids had first arrived in a bunch, worked their way into teachers' hearts, and then disappeared into the jungle. She worried, too, about all the disquieting articles. If things were so bad in the Church right here, what was happening to the kids in Guyana? Why had no one received a single letter? She thought especially about Mark—such a sensitive kid, stuck between two parents, forced to go against his will to a place that sounded inhospitable.

She thought about how, shortly after Jones had spoken at Opportunity, Bebelaar suggested to her daughter Kristy that they go to the Temple some Sunday. Though Bebelaar had grown up going to church, she had stopped when she entered college. When she had heard Jones speak, and when she learned about the dancing and singing, she'd thought this might be a church she and her daughter would like.

After reading all the articles over the summer, though, Bebelaar wasn't sure whether she wished she had gone to the Church, perhaps learning more about what was going on there, or whether she felt glad she hadn't gone.

The inner argument continued, both sides rallying in her head. Surely the defectors were exaggerating. Though the Temple kids may have been a little tired sometimes, they seemed no more so than other teenagers who stayed up late, doing things far less profitable than attending church. Always at school on time, their bag lunches and homework in hand, the Temple youngsters just seemed like somewhat serious but basically happy kids. These kids didn't seem to have painful stories they needed to share, as many of the old students did: stories of dysfunctional families, or with no one at home; time spent in jail, on drugs, or out on the streets. The Temple youngsters were more like the teachers and some of the more socially conscious students. Like Dorothy, they were people concerned about *doing* something about poverty and social injustice.

But what if the Temple kids had stories they were forbidden to tell? Mondo's poem, in which he worried he "might say the wrong thing" even when talking to himself, took on a terrible new meaning.

Perhaps, Bebelaar speculated, the Left could be just as blind as they often believed the Right to be. She used to believe that Opportunity belonged to the teachers who had created it, and that when they revised the school as Opportunity II they had a better plan. They would just keep following the original dream, perfecting their procedures along the way, and they would eventually succeed with these kids. But the school wasn't following the original plan. Golden had changed that.

After Perlstein left, and at other times since then, it had occurred to Bebelaar to leave also, transfer to another school, where she could just concentrate on teaching kids creative writing and making English classes more exciting. Not yet, she had always told herself. She would give it one more year. And the California Arts Council grant she and five poets had just secured would pay the visiting poets and provide funds for a book of kids' poetry—that was something to stay for as well.

Maybe, she thought hopefully, this publicity about the Temple would have a positive effect, and the Temple kids who had left would be brought back.

Yet she couldn't help thinking of them. She'd imagined Joyce would be the editor of the poetry book she and her students would produce thanks to the grant, and she thought about how the kids would enjoy working with the five poets: the "Nuyorican" Victor Hernandez Cruz; rising young Filipina writer Jessica Hagedorn; Nicaraguan Roberto Vargas; Simon Ortiz, a celebrated Acoma Pueblo Indian writer; and Herb Middleton, a young black poet who had been in prison.

The program was a big hit. Victor Hernandez Cruz's hilarious poem "The Latest Latin Dance Craze" begins with a long list of directions—throw your head back, jump onto the floor like a kangaroo, do a "mambo-minuet," among other wild movements, and finally ends with, "You have just completed your first / Step." When he read it for the Creative Writing class, the kids exploded with finger snaps and laughter. It was in this spirit that Raymond Berrios wrote his homage to Victor, "Conga," which begins:

Be free, think clear
Feel the percussion rhythm of the conga
let the beat join the rhythm of your heart
mambo dance dance dance guaguanco juega
la cache caliente, maracas, tocan la música
Chévere—Communication
Through rhythmic air sounds
Travel through my heart mind . . .

There were still a few Temple kids at Opportunity, but only Monica Bagby, a quiet girl, was in Bebelaar's Creative Writing class. Two other Temple girls, Sonje Regina Duncan and Lisa Lewis, were new to the school. Opportunity's new teacher Danny Hallinan said they liked to come to his room at lunchtime to giggle and gossip. Sonje was slender, and had a sweet, warm smile and almond-shaped dark eyes. Lisa had a usually smiling, round face framed with a big Afro. But their time at the school was short-lived. In the spring Sonje's mother withdrew her daughter, pregnant, from school and sent her to Jonestown. Lisa joined her soon after when her mother left Mr. Lewis and took their seven children to start a new life in Guyana.

Sonje Regina Duncan

Lisa Lewis

Just as the Temple kids had left Opportunity one by one, many teachers, discouraged and disillusioned, did too. The first to leave, Hal Abercrombie, summed up the collective feelings of what the teachers had lost: "I'll miss Opportunity, but—it's just not the same anymore. Just doesn't have the old spark. All this Jonestown stuff, the Temple kids gone, and the district seems to be sending us only kids they don't know what else to do with. Fewer kids like those we got in the old days seem to be applying too." Not long after, math teacher Fong Ha followed suit; and Anna Wong, the art and reading teacher, left soon thereafter. The Opportunity that had been was disappearing from view.

As for the Cobras, in the end they proved to be no match against the other teams. They were defeated in every game, with scores of 21–1, 28–4, 30–1, 30–0, 33–1. After being pounded into the ground, they finally forfeited the rest of the season.

It seemed to Cabral that the losses hit Manny, the team leader, the hardest. After one particularly painful defeat, Cabral had seen Manny sobbing on the bench in his catching gear. He must have bitterly felt the absence of his fellow Cobras, who would have made the team a match in this varsity league, and no doubt a mix of other emotions: sadness at the end of the team, relief at not being in Jonestown himself, and worry about his friends.

Manny wrote this poem, "Soul," that year:

> Fire
> Solar energy
> The power of the universal
> Which has held power
> For billions of years
> The heat is a reflection of loneliness
> Empty space
> The realm of blessed silence
> Red is a reflection
> Of the first man on earth
> The black drifting space is
> The soul
> Of what we now know
> And what the mind
> Can never achieve
> The sunset is a virgin smile
> Untouched by human hands.

With no baseball team, Cabral had no reason at all to stay at Opportunity. He left in April when he was asked to help head the district's summer school office, then was assigned to be summer school principal at Galileo.

Bebelaar's class poetry book, *Fire*, was published, and a successful poetry assembly capped the year, then she too considered it time to move on. She accepted a job at Galileo, enticed by a special class, funded by a grant written by San Francisco artist Ruth Asawa, in which Bebelaar and an artist would collaborate in creating an illustrated poetry anthology.

In the fall of 1978, Opportunity moved once more, to Alamo Square, atop a hill in the Western Addition. Only five Opportunity teachers followed Golden there. Of the five, Hallinan, Liu-Klein, and Andrea Lyons would leave within the year.

Still, none of the teachers forgot about the Temple kids, and, like Bebelaar and Cabral, all continued to wonder and worry about their former students.

Fire literary magazine, with cover designed by Susan Perkins

Welcome to Jonestown
Peoples Temple Agricultural Project

Chapter 9

Behind the Scenes

The People, The Preacher

t was at first hard for the teachers at Opportunity to know what to believe about the Peoples Temple and their Guyana settlement. The exposés and articles they'd read in the summer of 1977 left them confused about what to believe, and worried. The students they cared about were now completely in the hands of the Church and far from home; Bebelaar, Cabral, and the others wanted to believe the teenagers would be safe—that they would somehow thrive and be happy. It was only much later that what had been going on behind the scenes in their young lives began to come out.

It is clear to many that what happened in Jonestown resulted primarily from the destructive control that Jim Jones held over his Temple members— followers, detractors, and family members alike. But before Jones proved himself a tyrant, he had been a strongly charismatic leader who inspired hundreds of devoted followers.

What had attracted them to the Temple? What did Jones offer them? Did people always "choose" to join the Temple, or did the Temple sometimes choose them? Of course, the children and teenagers who went to Guyana— including those in guardianship custody—had little choice in the matter. What had led to the genesis of Jonestown in the first place? No one can fully understand just how it was that so many good people came to such a tragic end. Even with so much that can't be known, however, it does help to understand at least a bit about some of the figures involved, especially the students whom the teachers at Opportunity had actually come to know—to the extent they had indeed let others get to know them.

The Vision of Jonestown

Originally called the Peoples Temple Agricultural Project, Jonestown began as a noble enterprise, at least in the eyes of the people who made up the Church. Years before, Jones had sold his congregation on the idea of a paradise in the jungle that would be free of racism and sexism, a place where elders would be honored, children would grow up in equality, and people would live on the agricultural fruits of their own labor.

Having determined that the necessary sanctuary for the Peoples Temple was not to be found in the United States, Jones had sought wider locales, ultimately settling on Guyana. (It's likely that he also deemed it appropriate that his predominantly black Church find peace in a black country.)

The impetus for establishing the mission originally stemmed from the high-profile 1973 defection of eight young people, including Opportunity student Johnny Cobb's older brother Jim Cobb, Jr. When Johnny was about fourteen, Jim defiantly left the Church with his girlfriend and three other young, interracial couples (as the summer *New West* article had reported). Some of the defectors served as high-level security for the Church, and some were members of the Temple's esteemed Planning Commission. Jones—who labeled the group the "Gang of Eight"—saw the defection as a betrayal and sent a search party in a small plane to find them, but the defectors drove to Montana and evaded discovery. Losing so many high-ranking young people was an enormous blow to Jones, and soon after the "Gang of Eight" defected, the Temple leadership began to make plans that included establishing a "Caribbean missionary post." On October 8, 1973, the Church's governing body—the Planning Commission—made the decision that such a mission would be set up in Guyana.[1]

Jones described a "Caribbean paradise with ripe fruit bursting from every tree,"[2] and showed his congregation enticing films crafted to prove his words true. Temple member Deborah Layton described seeing a film with "beautiful greenery" and imagining the "beautiful wood cabins" she'd been told about that were "scattered throughout the countryside."[3] In one Temple film, Jones displayed a bounty of fruit supposedly grown by Jonestown settlers, though the paper bag from the store in Georgetown where the fruit had been purchased is in the shot as well. Indeed, a "visitor [to Jonestown in December 1974] who took Jones at his word expected to find lush tropical fruit growing wild everywhere and more nuts than he could eat. When he got to Port Kaituma, he asked Charlie Touchette where the bounty was. 'There ain't any,' came the reply. 'You could go into the jungle and starve.'"[4]

After a few years of planning, in 1974 the dream of Jonestown started to become reality with the arrival of twenty founding pioneers, who settled temporarily in Port Kaituma while a "road into Jonestown and the first thirty acres were hand-cleared by Guyanese workers." The Jonestown Institute reports:

The first residents of Jonestown proper had no electricity, no running water, and no toilet. They cooked on a modified fifty-five-gallon drum that had been converted into a stove. They used kerosene "wickies" (lamps) for light at night. They hauled water from a spring, until they put galvanized roofs on the buildings and collected the runoff from the rain.[5]

The hard-working settlers had much to do to develop a camp into a bona fide one hundred-acre "agricultural project": clearing the jungle for planting, a task impeded by thick bush and huge trees, and experimenting with fertilizers to amend the rock-hard jungle dirt—all the while battling tropical heat and torrential rains that often "wash[ed] away the thin topsoil."[6]

Two of these ground-breakers were Charlie Touchette and his wife, Joyce, who had been with the Church since its beginnings. Joyce was in charge of supplies, the kitchen, and laundry; her husband managed construction, mechanics, and the wood and machine shops.

Stephan felt particularly connected to the Touchettes, as he and their son Mike were good friends, and their daughter Michelle, not yet in Jonestown, was his girlfriend. These early settlers were no doubt very courageous and capable people, in part because they did so much of this difficult early work on their own. Stephan visited at least twice in those early days.[7] By the time he settled there in February of 1977, he joined a population of only fifty.[8]

From its earliest days in Indiana in the mid-fifties, the Peoples Temple was known for its good works. The Temple actively reached out to the poor, opening a soup kitchen and a nursing home; the latter began in the Jones's own home, and was run by Marceline, a trained nurse. The Church even offered trips to the zoo for black children.[9] The Temple was also known for its liberal beliefs, especially in breaking down the barriers of race and class and integrating all kinds of people into one loving family.

As the result of Jones's active recruitment of black people, the Peoples Temple became the first Church in segregated Indianapolis to be truly integrated. The young minister also invited Archie Ijames, a black man who would follow Jones all the way to Guyana, to be an associate pastor in his Church. The Temple promoted integration in other areas as well: lunch counters, movie theaters, employment. In response to all this activism Jones claimed to receive tremendous push-back: hate mail and anonymous phone calls, death threats, bomb scares, even murder attempts (allegedly via glass in his food)—much of which he conspicuously reported to local papers, though little evidence backed up his claims.[10]

By the early sixties, Jones had started preaching that "the world soon would be destroyed by nuclear holocaust, and that the surviving elect would then create a new socialist Eden on earth."[11] Claiming that Northern California was one of the world's few locations safe from nuclear fallout, Jones moved the Church to Ukiah, California, in the summer of 1965. Approximately 140 members followed him there from Indiana.[12] By 1967 or so, Jones had established the Church in nearby Redwood Valley. By 1972 they considered it their "'mother church' of a statewide religious movement," as that year also saw the dedication of a temple in Los Angeles.[13] So as to expand their flock ever larger, in 1975 the Peoples Temple officially moved its headquarters to San Francisco, where it would soon get the attention of activists and politicians. The families of Temple youngsters that Opportunity teachers knew had joined the Church at various stages in this history.

Rainbow Family: The Jones Children

Jones demonstrated the very equality he preached by adopting five non-white children. Indeed, when Jim and Marceline adopted a boy they named Jim Jones Jr. (known at Opportunity as Jimmy), they became the first white couple in Indiana to adopt a black child.[14]

Stephan Jones was the only biological child of Marceline and Jim Jones, although the couple legally adopted three other boys and three girls. Agnes, a nine-year old of Native American descent, had appeared at the Jones's front door in Indiana one day in 1954, ragged and proffering a small bouquet of flowers, telling Jones in a halting stutter that she loved him. The girl's

Jones's Rainbow Family (in back, Stephan, Jimmy, Lew, Tim; in front, Marceline and Jim Jones)

mother allowed the couple to adopt the girl. [15] Lew, the oldest boy, was one of two Korean war orphans adopted in 1958. At two, Lew suffered from malnutrition. Stephanie, the other Korean child, was a beautiful little girl of four. Stephanie died the next year in a terrible car accident coming back from a church trip, an accident in which five others also perished.[16]

Stephan, born in 1959, was named after Stephanie. Jim Jr., called Jimmy, was a year younger than Stephan, and was adopted when Stephan was a toddler. Tim, younger than Lew and slightly older than Stephan, had begun living with the family in Ukiah but was not formally adopted until later. Tim's biological mother, Rita Tupper, had joined Peoples Temple in 1969 when the Church was in Redwood Valley. She had come from Iowa and was married with seven children, but she and Tim's father soon divorced.[17]

Stephan and Tim, "a big blond kid, tall and skinny, with a knotted chin and deep-set blue eyes under a brow that became red under the sun," quickly became best friends. Where "Stephan was sullen, Tim was outgoing and talkative." After the divorce, two of Rita's four boys remained with their father, but Tim, though he described himself as a "real daddy's boy," chose to stay with the Jones family and his mother, along with his three sisters. Tim was only eleven at the time. The Joneses officially adopted Tim just before he went to Jonestown, but he had begun calling himself Tim Jones long before that.[18]

One other adoptee joined Jones's "rainbow family": Suzanne was a Korean orphan whom Stephanie had met shortly before the deadly accident—Stephanie had told Marceline that she wished her friend in the orphanage could have a good mother and father too. Marceline contacted the orphanage the day of Stephanie's funeral.[19]

Stephan and his Father

The relationship between Stephan and Jim Jones was difficult and complicated, much more so than for many fathers and sons. Stephan always had a great deal of competition for Jones's attention, and he had long grappled with insecurity about his father's love for him.

Stephan had been named after his late sister, but Jones gave his *new* son his own full name: James Warren Jones Jr. Jimmy was a bright and beautiful child whose adoption happened to embody Jones's commitment to equality and inclusiveness.

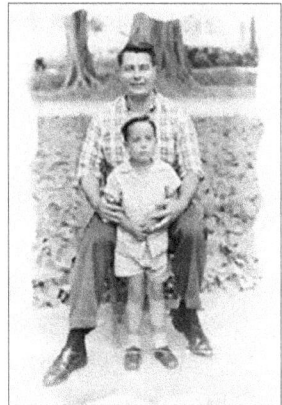

Jim Jones and Stephan

As Stephan grew, a rift between him and his father developed, and began to widen when the Church moved from Indiana to Redwood Valley. Neva Sly later said her sympathy often went to Stephan during that time, when it seemed obvious to all that his father's attention was so often drawn to Jimmy. When Stephan was ten, he was introduced to his father's mistress, Carolyn Layton, for the first time. In an article called "Like Father, Like Son," Stephan writes about the meeting that Jones orchestrated:

> *I'm standing outside a house I've never seen before, bathed by the light coming through the open front door. Dad is straddling the threshold, beckoning to me, pulling at the cold air between us. He's drawing me toward a woman standing about six feet inside the house. She is facing me, smiling nervously. She is a stranger. His eyes are smiling, his lips are moving; I hear nothing. I know that I'm being introduced to a very special person. Special because she is special to Dad.*
>
> *His warmth and excitement for this woman are obvious. He is giddy, like he's showing me his new bike. . . . I don't know her, but I am already jealous of her, for my mother and myself. I want what she has. Dad never looks that way when he speaks of me. . . . I don't remember him dragging anyone over to meet me. Mom seems only a burden to him, weak and old. We are facts of his life. This woman is the highlight.*
>
> *Her name was Carolyn, a woman in her mid-twenties. I wanted to please Dad by liking her, but I couldn't. It took all I had to breathe. I wanted this important person to like me, but most of all I wanted her to stay in her world and leave me and Dad in mine. . . . I was repulsed and drawn. I did not want to be infected like Dad was, but I wanted to know how she did it. What was it about her that held Dad's attention so completely? I couldn't see it. To me she looked willowy and plain, hair brown and limp, face pale, posture poor. Held against Dad's exhilaration, her nervous apprehension intensified her mousy appearance, but I was a tough audience, far preferring the woman who'd been given the part before her. I think my father saw a young, idealistic, and vulnerable woman with a genuine sweetness about her. That sweetness would sadly fade over the years, washed away by the tempest of Jim Jones's character.[20]*

Jones occasionally brought Stephan to visit his mistress, experiences Stephan found increasingly difficult. The meals Carolyn prepared—featuring vegetables, often raw—were nothing like his mother's Midwestern cooking. And at night he heard strange, frightening noises coming from the bedroom on the other side of the wall.

Even worse than his guilt and confusion at being privy to this relationship was witnessing his mother's anguish when he went home—cruelly, Jones had told his wife all about Carolyn. Feeling that his mother was suffering because of his own inability to stop his father, Stephan felt he "had been too afraid, hurt, and *proud* to act." For this he felt "soiled, terrified that someone would surely smell the betrayal that dripped from me." Stephan began to hide out from his family, spending more time alone in his room and in the nearby woods of Redwood Valley, just as he would later try to find time to explore the jungle outside Jonestown.[21]

Despite Jones's admission, Marceline continued to be a good minister's wife, a good mother to Stephan and the other kids, though she was hurting both emotionally and physically—she was troubled by back pain and often bedridden, in traction. Taking advantage of her weakened state, Jones worked to get his wife committed to a mental institution so he could continue his affair with Carolyn Layton. Ever the manipulator, he tried to convince his wife's parents and sister that Marceline was both insane and suicidal. To tend to their daughter, Marceline's parents drove nonstop from Indiana to California, only to realize upon arriving that Jones had deceived them.

Marceline knew nothing of this at first. But soon thereafter she determined she must leave Jones, taking the children with her. She found a surprising ally in Jones's mother, Lynetta, who disapproved of her son's liaison with Carolyn and agreed to help with the escape. But one of the boys learned about the plan and told Jones. Jones subsequently informed his children: "Your mother's going to ask you if you want to go with her. . . . You're going to say no. Your mother loves you, but that's not the best thing for you." He convinced them *he* was the one holding the family together, that it was Marceline who was trying to break it up.

So when Marceline announced her plan to the assembled family, she encountered unexpected resistance. She wept and pleaded with her children to leave with her. Unfortunately, her despair served to make what Jones had claimed about her appear to be true. She *seemed* crazy, so they refused to go. Jones then acted as family "healer," and convinced Marceline to stay.[22]

Stephan has written of other examples of his father's manipulation, the extremes to which he would go just to get Marceline's attention. Occasionally Marceline would get fed up and ignore her husband. "This was more than [Jones] could take. He was starved for acknowledgment, but it had to come from an adult, preferably female." This was a pattern of behavior with which Stephan would become more and more familiar, and which he would grow to hate.

One of Jones's regular stunts would be to collapse, feigning insulin shock. Every time this happened, Stephan and the other children were terrified that their father was dying; and every time, Marceline could be counted on to respond as dutiful wife and nurse to bring him back. But the repetition of this behavior—staging attacks, pretending to fall desperately ill—started "losing its luster" for Stephan, even at a young age. It "seemed like we were always fearing for our lives, or his, or both, and I was growing tired of it. My hardening eyes had glimpsed the buffoon, had spied the brat who took the tummy-ache-for-attention to new heights."

Stephan learned to mimic his father's performances, and nearly killed himself—unintentionally—more than once.

> I was around twelve the first time I took more than enough Quaaludes to kill me. I didn't want to die. I just wanted to be telling the truth when I told Mom that I didn't feel well enough to attend the regular Wednesday night marathon meeting. . . . I snuck home. . ., and popped a couple of the capsules from the full bottle I found on top of Dad's dresser. I waited a minute and, having felt nothing, downed a couple more. . . . In this fashion, I [took] fourteen [pills] in short order before examining the bottle, which instructed the user to take one capsule thirty minutes before bedtime.
>
> Well, I figured from this discovery that I might be stretching things a bit. So, still quite sober, I walked back to the Temple, eased my way back inside, risked the exposure of crossing the auditorium, and slipped up behind Mom where she sat behind Dad on the small, carpeted, plywood platform we called The Stage, and whispered in her ear as Dad droned on, "Mom?" Her eyes never left Dad, and that serene, warm, faithful-servant expression did not falter as she leaned toward me slightly, "Yes, Honey?"
>
> "What's an overdose of Quaaludes?"
>
> "Oh, three or four I guess. Why do you ask, Honey?" Mom was more concerned with remaining unnoticed by Dad and his congregation than she was with what I was telling her. That, combined with her coping-disconnectedness at meetings and my tendency toward eccentric curiosity, blinded her to the red flags of the moment.
>
> "I don't know. Just curious." It took everything I had to not gargle the words.
>
> My only exposure to overdose was through stories of dead heroin addicts, so to me overdose meant death.[23]

Stephan ran back to the house, which only sped up the course of the drug. But, fortunately Tim was there, having decided to escape church too. Stephan, by now really frightened, told his brother to go tell their mother he'd overdosed.

After rushing back to the house and plying Stephan with coffee and syrup of ipecac, his mother drove him to the hospital in Ukiah. Later he woke to her by his side.

Dad was there somewhere too. I knew it instantly. It was something about Mom's carriage—an apprehension, a slight distractedness. He was also in the air. He affected people and places, and I always had my maybe-this-time-radar going: Maybe this time he'll place me on top of his list of to-dos, make me the most important person to influence. Maybe this time he'll notice what a good woman Mom is, what a good family he's got. Maybe this time he'll pull himself from in front of the viewfinder and place there those that adore him. Maybe this time he'll keep it simple and safe. Maybe we'll all be enough. Maybe we'll all heal together.[24]

But Jones was obviously also proud and fond of Stephan. In his article in the *New Yorker*, "Orphans of Jonestown," Lawrence Wright has described some of the nuances of their relationship. Stephan told him, "There was a tenderness about [Jones] that was unique for men his age." Wright described how "sometimes Jones would pull Stephan aside and tell him that the two of them were special in the universe, and that Stephan would inherit his psychic gifts, because their genes were so closely linked. Despite his growing disaffection with his father, Stephan still wanted to believe that."

Stephan told Wright: "It was a strange relationship. . . . I still wanted his approval. I wanted his time. I wanted to love him. I always felt he loved me—I felt that, if nothing else, he was proud of me. But I fought him. And it wasn't out of any bravery or enlightenment—it was just that, one, I saw things that other people didn't see, and, two, I could get away with it. I was his son."[25]

Stephan tried "overdosing" at least two more times: "Once I got a taste of the attention I got after that first overdose, I had to try it again."[26] Meanwhile, his relationship with Jones had grown into a nightmarish dilemma. He loved his father, and yet he also saw the manipulator, the betrayer, the "buffoon." Stephan also loved his mother, who had been among the first to be betrayed—and he felt he had betrayed her too. Not surprisingly, having such complicated relationships with his role models, Stephan struggled in trying to find an identity for himself.

It was no wonder Stephan seemed withdrawn and tired when Bebelaar first met him at Opportunity.

Opportunity's Other Temple Families: Hidden History

At the time, the teachers at Opportunity only knew what they could observe at school of their well-behaved Temple students. There was so much going on behind the scenes that affected the young people—not just within the Temple, but within families too. Jones made sure to exploit existing family rifts and even engineer new ones. And many families came to the Temple in the first place as the result (or cause) of family arguments or splits.

In the process, a few Temple students managed to leave the Church or otherwise avoid being sent to Jonestown, while others were not so lucky.

Teddy McMurry

Like so many others, Cobra player Teddy McMurry was drawn to the Temple, and then to Jonestown, to escape an unhappy family situation. One of six children, Teddy was the youngest of four brothers. His parents separated, after which the children didn't see much of their father, who was stationed in Korea. Their mother, Delores, lived in East Oakland with the children and remarried. The new house-hold was not a placid one. Teddy's sister Renee talked about

Teddy McMurry

her stepfather being "mad" at both her and her mother; she felt her stepfather was jealous of the attention Delores gave her.

Seeking escape, several of the McMurry kids—Carl, Teddy, Sebastian, and Renee—began attending Temple services after hearing about the Church from an aunt. Drawn by the loving family atmosphere he found there, Teddy was the first to leave home, accepting an invitation to live with Church members in Redwood Valley. His big brother Carl found another way out: he followed in his father's footsteps and signed up for the Army. Renee joined the Temple on her first visit, attracted by the lively services and fascinated by the preacher's "cussing."

When Renee was accidentally shot through the neck, the doctor told her she would not walk again. Teddy came to the hospital, bringing her a picture of Jim Jones. Later, the minister himself came to visit. Renee believed that, because he sat on her bed, she was healed, as she found she could move her legs a little starting the next day.[27]

Marilee and the Bogue Family

It was a camping trip from years earlier that had brought Marilee Bogue's family to join the Temple, according to Julia Scheeres in her book, *A Thousand Lives: The Untold Story of Hope, Deception, and Survival at Jonestown*. One night James Bogue took his three daughters to watch fishermen catching night smelt as the silvery fish spawned on the beach. Tommy, a baby, and Jonathon, a toddler, were in the tent with their mother. Jonathon must have wandered out to follow the others; his mother apparently thought the child was with his father and sisters. It was only when James and the girls returned that they made the terrible realization that Jonathon was missing. With the help of fishermen and other campers, they searched for hours, frantic. Finally they found his little body on the beach a mile or so south. Marilee was only nine at the time; Jonathon, two.

Marilee Bogue

After the tragedy, James Bogue desperately sought some way to communicate with his dead boy, talking with a clairvoyant and a Buddhist priest, reading books about "ESP and paranormal activity." When he heard about Jim Jones's touted powers, he brought his family to hear the preacher in Redwood Valley, and soon the family was part of the Temple. Of all the family, Marilee and her mother felt the strongest attraction to the Church, and remained steadfast devotees thereafter.

Scheeres describes how the ritual of having Temple members sign false "confessions"—as reported in the news articles over the summer of 1977—led to a rift in the Bogue family when James was coerced into signing a statement that he had abused his three daughters, then later regretted it and wanted to leave the Church. When he told his wife, Edith Bogue, she went directly to Jones, and James was told such signed statements were "meant for situations like these, where members tried to betray the Church by leaving." So, for the love of his family, James returned to the fold, until Jones sent him to Jonestown on July 23, 1974. Though he was told his family would follow him "soon," it was nearly two years before any of them did. What did happen soon was his wife took as her new partner Harold Cordell, Cindy and Candy's father.[28]

After James Bogue left for Jonestown, Marilee's brother Tommy lived in the Church, in a supply closet he shared with fourteen-year-old Brian

Davis, who'd been made a ward of the Temple when his mother decided she couldn't control him. The boys quickly became best buddies.

One day, according to Scheeres, Tommy took Brian to visit an aunt and uncle—which violated the Temple rule of not associating with outsiders. As punishment, Tommy was forbidden to be with his friend; they were assigned to different rooms, weren't allowed even to speak to each other. By this time Tommy was beginning to hate life in the Temple. During one of the many trips to the Los Angeles temple aimed at recruiting new members, he escaped by hiding in a rest stop bathroom. After a few days of camping there, fed by a sympathetic transportation worker, the police delivered him to his aunt and uncle. Though Tommy told them about "everything: the beatings, the fear, the control," his mother claimed he was exaggerating, and had him sent back to the Church.[29]

Tommy was given a choice: he could live in Alaska with relatives he didn't know, or he could join his father in Jonestown. Tommy loved his dad, and believed, from the glowing films shown at the Temple, that going to Guyana would be an adventure, so off to Jonestown he went. He arrived July 24, 1976, almost two years to the day after his father. He was fifteen.

Marilee was—and remained—fervently committed to Jones. Soon after her arrival, she and her brother Tommy were standing near the warehouse and Tommy shared with her how easy it would be to break in and take a new pair of sneakers as his own were falling apart. Marilee went right in and told the man assigned to watch the store, "My brother's fixing to steal [from] here, so I figure I'd best tell you." Fortunately for Tommy, the man ignored Marilee's warning. Tommy wouldn't speak to Marilee ever again.[30] It seems that Marilee separated herself from the rest of her family too.

Mark Sly

Mark had shared with Cabral his reluctance to go to Guyana. But there was much more that he didn't share with anyone at school.

Mark, who had been adopted by Neva and Don Sly when he was only seven and a half months old, had hated Jones since his early childhood in Ukiah. Neva and Don, devoted Temple members, decided that Mark's aversion to Jim had to do with his having been badly beaten as an infant, probably by a man. At first Mark had screamed whenever his father came into the room, though he soon got over that. But he never got over his dislike for Jim Jones.[31]

Neva's view of Jones and the Temple would come to match Mark's early instinctive feelings. The turning point for Sly concerned the brutality of the Temple's catharsis sessions, supposed tools of healthy "collectivism" that became nothing more than grievous abuse and domination. In a Temple meeting in February 1976, Sly was beaten with a rubber hose that left horrible welts on her legs. With the help of her boss, manager of KFRC radio, she left the Temple and went into hiding.

Mark Sly

For fear of the safety of her son, Sly didn't dare inform Mark of her whereabouts. Though he somehow managed to find her, she was afraid to have him stay there. What might happen to him if he was found with a defector? And, indeed, she soon discovered her phone had been tapped. She hired a private investigator to try to help her rescue Mark, but nothing came of it, and she later found out the investigator "was answering to Jim Jones."[32] This likely happened in the months before the Temple youngsters came to Opportunity.

Linda Mertle Escapes

Linda Mertle was one of at least three Opportunity students who managed to escape the Church before she too would have been sent to Guyana. Three decades after these events, Linda, by then a confident, straightforward young woman with short brown hair and a warm smile, described to Bebelaar how she left—not to join her parents in Berkeley, as those at Opportunity had thought, but on her own.

Linda explained that Deanna Mertle (Jeannie Mills) was actually her stepmother, her father's second wife. When Linda's father remarried, Elmer and Deanna joined the Temple, in 1969. Linda; her younger sister, Diana, or "Turtle"; and her brother, Steve, continued to live with their mother, Zoanna. When Linda's father and stepmother later moved to Redwood Valley with Deanna's children, Eddie and Daphine, Steve opted to move with them.

Linda might never have joined the Church. But during an Easter break, Linda and her little sister Turtle traveled to Redwood Valley for a family visit. There they went to some Church meetings, made many new friends, and in general "had a fantastic time."

Even though it was hard to be a child in the Temple, in some ways children were also the center of everything—at least in those earlier days. Life was good in Redwood Valley. Much of the food was home grown and the cooks were skilled. There was a swimming pool, the beautiful outdoors, good friends. And Linda found her first boyfriend in Ukiah: Jimmy Jones.

But the "fantastic time" ended with a devastating piece of information: Linda's father told Linda and Turtle that Zoanna didn't want them, and that she was an "unfit mother." He said the girls would now live with their Temple family in Redwood Valley.

Hurt and confused, Linda wrote letters to her mother explaining how she and Turtle were both homesick, asking if they could come home. But as she never received an answer, she took that as painful proof her mother indeed didn't love them. When Turtle found Linda crying as she wrote their mom yet another letter, the little girl tried writing too. But no letter came for them. Linda found solace in the Church, and grew to love it in many ways.

Several years later, in 1975, Linda and Steve moved to a Temple commune on Van Ness Avenue near Geary. Most of the Temple kids lived in communes with other children—some their own age, some younger and older—with a couple chosen by Jones to be substitute parents. Linda "was fine with living in a commune. It was like a big family." Melanie Breidenbach, Wesley's sister, was Linda's best friend. Her roommate, Bertha Ford, was part of the Los Angeles temple. To this day Linda has fond memories of life in the Church. "When I think back," she told Bebelaar, "I loved the experience. I loved the camaraderie. But when the punishments started getting really weird, I started wondering."[33]

Linda had been punished often in the Church. Her "weirdest" punishment took place in Ukiah in 1974 when she was sixteen—the paddling the *New West* article had described, which was administered using the Temple's infamous "board of education." She said that afterward she "couldn't sit down for at least a week and a half,"[34] and other problems stemming from this beating plague her to this day.

Even though Linda's father and stepmother later claimed they left in part because of this abuse, when the Mertles defected from the Church in December of 1975—something San Francisco would read about in the summer of 1977—they did not tell Linda about their plans. It was a week before she even realized they were gone—after she noticed they hadn't come to church. Soon after, she was assigned to care for a toddler, Tiffany, one of a few dozen children fostered by or under the guardianship of the Temple.[35]

Linda adored Tiffany; that Tiffany needed her love in return helped Linda cope with her feelings of having been left behind for a second time.

Linda explained to Bebelaar that even separate from its punishments, Temple life was hard work, for the kids as well as for the adults. Kids could not miss school, and their homework had to be done. After school they passed out Church leaflets and collected donations. Two or three times a week they were required to attend evening meetings that often lasted until past midnight, sometimes until 3:00 or 4:00 AM.

Before she came to Opportunity Linda had gone to Washington High, as had many Temple kids. At Washington she found a friend in the school nurse, who let her nap in her office when Linda was too exhausted to stay awake in class. And she wasn't the only one who noticed the stress Linda was under. One day, Maya Angelou was a guest speaker in Linda's Black Literature class. Afterward, Angelou took Linda aside. She had noticed something about Linda, maybe the dark circles under her eyes. Angelou told her, "Whatever you're into right now, it's not good for you. You have to get out of it."

The Temple kids weren't like ordinary teenagers, according to Linda. They had been molded to think and to be as Jones wanted. They were taught not to trust anyone. They must protect the Church, at all costs. The children were told not to reveal anything about the Temple to strangers, because they might say "the wrong thing," which casts new light on Mondo's poem about "sitting in the dark," afraid even to talk to himself "because I might say the wrong thing."

No one could talk about the punishments members, including children, endured: the "board of education" beatings, or the forced boxing matches, with a larger person pitted against a smaller one. Jones said the punishments were necessary. Even a minor offense, for kids—being caught smoking a cigarette, or failing to raise $100 while begging for the Church on the city streets—could merit punishment. "Everything was fear based," Linda told Bebelaar. One reason the Temple students at Opportunity were so well behaved was because if they weren't, or if they got bad grades, they would have been "brought up" in front of the congregation for criticism or worse.

At first Linda believed the punishments were necessary, and thought of beatings as "character building." She hated it, though, when she was forced to box with someone smaller. She thinks it may have been one of those boxing matches that had caused her bruises that Cabral reported to Golden—who had told him not to worry about it, that she'd "take care of it."

Linda says she owes her life to an older woman in the Temple, Kay Henderson, who was a sort of guardian to her after her parents left. A member of the elite Planning Commission, Kay had taken Linda aside to warn her that when she soon turned eighteen Jones planned to have her drugged and sent to Jonestown. Why? To separate Linda from Cynthia Davis, the young woman she loved. But Kay believed Linda should have the choice: go to Guyana, or leave the Church with Cynthia.

Linda and Cynthia had often talked about leaving the Church so they could live together, supporting themselves. But because Linda was not yet eighteen, they had always put off the plan; they worried that Jones would attack Cynthia, who was twenty-eight, with charges of corrupting a minor, or even of statutory rape. When Linda told Cynthia what Kay had revealed to her—asking Cynthia to promise not to tell anyone—the two finally made plans to leave the Temple.

But Cynthia, truly believing that Jones had the power to read her mind, ended up confessing to him. It could be that Jones tricked Cynthia into admitting to what he suspected. Now, Linda feared, Jones would certainly send her to Guyana. This was a horrible prospect for her: She feared the jungle and had a phobia of spiders. And since she had planned to escape, she'd be labeled a traitor, which exacted the worst punishments the Temple doled out. Linda also agonized about what would happen to Cynthia if she, Linda, escaped—and the thought of leaving Tiffany, the little girl she cared for, "ripped her heart out." But she knew she didn't have much choice, and that she didn't have long to decide.

Even after all the time that had passed since she'd lived with her birth mother—seven years—Linda still had her mother's phone number and address. She feared her mother wouldn't want her, but she didn't want to appeal to her father either. She took a chance, went to a pay phone, and dialed. If her mother wouldn't take her in, she decided, she'd just go back to the Church and go to Jonestown.

A familiar voice said, "Hello, this is Zo."

Linda blurted out, "I don't know if you remember me, but I'm your daughter Linda. I'm leaving the Temple, and I'd like to come live with you, if that's okay. I don't know what I did, Mom, but I'd like to come home." Linda held her breath.

"Oh, Honey! You don't know how long I've waited for this phone call." Linda's mother had intentionally kept the same number, just in case her daughters ever reached out to her. Linda was to learn later that her father or stepmother had kept from her the letters her mother had sent. Zoanna had answered all the letters Linda had written, and had kept them in a bundle, along with copies she'd made of her own replies.

Zoanna said she could be in San Francisco in two hours. Linda said she'd be waiting, hiding on a fire escape on Myrtle Street, an alley not far from the commune.

Linda ran the five or six blocks to the Temple as fast as she could. She searched everywhere for Cynthia, but could not find her. As she headed out of the Temple for the last time, she spotted a woman near the door. This woman had reported Linda's "infractions" many times, including the kiss that had brought on the terrible beating in Ukiah. Without a moment's thought, Linda punched the woman as hard as she could and kept going, running back toward the commune. She grabbed a change of clothing and three photographs and ran to the alley.

Shortly after she arrived, breathless and terrified, her mother drove up. Linda jumped down from the fire escape, and they left for Zoanna's home across the Bay. Linda was shaking. What would happen to Cynthia? How could she explain to her mother that she was gay? Would people come after her?

Linda mostly slept for the first two weeks after her escape. In reconnecting with her mother she told her she was a lesbian, and about Cynthia. Her mother was not surprised, and told Linda she would welcome Cynthia too. But it was too late for Cynthia. Upon learning of Linda's escape—no doubt reported by the woman she had punched—Jones had almost immediately sent Cynthia to Jonestown.

After her escape, just to be safe, Linda moved every two years or so, always returning again to her mother. She missed Cynthia terribly, and later would come to feel she could never forgive herself for leaving her and Tiffany in the Church. [36]

Manny Slips Out

It turned out that Cobra and poet Manny Blackwell was another Temple escapee who avoided Jonestown. Manny had told Cabral he was "just friends" with the Temple students. Indeed, it seemed to his teachers that

Manny knew how to get along with everyone. None of the teachers had known his history with the Temple

Manny, his mother, and his sister had been Temple members for years, but he had become increasingly uncomfortable with what he saw happening in the Church. He also believed his family would probably be sent to Jonestown. He didn't want to go there—and he knew that Guyana was the wrong place for his troubled sister, who'd only recently overcome drug problems.

Much later, Manny wrote:

> *There was a lot of apprehension and fear, but that was squelched on Wednesday nights, when the 'beatings' intensified . . . with Jim overseeing and being the ringmaster of the circus. My sister was a nonconformist, so I wasn't going to leave without her, and my mother wanted to go but wouldn't leave her children behind. We started backing away when Jim went ahead to oversee the transition from the U.S. to Jonestown and mother Jones was going about fleecing the remaining flock of all their worldly possessions, leaving us without options and dependent upon the church for all our needs. Great plan: strip you of all your friends, and make you paranoid and fearful of everyone and everything not church related. Not very many wanted to go and leave our new friends and family outside the church and go to a country we knew nothing about and start over.*
>
> *When Marceline began to leave for Jonestown more and more often, that was the end for us. No reason to go to church anymore, so we lost contact.*

He convinced his mom and sister to leave quietly—to just gradually stop going to services. Unlike with previous stragglers, Church members weren't sent to bring them back into the fold: by this time Marceline had taken over many of Jones's duties in San Francisco, and Manny said she was not one to track down people who left.

It was likely just a coincidence that Manny had entered Opportunity right before the Temple students arrived; a middle school counselor had arranged for Manny's transfer to get him away from school bullies. Manny later said there were other Opportunity teenagers who—probably because Jones decreed it—had hidden their Temple association. "They were under the radar."[37]

Three Who Didn't Want to Go

Carl and Ronnie Ross were two Opportunity students who were not in the Temple but had tried to break through the Temple kids' barriers. Ronnie, the spunky and outspoken student who had demanded Jim Jones take off his dark glasses at an Opportunity assembly, was nonetheless a favorite of the teachers. (Except, that is, for Golden, who demanded Ronnie head in the opposite direction whenever he saw Jim Jones at Opportunity.)

Carl, Ronnie's brother, was handsome, shy, hardworking, and responsible; his mother sent Carl to Opportunity because Ronnie was there and loved the school—though she probably also hoped Carl would be a good influence on his brother. Carl and Ronnie had known some of the Temple kids from elementary school days, or junior high. Still, most of the kids would not open up. When pressed, the Temple kids would say they would "get in trouble—not now, but later, at services. We all watch each other. Talk a little too long to someone, and we'll get in trouble."

When Ronnie would ask, "What are they gonna do to you?" they would "shut off," he said. That told him something was wrong. Sometimes, though, a girl or boy would accept his offer of a ride on his Honda 350—apparently an opportunity too great to pass up.

Ronnie and Carl lived near the Griffiths, Mondo's family. Carl delivered their paper. "It was a nice house," he said. Then suddenly, one day the house was empty.

Carl was "crazy" about Temple member Kim Fye, whom he called Kimberly. Kimberly, of course, would have been in trouble at the Church had anyone known they were boyfriend and girlfriend. Carl and Kimberly "started to like each other" soon after they first met. When they could, they'd meet in the darkened, empty art room—a favorite place for secret couples—where they'd talk, "hug a little," maybe steal a kiss. Carl asked Kimberly about the Temple, to tell him what it was like, why the other Temple kids seemed to close up when asked questions about it. She replied, "Carl, there's a lot of stuff going on there." When he asked for details, she invited him to come see for himself, but warned him he'd be searched, maybe asked to "drink something or smoke something." He never did go, and Kimberly didn't tell him much more about the Church.

On the last day of school in 1977, at a picnic in Golden Gate Park, Kimberly asked Carl to meet her back at school later. She had an emergency and needed some money—immediately—but she'd give it back that same evening. He managed to scrape some together and they met at school. Kimberly promised to call him later. On the same day, Carl ran into two other Temple kids he knew: Donald Marshall, and Cleve Garcia, "a shy kid, a really great guy. He had a huge Afro, I remember." Both of them told Carl, "We gotta go someplace, tomorrow." They didn't seem eager. Carl was on his way to a summer job interview and invited the two to come along. Carl's invitation turned out to be a life-changing moment for the two boys. Donald chose to go with Carl and ended up getting the job—and avoided going to Jonestown. But Cleve replied he had to get back to the Church. Carl never saw Cleve again, nor Kimberly.[38]

The way Kimberly had dropped out from Carl's life broke his heart.

Part II

Jonestown

The Cudjoe, the Temple's boat at Jonestown (photo prepared by Ana Gregoriu)

Chapter 10

Entering the Jungle

Spring 1977

Welcome to Guyana

he jungle is an ancient symbol—in dream interpretation, in artists' paintings, in literature, in common parlance—for the beauty of wildness and also for a tangle, a ruthless situation, the unknown, or the wild within.

Guyana is a small country tucked between Venezuela and the tiny nation of Suriname. On its ragged southern border lies Brazil. The weather is hot, with high humidity and frequent rain. The country is home to palms, wild banana, Brazil nut, guava, balsa wood, and, in its deep rainforest, giant mahogany. Near Jonestown the actual jungle, or bush, is a triple-canopy rainforest. Tree branches are draped with lianas; mosses, ferns, and orchids grow in damper, wilder places. In some ponds and lakes float water lilies with pads big enough to support a child. Named *Victoria regia* by a German botanist in 1837, the enormous floating flowers were called "naia" by the indigenous Arawak, after a young girl who, in legend, drowned trying to touch the moon reflected in the river, and the moon transformed her into a beautiful flower.

The blue-backed grass bird, the Guyana redbreast, toucans, and the bright orange cock-of-the-rock are among the many colorful birds; a flock of "curri-curri" (scarlet ibis) in flight is said to be a beautiful sight. Guyana is also home to African violets, gentians, yellow-eyed grass, bright pink and purple bromeliads, and numerous species of passion flower.[1] Joyce, the Opportunity poet who wrote about "the tropic island" and "the small creatures hiding from the rain," would have sought out beautiful things in Guyana, her teacher was sure.

The jungle offered plenty to fear, too. Former Temple member Eugene Smith (the husband of Opportunity student Ollie Smith) spoke of poisonous plants like deadly nightshade, snakes that bite, bees that sting multiple times, and how it was "nighttime all day."[2] But Jones created a figurative jungle as well, turning the bush, with his words, into ominous, impenetrable prison walls.

peppered decoration

During the spring of 1977, Jonestown averaged about twenty new arrivals a month, and at least five of those spring arrivals were Opportunity students.[3] But as pressures mounted back in California from continued defections and bad press, Jones began to speed up the exodus from San Francisco, and it was during the summer and fall of 1977 that the full-blown migration of people from the San Francisco Temple took place. Between April and September of 1977, the Jonestown population grew from 65 to 630. One hundred forty-five arrived in July and 358 more in August. After that the community continued to grow steadily, averaging 25 new arrivals each month.[4] Ultimately, there would be more than nine hundred listed as residents of Jonestown by November 1978.

The exact number of Opportunity Temple students who were among those in Jonestown is uncertain. Out of ninety Jonestown residents listed on the Jonestown Institute's website (*Alternative Considerations of Jonestown and Peoples Temple*, www.jonestown.sdsu.edu) who would have been high school age in 1976, forty-six were young people Bebelaar and Cabral had known, or whose names seemed familiar. When the teachers contacted the San Francisco school district for help identifying students who might have attended Opportunity, a lawyer said the district could not release such records because of state and federal laws.[5]

This account follows the twenty-four students who went to Jonestown that Bebelaar and Cabral (and other Opportunity teachers) identified and focuses on those they knew best. Of the young people listed among the Jonestown arrivals in this chapter and the next, those who had been Opportunity students are marked with an asterisk. Other young people are included in this account because of a special relationship to an Opportunity student. It seems that Jones sent most young people to Guyana with at least one relative or friend, perhaps as part of a strategy to help ensure their compliance, so those with whom each young person entered are noted as well.

Though Jones saw to it that copious records were kept at Jonestown, they are not always accurate, and there are many discrepancies between the two Jonestown entry lists: one that shows arrivals by name, alphabetically, and the other by date, showing the groups who arrived together. Not everyone is on both lists. Some, like Jones himself, his wife Marceline, Stephan, Tim, and

Jimmy, entered more than once, but entry dates are often only recorded once (and not always on the date of the first entry).

The Journey to Jonestown

As more and more Temple incomers arrived in Guyana, their dreams of a jungle paradise began to erode on the long journey into Jonestown. Such was the experience for Temple member Deborah Layton. Deborah had joined the Church as a teenager; she was twenty-four when she came to Guyana, accompanying her mother, Lisa, who was ill with cancer. Believing Jones could cure her, Deborah's mother came to Jonestown to be near him. Deborah describes her and her mother's arrival at the Georgetown airport:

Deborah Layton

> *It was five in the evening and I could feel the heat radiating up from the old cement runway, trying to melt the soles of my shoes. A sign glued to a window of an old, dilapidated building read, "Welcome to Guyana." We entered the terminal through thick glass doors. The building reminded me of a World War II airplane hangar . . . long, old, dark, and noisy. . . . The ride from the airport was long and frightening. The road was narrow. Little, run-down, flimsy taxis honked and sped by, even if there was an oncoming car. . . . Everything was old, shabby, and neglected. There were pathetic sheds along the road, each with a sign in the front window announcing that they, too, sold Coca-Cola. . . . After an hour and a half of bouncing down the road, past empty fields and desolate countryside, we slowed and entered a decaying township. The main thoroughfare was one-lane wide, but the buildings on either side of the road had once been elegant Victorian homes.*[6]

Eugene Smith said this of his first sight of Guyana:

> *A Third World country, shacks, barren patches of brown grass, people, villagers doing the best they could to survive. I saw the first and last person in my life afflicted with Elephantiasis. . . . The people looked desperate and very tired.*[7]

From Georgetown, most new arrivals made the journey to the jungle interior on the Temple boat, the *Cudjoe*. Smith described the boat trip from Georgetown to Port Kaituma as a wild, scary journey, the deck covered with vomit, and Guyana's heat as hammering.[8]

Deborah's description is equally vivid:

> *We sailed out into the Caribbean for the twenty-five-hour voyage to the mouth of the Kaituma River. The seas were rough and no one was spared the ocean's wrath. We stayed in our places, hanging on tightly, heads bobbing, stomachs*

croaking. We heaved ceaselessly into the waves, which crashed onto the deck and drenched us. As our bodies slumped down on the dirty barge deck, the day turned dark and I was no longer able to decipher time, nor did I care to. The swells continued to rise above the sides of the tug, the ocean's salty mist splashing over my face and lips, stinging my swollen, unopened eyes. My clothes were soaked with seawater and vomit. . . . As the night crept on and turned to dawn, my body was transformed into one enormous cramp.

"Only eight more hours to go!" yelled a crew member as the Cudjoe entered the mouth of the Kaituma. My stomach settled as we made our way into the calmer river waters. . . . The jungle river was thick with life, snakes, piranha, and curious debris from the rain's torrential runoff. Its root-beer-colored water shwooshed past us, carrying felled trees and other plant life uprooted from its banks.[9]

Most of the Opportunity students had likely never been on a boat before this—and might have believed they were going on a trip to a tropical wonderland. During the early days of Jonestown, according to Michael Touchette, on one trip from Guyana to Florida in order to collect supplies and twenty-four passengers, the seas were so rough that some of the windows in the pilot house were smashed. And the men Jones had selected to pilot the boat had no experience navigating a boat in the open ocean.[10]

Deborah names the Caribbean in her account of the boat trip, but it was actually the Atlantic that the immigrants entered on the trip from Georgetown (although Caribbean waters mingle with the Atlantic there). "When I was on the *Cudjoe*," Eugene Smith writes, "the waves were breaking over the bow. The Atlantic is a lot more turbulent than the Pacific. Then when you add the fact that [the boat] was overloaded and the young folks were sleeping on the deck, sea travel took on a whole new view!!"[11]

When they finally reached Port Kaituma, the voyagers could look forward to a beautiful, peaceful ride up the river. But then they had yet another difficult leg of the trip. Deborah writes:

The following ride in the truck was agonizing. We sank into deep troughs and struggled back out as the truck sputtered on, taking us farther and farther into the jungle. After two exhausting hours, I suddenly heard oohing and ahhing and sat up. Not too far in the distance I saw lights. It seemed as though we were nearing an enchanted city. The halo illuminating the sky ahead of us was captivating.[12]

For Smith the trip was a leap into a strange new world:

It's raining like hell, and it's still hot, muddy, bumpy, miserable, exciting, edgy, crazy, risky, momentous, frightening, anxious, hopeful . . .

I could see this eerie light in the distance a glow. Then I hear the people, voices, screaming, and singing. At the moment it is Monsoon season and I'm behind a farm tractor, being pulled down the road in a metal trailer, hanging, holding on as best as one could. I have never seen potholes the size of these in my life, and [we] drive through them. We managed to hit, fall into, and climb out of, every hole there was only to do it again and again for miles and for the next couple of hours. But the real relevant point is that it's dark, real dark. The jungle is there, you just can't see it.[13]

Stephan Arrives* [Asterisks indicate Opportunity students.]

It was into this strange country that Stephan entered for the long term on February 15, 1977, though he had visited at least twice in earlier days.[14] By the time he settled there in February, he joined a population of only fifty.[15] In the photograph from his entry passport, Stephan's face is that of a very young exile. His dark eyes are guarded, with a hardness revealing both intense anger and sadness.

Stephan traveled to Port Kaituma from Georgetown by plane when he came in February 1977 (although he did end up traveling to and from Georgetown on the *Cudjoe* several times and knew what a long and miserable part of the trip the ocean journey could be).[16]

In an article in the *New Yorker*, "Orphans of Jonestown," Lawrence Wright describes Stephan's arrival in Guyana's capital and his first impressions of Jonestown:

After landing in Georgetown, 135 miles from Jonestown, Stephan caught a flight up the coast, on an alarmingly rickety military cargo plane. Through the window he could see the jungle stretching endlessly below him. The only breaks in the canopy were vast rivers that cut through the bush. There were no roads, no towns—no human mark visible in the entire expanse.... The airport consisted of the strip and a shed with a dirt floor.... The sounds of Marvin Gaye's "Let's Get It On" drifted across the village from a tiny hut that called itself a nightclub. Barefoot Indian children ran up to Stephan and looked at him with fascination. Six feet five, with wide cheekbones and his father's fiery eyes, Stephan Jones, at the age of seventeen, was already an imposing figure....

Roughly half of the fifty settlers were inner-city kids who had been taken in by the Temple and the other half consisted of long-time church members who had the skills Jones needed to build the settlement.

The kids were mostly troublemakers in the Temple membership, who had been sent by Jim Jones to Guyana either as punishment or to put them beyond the reach of the law. They were working from before dawn to nearly midnight every day clearing brush, and it was formidable work—especially cutting the hardwoods, which were so dense that they could deflect an iron axe head. They left the fallen trees to dry for months, then ran through in teams of two, one boy carrying kerosene and the other a torch, and set fire to huge swaths of brush. "We howled at the top of our lungs, pouring kerosene and lighting fires," Stephan remembers. "It was quite a romp." Ahead of them would be a rush of wild-life—iguanas, monkeys, lizards. The ruined forest would burn for days, and while it was still smoldering Stephan and two other colonists would come in with bulldozers and push the embers into ravines. They loved to do this work at night: when coals hit the bottom of a ravine there would be an explosion of sparks. The boys would come back with their faces black with soot and their hair singed. In this fashion, they cleared three hundred acres. [17]

The Jonestown Stephan encountered was peopled by many he had come to know as a child growing up in the Church: good, steady, brave, committed

Stephan Jones and Marceline Jones in Jonestown

folk whom Jones had chosen for their intelligence and their capabilities—the kind of people who used to be called the Salt of the Earth. Stephan surely also liked the young people there, the "troublemak-ers"—kids like he'd met at Opportunity but wasn't allowed to fraternize with, kids who, in a way, were much like him: rebellious but likable, and smart. And although the work was hard and the weather inhospitable much of the time, because Jones hadn't settled there full time yet, the ground rules and the basic setup were more humane, created more for the safety and comfort of those who came to populate the settlement. Though Stephan hadn't wanted to go, Jonestown was nonetheless an escape from his father. And since Marceline divided her time between San Francisco and Jonestown, oversee-ing children and their care, and the overall health of Jonestowners, Stephan was also able to still feel connected to his mother.[18]

Though many found Jonestown a challenge, Stephan thrived on the hard work and the beauty of the wilderness. He ventured into the bush and learned to love it, as he had the woods in Ukiah. Here, too, the wilds became his refuge. He had an anaconda and emerald tree boas as pets in his cottage, and he would walk around with one of them wrapped around him. "When the natives saw that, they freaked out," Stephan told Wright. "They thought I was some kind of demon."[19]

Even if Stephan was not the willing pioneer that many were, he did find a way to enjoy several months in Guyana before his father established permanent residency there. Stephan later said these early adventurous times were his best days in Jonestown; indeed, they were the best in his life up to that point.[20]

According to Lawrence Wright, Jones saw Stephan as "a natural leader, like himself," and made his son the chief administrator of the entire project,"perhaps hoping to bring him back into the fold."[21]

Almost as soon as he arrived, Stephan was encouraged by the settlers to stay permanently. He didn't want to seem selfish to the people he'd grown up with and loved—all of them having sacrificed so much and worked so hard to build Jonestown. But, he says, his feelings were beside the point; he wasn't given a choice.[22]

Tim Jones*

Tim came to Jonestown for what was likely an early visit on March 9, 1977 (Marceline didn't pull him out of Opportunity until March 25), then arrived permanently sometime in late March.[23]

Jim Jones considered Tim "intensely loyal and courageous," and made Tim one of his personal bodyguards in Jonestown as well as one of the top leaders of the security team, which was composed of almost all the young men and some young women in Jonestown.[24] As the weeks passed, Tim spent more of his time "tending to Jones's nocturnal whims and fetching people" Jones wanted to meet with. "A squire—I was like a squire," Tim says in the *New Yorker*. He had learned to avoid thinking about it too much. According to Stephan, "Tim had sworn an oath to my father. I equate it to a military oath. The guy said, 'Look, I'm in. You're my *leader*. And with that I sacrifice some of my own thought processes and defer to you.'"[25]

Tim did not share Stephan's love for the jungle. In fact, from the moment of his arrival he hated Jonestown. He missed life in the city and his friends at Opportunity.[26] He may have been thinking of finishing the baseball season with the Cobras, pitching the team to more wins and moving the Cobras up to varsity status, thus helping ensure for himself a spot on Cal's team.

Tim would also have been missing his girlfriend—by then his fiancée and pregnant with his child—Sandy Cobb (a sister of Opportunity student Johnny), who was still back in San Francisco. Bebelaar suspects Sandy was the girl he wrote a poem about in class, whose face Tim said "reminds me of night that comes / And settles down / Over the world."

In July, Tim returned to San Francisco to bring Sandy to Guyana, along with the remaining members of the Tupper family: his brother Larry and sisters Janet, Mary, and Ruth. (His birth mother arrived on June 29, 1977.) Tim and Sandy were wed in Georgetown on July 17, the day they landed together in Guyana. Sandy stayed in Georgetown until the baby was born. But even in the capital city the facilities were primitive, and their baby died.[27]

Tim Jones and Jim Jones at I-Hotel protest in San Francisco

Jimmy Jones*

Jimmy's entry date is listed as June 17, 1977, but he too would have actually entered earlier, as Jones began to call his sons to Jonestown. Jimmy, like Tim, held a high ranking, as Jonestown's "communication officer." Many of the less privileged members of the Jonestown community were both afraid and resentful of Tim and Jimmy. "We were the Gestapo, the elite, and we treated ourselves that way," Jimmy admitted much later.[28]

Cornelius Truss*

Cornelius Truss had been an Opportunity student, and records show he arrived in Jonestown on April 5, 1977. Cornelius, who was black, was inseparable from his friend Vance White, who was very fair with longish straight blond-brown hair. Bebelaar remembers Cornelius well partly because of this friendship—the two embodied the quality of color-blindness the teachers found so appealing about Temple kids.

Cornelius and Vance were in Bebelaar's reading class, and asked to work together on a project for which students were to choose a book to read and then write an essay or a letter to the author. They chose *The Cay*, by Theodore Taylor. The story is about a young white boy who has been taught black people are inferior and not to be trusted. After the boy is blinded in a shipwreck, he is saved by an older man whom he comes to love. He only later discovers the man is black. Theodore Taylor answered Cornelius and Vance's letter, which Bebelaar read to the class.

> *Yes, I think that everyone on earth, of all colors, could be helped by a tiny bit of color blindness. . . . Touch someone with your eyes closed and you don't know if they're black, white or polka-dot. I feel that we older people have failed and it is up to younger people like yourselves to turn the world around. I also feel confident you will do it.*[29]

Vance did not go to Guyana; perhaps he was one of those who managed to avoid it. Bebelaar and Cabral have not been able to find a trace of him.

Michelle Touchette

Michelle was, off and on, Stephan's girlfriend both in San Francisco and Jonestown, but, as Stephan writes in his heartfelt essay about her, "Reunion," she was his "first love." Michelle came to Jonestown before Stephan did; though her official entry date is April 28, 1977, Stephan says that must have been a re-entry date.

A slender girl with long brown hair and a shy smile, Michelle wore glasses that belied her prettiness. She did not attend Opportunity.

When Michelle had left for Jonestown, Stephan heard she was dating Emmett Griffith, Mondo's brother, and Stephan began seeing someone else in San Francisco. She didn't know that, and Stephan didn't tell her.

Though he "always made sure [he] broke up with her" before seeing another girl, he knows he also broke her heart—and more than once.[30]

Wesley Breidenbach*

Wesley Breidenbach, the first Cobra replacement pitcher for Tim, arrived in Jonestown on April 24, 1977.[31] That he was sent there so early may indicate his importance to the project, and the jobs he held were ones Jones gave only to those who were trusted and capable. For one, he was a radio operator on the system that connected Jonestown with Georgetown and San Francisco—the system through which Jones had communicated with Golden. He also drove the tractor and even operated the *Cudjoe* on which newcomers were transported from Georgetown to Port Kaituma. And like all the young men, he was also part of the security force protecting Jones.

Wesley's sister, Melanie, joined him on April 28, 1977, and his mother later that fall.[32] According to the Jonestown records, Wesley had a "partner"

Wesley Breidenbach (left) and Donny Casanova working in Jonestown

(meaning "spouse," whether actually married or not), Avis Jocelyn Garcia, who wouldn't arrive until August. Avis, born in Belize, had sparkling, dark, earnest eyes and was a year older than Wesley.

Though Wesley and Avis were partners, once she arrived they apparently did not live in the same cottage: records indicate Avis lived in cottage 18, Wesley in cottage 33 with eighteen others, including Tim Jones and, later, Opportunity poet Joyce Polk Brown.[33] Such living arrangements were not unusual even among couples who were actually married: Marriages were often arranged by Jones and could be rather loose relationships, which Jones might decide to rearrange. Also, Jonestown residents were moved around fairly often, especially when the encampment became more crowded, so Wesley and Avis may have lived together at times. Though in theory the Relationship Committee also decided who could be together, as with everything else it was Jim Jones who had the last say. Jones may well have arranged this marriage as he often brought couples together—or caused families to break apart.

Candy Cordell

Candy Cordell, older sister of Opportunity student Cindy, came to Jonestown on May 29, 1977. She either arrived with her older brother, Christopher Mark, or he had preceded her.

Candy wrote a letter to Angela Davis that remains a poignant artifact from Jonestown. Even if she was assigned to write the letter, with instructions to paint a glowing picture of the settlement, there is likely at least some truth in what she wrote. Either way, she conveyed the Jonestown that Jones wanted the world to believe, the "paradise" he had claimed it to be, and likely what she wanted it to be (and perhaps even experienced, for a while).

Hello Comrade! I am a member of Jonestown. I am 17 years of age and in High School. I have listened to you speak at the San Francisco Temple and have read your book. I enjoyed your speeches and appreciated hearing you speak about Black Liberation and the Peoples Freedom. All my life I have wondered if there would be any place in the world where Blacks, Indians, or minority people could go and really be free. Well, I never found the place until I came to Jonestown, Guyana. Because in the states all I saw was young people going to drugs or jail and even being killed. But here in Jonestown there is none of that. It is a very beautiful community and I would like to tell you just a little bit about it.

In Jonestown we have five large buildings we call dorms, about 60 cottages, a large kitchen, and a main dining area where we all eat. Surrounding Jonestown are miles and miles of jungle. It is so beautiful to look out and see nature as it should be, not infiltrated with smog and pollution—much less racism and fascism. We have about 50 dogs, 3 beautiful birds, 2 small monkeys—plus Mr. Muggs (the chimpanzee), 2 horses, 16 cows, 100 pigs, 2000 chickens, 1 anteater, and many others. We serve 3 meals a day, also 3 mid-time meals (snacks). And many 100s of acres of food planted: Bananas, fruits, eddoes, papayas, lettuce, carrots, cucumbers, sweet potatoes, just so many for me to even think of. We also have a large Cassava Mill, Piggery, Chicken House, Sawmill, Tent, Mechanic Shop and other productive things.

We also have a very beautiful nursery—for the babies. There are three different rooms—one room is for the babies 0–8 months, the next room is for 8–18 months, and the last room is 18 months–three years. The parents can leave the babies in the nursery if they want to while they go out to work. All of the babies here are very healthy. As a matter of fact, in Jonestown, a community of about 900 citizens, we have maybe only a couple of people that are not to the best of health. The climate is nice and warm but there is always a cool breeze blowing. No money in the world could ever pay for this kind of a life. Many people coming from the states that are here did not know anything about agriculture, including myself. But we have caught on and learned that I really love working in the warm sun; Planting, weeding and picking the food. Which really makes me feel good because I know I am doing it for myself and I can actually see what I have produced it and eat it! Jonestown is undescribably beautiful. Thanks to my leader, Jim Jones, who paid my way over here, I can now live with comrades that care for me. I work in the nursery with the babies, 0–8 months, and enjoy it very much. I hope that you will write us back in response to our letters.

We are determined to keep our land free and committed to defending our land.

We really have a beautiful land to defend and we're not going to let the Capitalists come in and take over our land.

Thinking of You Always,
Your Comrade Sister,
Candace Cordell[34]

The rest of Candy's large family—four sisters, two more brothers, mother and father—would arrive during the summer.

~❧~

At least twenty Opportunity students arrived in Jonestown, along with many adults and elders, just as the "great experiment" was breaking down: just as housing was becoming more crowded, food was growing scarcer, and Jones was beginning to spiral out of control.

Scarlet ibis in flight

Chapter 11

Children of Paradise

Summer 1977

Dreams Deferred

> *What happens to a dream deferred?*
> *Does it dry up*
> *like a raisin in the sun?*
> *Or fester like a sore—*
> *And then run?*

angston Hughes's poem, "Harlem" (later titled "Dream Deferred") ends with "Or does it explode?"

For those who entered Jonestown earlier in 1977—including Opportunity students Stephan, Tim, Jimmy, Cornelius, and Wesley—the conditions in the settlement were considerably better than for those who came later, after Jones settled in permanently in the late summer of 1977. Before then, the atmosphere was generally relaxed. Yes, the settlers all worked hard, but it was Peoples Temple, after all, with music, singing, dancing, and general enjoyment of each other. It was Jones who later instigated the harsh, disciplinary side of Temple life. Until then, they still had some free time. It was a hard life, but it was one without their "father."

The mindset of the earliest settlers was one of working together for their common mission. While they did hold regular meetings—as Peoples Temple always had—they met only once a week, usually on Sundays, and addressed important topics in a "civil" manner, with no harsh punishments or community shaming. "They had decided . . . games and browbeating would only hurt the project," as Tim Reiterman writes in *Raven*.[1]

People in the settlement's kitchen were good cooks. Records describe rather healthy meals at first: rice and okra, pineapple, mangos, and fried fish; curried chicken with chicken necks and pork bones, rice, pumpkin, and a roll; fish cakes and rice; and on Sundays, chicken raised in Jonestown—though the chicken would soon be off the menu at Jones's order, so as to

Joyce Polk Brown, Eileen McCann and other young women on kitchen crew in Jonestown

sell the birds that managed to survive.[2] Over time, meals became more spartan in general—at least for most of the rank and file.

The population in Jonestown grew tenfold between April and September of 1977, and the influx meant that food was doled out in smaller portions and cottages and dorms became even more crowded. In Mark Sly's cottage, which was designed for four residents, fifteen squeezed into a fifteen-by-thirty-foot space. Overall, about fifty cottages each held anywhere from two to nineteen settlers—usually eight to twelve; the dorms housed between thirty and fifty people. Marceline lived in one of the six smaller cottages, their walls woven with troolie palm leaves. Jones had a larger cottage, more like a small house, for himself—and his mistresses—known as the West House, which was set at a distance from the other cottages.[3]

Although several of the early settlers were experienced in farm work, carpentry, and building, many of those just entering didn't have the skills or knowledge to help with the extra work that was required to maintain such a large community. More people just meant more people to feed, more children to tend, more illness and injury. And although Marceline was a good nurse, the only Temple "doctor" was Larry Schact, a former drug addict whom Jones had put through medical school but whose internship Jones cut short to go to Jonestown.[4]

Summer 1977

Everything Changes

Jim Jones's official entry date is listed as June 17, 1977.[5] It is not clear exactly when he came to stay permanently in Jonestown, but it was likely sometime in the late summer of 1977, after the *New West* exposé came out.

Exact dates of events that took place in the settlement are often difficult to chronicle, especially before Edith Roller, the sixty-two-year-old Temple scribe (who kept the only known journal of life in Jonestown), arrived in early 1978. There were no calendars in Jonestown, Deborah Layton explains; radios were not allowed, nor were newspapers or magazines, save for the torn pieces used for toilet paper in the latrines. Indeed, holidays like Thanksgiving, Christmas, and even everyone's birthdays "went forgotten."[6]

Jones had traveled to Guyana three or four times in 1975 and 1976. Each time most of the settlers were relieved to see him go since he always reinstituted the manipulative public catharsis sessions that he had led in the San Francisco Temple. These exhausting meetings replaced the evenings previously enjoyed watching rented movies, playing cards, reading, or talking to friends.[7]

The records do not always indicate the comings and goings of Jones family members and some others who travelled to and from Jonestown. Marceline travelled back and forth from California, tending to the children and those in the infirmary in Jonestown then returning to the San Francisco Temple to see to matters there, but the only entry date listed for her is March 29, 1977.[8]

It was during the late summer and early fall of that year, as Jones began to spend more time in the camp and eventually settled in for good—when things really began to change for the worse. His increasing presence corresponded with the deterioration of the situation there, and, as time went on, as his own mental and physical state went into a downward spiral, so did conditions in Jonestown. The drugs he was taking no doubt contributed to his degeneration: amphetamines alternating with Percodan, antidepressants like Elavil, and perhaps heroin.[9]

Stephan said of his first months in Jonestown, "We worked long hours, but when we were off, our time was our time." The settlers were proud to be building a town for the new community, and they "played and worked hard." Whenever Jones arrived, things changed "overnight." Now when people got off work, Stephan said, "your time was his time."[10]

Both new and established Jonestowners only learned of the happenings in the world outside their "jungle paradise" in meetings and through the news reports Jones regularly provided over the public address system. The information offered, of both national and international concerns, was culled from radio news services and supplemented by the magazines and newspapers newcomers brought with them from the States. Of course, Jones didn't read just any news; the reports were selectively chosen, and those he did read often included his own biased commentaries.[11]

Evening meetings or "rallies" were held at the pavilion more often, increasing to three times a week: two on weekends and one midweek (or even more if "needed," as determined by Jones and dependent on his level of paranoia at the time). Rallies usually included a discussion of matters related to agriculture, some kind of entertainment, and "Discipline and Praise"—as time went on, more discipline than praise.

Jonestowners were also tested on the news reports that Jones had read over public address system and on socialism taught in the "Enlightenment classes." Whoever failed the tests might be forced to attend additional classes or even forgo "the next meal" until they retook the test. [12]

Jones's growing concern that things were falling apart resulted in a tighter, more paranoid grasp on his power over the Jonestown residents. Deborah was dismayed to discover that the letters travelers had brought to Jonestown residents were confiscated, "to be reviewed by the Clearing Committee."[13] All passports, too, had been collected to be kept in Georgetown. There were more rules and harsher, more frequent punishments.

On top of that, the humidity and heat are high at the end of summer in Guyana, and the rain is still heavy—nothing like summer in San Francisco, where the foggy cool turns warmer as September approaches. The weather in Jonestown would have been hard on teenagers in particular, and the emotional atmosphere even more stressful. Jonestown was full of tension and fear when most Opportunity teenagers, including those listed below, entered in the summer and fall of 1977.

Opportunity Influx

It was just as living conditions were rapidly declining that most of the former Opportunity students were entering Jonestown to begin their new lives. Mark Sly* arrived July 17, 1977, along with Johnny Cobb* and the four members of Tim's family, the Tuppers, with whom Mark had grown up. Mark's father Don Sly did not arrive until October or November 1977.[14] His mother, Neva, had become known as a "traitor" to the Temple and Jones, while Don remained a devout member. His father's arrival may not have been much comfort to Mark. Their relationship was likely troubled by then, as Mark was very close to his mother. It is possible that Jones had realized that Mark was a minor without a representative parent or legal guardian in Jonestown, and for this reason ordered Mark's father to Guyana.

꒜

Billy Oliver* and Ricky Johnson* entered Jonestown on July 27, and lived in the sawmill with Cornelius Truss, which meant that Cornelius had two Opportunity buddies with whom to share his experiences. Billy's handsome, square-jawed older brother Bruce, and Bruce's lively and beautiful wife, Shanda, also came then.[15]

Billy Oliver

Bruce Oliver

The Olivers' father, Howard, and their mother, Beverly—another Temple member who had left the Church—had given their permission for the boys to *visit* Jonestown. But when

Shanda Oliver

Ricky Johnson

the exodus began, they feared "their sons were gone for good." Bruce and Billy wrote letters home about the wonders of Jonestown, but Beverly was skeptical. Billy was still a minor so the Olivers obtained a court order demanding his return, but he was about to turn eighteen—they were running out of time. Later that year, the Olivers set off for Guyana; for eight days they did everything possible to see their sons, going to the U.S. embassy and even seeking an audience with the prime minister, but the Temple kept finding ways to postpone the visit. Finally news came from Jonestown that the Church council had decided the couple could not see their sons. Exhausted and terribly disappointed, the Olivers returned home. But they would try again, borrowing money for the airfare to get to Guyana, up until the very end.[16]

꒜

Linda Mertle's beloved Tiffany La Trice Garcia, the child she was asked to look after in San Francisco who was not yet three years old, was sent to Jonestown with her mother, Tanya Garcia. Separating children and parents was "a way of controlling people," Linda said much later.[17] Tiffany arrived a week before Linda's girlfriend, Cynthia, on July 23, 1977.[18]

꒜

Cindy Cordell*, who had written the report about the Temple for the *Natural High Express*, arrived on August 4, as did Cleve Garcia*, after he declined an interview for the job Opportunity student Carl Ross had told him about.

Cleve Garcia

≈⊌

Cobra player Calvin Douglas,* along with Opportunity poets Willie Thomas* and Rory Bargeman*, and Carl Ross's secret girlfriend Kimberly Fye*, arrived August 6. Mondo Griffith* arrived August 10 (along with Agnes Jones, adopted member of the Jones "rainbow family").[19]

≈⊌

Marilee Bogue* arrived on August 11. Her partner was Cardell Neal, a strong, serious-looking twenty-year-old black man, a Jonestown security guard. Marilee probably knew Cardell from the San Francisco Temple. Both were committed to Jones.[20]

≈⊌

Cobra Teddy McMurry* arrived August 14.[21] When Teddy was called to Jonestown, his sister Renee wanted to go too. But their mother, Delores, wouldn't give her permission as she had for Teddy. (Parental consent was required for all minors who weren't wards of the Church.) So Renee worked to make her mother "hate her," pestering her with various small annoyances to make her *want* to get rid of her. She apparently succeeded, because Renee and brother Sebastian followed Teddy to Jonestown, arriving on September 23, 1977. [22, 23]

The girl Teddy would marry, red-headed Eileen McCann, would enter then too. Eileen was pregnant, but she and Teddy did not make the journey together, although they were allowed to stay in the same cottage. Their child would be one of the many babies born in Jonestown.

Since Jones often divided couples and families, children—including Teddy and Eileen's baby—lived in a separate children's cottage, furnished thoughtfully by Marceline with pictures, books and toys. Many of the teenage girls no doubt chose to work there if they could. The children lived in their own cabin in order to allow the parents to wake early and go off to long, arduous workdays that lasted until dinnertime. In Jonestown, now, there was little time for either romance or one's own children.

≈⊌

Dorothy Buckley* and her mother, brother, and two sisters arrived August 22, along with Cobra Christopher Newell.*[24]

≈⊌

Later, in the next—and final—year of Jonestown, Monica Bagby and at least three other Opportunity students arrived.

Christopher Newell

On February 23, 1978, Ollie Smith*, the singer at Opportunity's open house, now married to Eugene Smith, arrived.[25] She was pregnant and wanted her child to be born in Jonestown, where he would be raised without sexism, racism, or ageism.

Ollie Smith

Stephanie Chacon* and Joyce Polk Brown* arrived on March 15, 1978. Joyce was accompanied by Lucy Crenshaw, named her "birth mother" on the entry list but who was actually her aunt.[26]

Stephanie Chacon

Monica Bagby*, who had been a student in Bebelaar's Creative Writing class, arrived in Guyana in the summer of 1978. The arrivals list on the *Alternative Considerations* website indicates she entered in 1977, but in another section of the site, Monica's Jonestown friend, Vernon Gosney, writes about her arrival in 1978.[27] And Monica's poem, "Darkness," appears in the spring 1978 issue of *Fire*, Opportunity's poetry magazine. It says much about her spirit:

> *I wish the sun had shined longer today*
> *But I knew that soon it would be taking*
> *A stroll down the back stairs of the earth*
> *Darkness is no bother,*
> *The moon is my sister, shining in full*
> *On the days marked on my calendar*
> *The moon's glow dances softly on the ocean*
> *Soon darkness will retire*
> *I must say goodbye to night*

Monica did not want to go to Guyana, but her mother had decided she must.[28]

Jonestown's School

The former Opportunity students—as well as elementary school-age children and adults—had a school in Jonestown. But the school, like Joyce's dream of a jungle adventure, was another dream deferred. Developed in late 1977, the school "building" consisted of two open-sided green-roofed long tents, which were located near the central pavilion where residents ate and attended meetings. Though permanent buildings to house the school and library had been planned, they were never built.[29]

In a letter to her mother dated September 19, 1977, Judy Houston—who, with her sister, Patty, had been spirited off to Guyana after the mysterious death of their father, Bob Houston—in a railyard under suspicious circumstances that some thought pointed to Temple wrongdoing—wrote, "We are getting ready to start a high school." (Judy and Patty were both too young to have attended Opportunity) In the letter was a school schedule that had been proposed.

7:00–8:00 AM	Breakfast
8:30–9:00 AM	Father's Time
8:00–8:30 AM	Karate And Exer[cises]
9:00–9:45 AM	Math
9:45–10:30 AM	Language Arts
10:30–10:45 AM	Break
10:45–11:30 AM	Spanish
11:30–11:45 AM	Logic
12:00–2:00 PM	Lunch & Rest Time
2:00–2:45 PM	Social Science
2:45–3:30 PM	Guyanese History & Pol[itical] Enlightenment
3:30–3:45 PM	Break
3:45–4:30 PM	Basic Science Experiments
4:30–5:30 PM	Break
5:30 PM	Dinner[30]

Later, Edith Roller, the Temple scribe who was also a former teacher, was summoned to Jonestown to get the school on track for accreditation from the Guyanese government. One of Roller's first journal entries after she arrived in Jonestown reads:

> *Students have classes in the morning and in afternoon from 12.00 to 3.00. Teachers have a preparation period from 5.00 to 6.00. . . . The level of student ability is low. . . . A project on science in relation to Guyanese development is planned. Instructional materials and office space are limited. . . . I warned Tom [the school director] that my age would limit the amount of work which I can do. . . . Language arts classes in the high school are taught by: himself, Dick Tropp, Jann Gurvich, Shirley Williams, and Barbara Walker.[31]*

Roller also taught language arts classes and, later, literacy and socialism classes for seniors. Ultimately, socialism classes were required of all, and included exams. Her main duty was to prepare the school for accreditation.

She approached this role assiduously, creating an extensive report on what the school would need by the following September. In this she detailed the need for a more appropriate learning environment, more academically rigorous curriculum, clarified teacher responsibilities—including stricter qualifications for teachers, attention to disciplinary problems, requests for additional materials and supplies—even a proposed budget.[32]

Later journal entries convey Roller's frustration that the school wasn't developing as she'd planned, that student attendance was flagging and teachers weren't showing up for meetings, and that getting a school accreditation was clearly not high on Jones's agenda. In theory, accreditation meant the Jonestown school would meet the standards for Guyana's schools. But Jones didn't allow her to maintain inviolable school hours: At any time he might interrupt with an announcement, calling people off to work in the fields, join the water brigade—which was watering the crops during dry spells—or attend a meeting.[33] It may have become apparent to Roller later that she had been brought to the settlement just to give the *appearance* of Jonestown having a formalized, appropriately rigorous school.

September 1977

The Six-Day Siege

The summer sweltered on—humidity hovering around 90 percent, hot sun for four to eight hours a day—followed by deluges as September began. Typically a brief respite would come at the end of September, usually followed by a second hot and rainy season beginning in November. For the residents, the emotional atmosphere in Jonestown was becoming as oppressive as the weather.

In his book, *Raven*, Tim Reiterman describes how, on the evening of September 5, 1977, Stephan was at his father's cottage along with some other Temple members when Jones suddenly pulled out a revolver—until that point Stephan hadn't known there were guns in Jonestown—and fired at a tree. Later, as they left Jones and headed back to the other buildings, Stephan and one of the top security guards, Johnny Brown Jones (who, at twenty-seven, was another member who'd been brought into the fold of Jones's family and name) heard another shot, then silence. They ran back and found Jones in his cabin, flat on the floor.

Jones claimed that he'd had a strong feeling that "enemies" were out in the bush and had moved away from the window just in time to avoid a gunshot that barely missed him. Stephan ran out the door with a shotgun, another weapon in his father's room, and fired into the jungle where Jones indicated the shot had come from. When Stephan returned, he found several of Jones's aides with him, and Stephan positioned himself and some of the others to guard Jones's cottage and the surrounding area. The scare was the beginning of what would be a "Six-Day Siege."

A few days before, Jim Jones had learned of a September 6 court date set in Georgetown for a hearing regarding the custody of Grace Stoen's son, John Victor (or "Jon Jon"), now five years old, who was in Jonestown and whom Jones claimed as his own son. Grace had defected from the Temple the year before, leaving her son behind, and Tim Stoen, her estranged husband and formerly the Temple attorney, had left in March 1977. Jones now considered the Stoens traitors.

Reiterman reports that the Stoens' lawyer, Jeff Haas, had traveled to Georgetown with a California order demanding that Jones return the boy to the Stoens. A justice in Georgetown ordered that Jones bring Jon Jon to a second hearing on September 8, and, barring any convincing argument against it, turn the boy over to his mother for good. Haas, along with a Guyanese Supreme Court marshal, then set off in a plane to Port Kaituma carrying a writ of habeus corpus for Jones. When they reached Jonestown, the lawyer was told Jones was out on the *Cudjoe* somewhere and could not be reached. But once back in Port Kaituma, Haas learned Jones had been there all the time. Undeterred, Haas made plans to return.

Meanwhile, Jonestown workers were brought in from the fields in the Temple truck, with guards yelling, "We're all going to die!" As the workers arrived back in camp, Jones was shouting over the speakers, "Alert! Alert! Alert!" Hearing the sirens blaring, Jonestowners knew they were being called to the pavilion, where they were frisked, then given knives and farm tools and told to spread out to the perimeters of the compound and stand looking away from the camp, into the jungle. Jones announced they were about to be attacked by soldiers hired by Tim Stoen, as well as by the Guyanese army. The children would be seized and removed from Jonestown. They were to rub mud on their faces as a kind of camouflage, and prepare to "fight to the death." They would eat (only rice) and sleep (very little) in the jungle. Anyone who ran away would be killed. Stephan and another man were posted at the front gate to stop and examine any car or truck, along with its occupants, that arrived at the camp.[34] "We don't stand a chance," Stephan thought, according to Wright, and felt "scared to death."[35] Jones had all his followers terrified.

During the "siege," Jones ordered fifty people to go to Port Kaituma, where he said the boat would take them to Cuba. In the panicked rush to board, a woman fell, breaking her hip. Jones escalated the fear level of the exhausted people with more histrionics. He cried dramatically that only he and his family and a few others would be allowed to escape on the boat, but that he would not go without all of them. The group returned unquestioningly to Jonestown.[36]

After a few days of such chaos, Stephan started to wonder about the "crisis." Others lost fervor after being told to go back to work only to be ordered again to grab their weapons and dash back into the jungle for yet another alert. Opportunity students, young and strong, were surely among those sent out with farm implements to fight "the enemy," their initial terror likely slowly dissolving into exhaustion, perhaps laced with anger—which they would not have been able to express for fear of reprisal.

Stephan, who was beginning to think of Jon Jon as his little brother, started to question the attacks, especially since his father seemed always to be the first one to "see" enemies in the bush. Then one day Cindy Cordell's older brother Mark burst into the shower where Stephan was, yelling, "They're trying to get Father. . . . I saw the bullets hit the ground!" Shoeless and with soap still clinging to him, Stephan rushed to the main road where people were gathering. This time, when Stephan went to the scene of the supposed attack on Jones, someone he trusted and who he knew was not a "blind follower," Al Simon, silently held up two fingers, indicating he'd seen two men, and gestured toward a line of sugar cane about one hundred feet away, in line with the window of Jones's cabin.[37]

⚓

In the meantime, Jeff Haas had returned from Georgetown with the judge's permission to serve the writ to Jones by putting it up somewhere in Jonestown. This time Jones took Jon Jon and hid in the jungle, in an out-of-sight place he had told Stephan to prepare for them. When Haas tried to present the writ to Harriet Tropp (the schoolmaster's wife, another of Jones's highly trusted members), she refused it and let it fall to the ground, kicking it in disgust. When Haas nailed a copy of the writ (others had been dropped from the plane) to a nearby building, Stephan tore it down and warned Haas not to "deface [their] property." Tropp warned Stephan not to say anything more, not wanting to risk a search that might turn up the guns. Having finished their job, Haas and his party left. The next day the Georgetown judge ordered that a bench warrant be issued to take Jon Jon, and that Jim Jones be held in contempt of court.

Feeling increasingly trapped, Jones kept referring to "revolutionary suicide," while Marceline pleaded with Jones over the radio from San Francisco, begging for more time to reach Ptolemy Reid, the Guyanese deputy prime minister and their best supporter there, who was traveling in the U.S. Marceline hoped she could convince Reid to prevent Jones's arrest, or the child being taken. She broke down, weeping, but Jones simply repeated his threat. "We will die unless we are given freedom from harassment and asylum somewhere."

Then Jones gave Jimmy the microphone. "Hello, Ma, this is Jimmy. I want to die."

"Jimmy," Marceline said, still crying. "It was not too bad a few days ago. If you and your dad could kind of hang on there. The other's so final, Jimmy."

Then Stephan came on. "Mom, don't get too emotional. Dad loves all of you there. We're the ones standing here, and he's holding up. He's trying as hard as possible, and you don't have to worry about me, because as I've told you before . . . all I've ever done in my eighteen years is to anticipate what would happen . . . and I know this is the way I want it."[38] Much later, Stephan admitted he was being "grandiose," saying only what he knew his father wanted to hear.[39]

In truth Jones was *not* holding up. He continually went without sleep and used more and more drugs to keep going. And no one else was holding up either: all were exhausted and alternately terrified or suspicious.

Later, in an exchange over the radio that was being broadcast into the Jonestown pavilion for all to hear, Jones told his wife, "Well, we're gonna die if anyone comes to arrest anyone. That's a vote of the people. . . . You are the most beautiful people in the world." The crowd cheered again and again.

Desperate, Marceline went to search for Deputy Prime Minister Reid in person. When she managed to find the prime minister's wife near Chicago, she was assured no one would be arrested. Marceline urgently informed Jones, and "revolutionary suicide" was averted—for the moment.[40]

Soon after the "siege," Jones wanted Stephan to fake a kidnapping of Jon Jon Stoen, after which he would pretend to save the boy following a struggle with the "kidnappers." Stephan thought the idea was crazy, and feared the boy would be traumatized. Maria Katsaris—another of Jones's mistresses, who took care of Jon Jon—agreed with Stephan, and urged him to talk his father out of the plan. Fortunately Stephan succeeded.[41]

From that point forward, whenever Stephan met new arrivals at Port Kaituma, he "secretly boarded the truck bringing them in with a loaded rifle in my arms and a pistol on my hip."[42]

⊸

The tension of the Six-Day Siege further heightened the fears, suspicion, and punishments, and the camp's conditions worsened through the rest of 1977. Stephan's friend Mike Touchette left in September to work at the Temple's house in Georgetown, known as Lamaha Gardens, which provided a sort of public relations headquarters in Guyana's capital. Jonestowners living there bought food and supplies for the settlement, met new arrivals, and coordinated shipments from San Francisco to Jonestown. When Touchette returned in December, he was shocked to find Jonestown had deteriorated considerably since he'd left in September. Jones regularly reminded the residents, now prisoners, of the dangers outside their settlement. The rallies and catharsis sessions were now up to three or four nights a week, with Jones railing and ranting doing his best to use the residents' own fear against them.[43]

The end of 1977 was marked as if by a death knell for the year as a whole when Jones's mother, Lynetta, died at age seventy-five. The especially rough trip up the Kaituma River earlier in March had been hard on her. On the first night of her arrival she was violently ill, and she was never well enough to leave her cabin for long after that. Her health deteriorated until ultimately a stroke and emphysema killed her in December.[44] This was decidedly another blow for Jones, as it must have been for those who had believed in—and possibly now were beginning to doubt—his notorious curative powers.

Perfect Comportment

The young people, who made up more than half the Jonestown population, bore both the brunt of the workload and the physical punishments—which were Jones's idea of "justice." One such form of punishment was Learning Crew, which had nothing to do with teaching. Learning Crew was re-education in the sense that Communist China used labor to re-educate "reactionaries" and "loafers." Those assigned to Learning Crew had to work double time at even harder work assignments: cleaning outhouses, digging latrines, chopping wood. Once one job was finished, they had to run to the next. They were not allowed to speak to anyone; they ate separately, and they slept in a special "punishment" dorm.[45] The Box was one of the worst forms of punishment handed out at rallies. The brainchild of head teacher Tom Grubbs, it was a four-foot-tall, six-foot-wide, ten-foot-long plywood shipping crate designed as a sensory isolation box, for "deprogramming" people. The Box was at first placed atop a hill near the settlement, but, since the prisoner could still hear the sounds of daily life, it was later moved to a ditch.

Jeff Carey was the first victim assigned this torture—on a separate occasion from the one mentioned above—for allegedly spreading a rumor that Jones's adopted Korean son, Lew (who was married and whose baby, Chaeoke, was the first to be born in Jonestown), was borrowing lots of money in Georgetown to take out white women.

After spending a week in the Box at Jones's decree, given only water and "mashed-up, unappetizing food," Jeff emerged, stiff, sore, and dirty. At the rally that night he said what he was expected to, that he'd been changed, that the Box was "great"—no doubt hoping to avoid an even longer sentence.[46]

Roller also wrote about a thirty-five-year-old, possibly mentally unstable woman, Michaeleen Brady, who was sent to the Box more than once. "I have seen [Michaeleen] several times since she was released from the isolation box. Her face looks very haggard and her eyes fearful."[47]

Marceline Jones was opposed to the Box. When she first discovered its existence, having just returned from one of her trips to San Francisco, she insisted nurses check the vital signs of anyone in the Box every two or three hours. She worried in particular about Michaeleen, and ordered some medical tests for her after each solitary confinement. Apparently that was the most Marceline felt she could do to help anyone assigned that punishment.[48]

⁓

Children were not exempt from being assigned to the Box—and they were often told there would be a wild creature locked into the darkness with them. Shonda Gaylor, a little girl of nine, and Mark Rhodes, a seven-year-old boy with huge brown eyes, were two examples.[49]

⁓

Even the polite, well-behaved students Opportunity staff knew did not escape the Box. Sonje Regina Duncan (known as Gina Bowser in Jonestown), pregnant, had been quickly pulled out of school and sent off to Jonestown; she was sent to the Box for three days after being assigned to Learning Crew. None of the teachers at Opportunity had seen Sonje Regina as a rebellious girl; what she had done to be sentenced to the Box is not known. It could have been something as simple as using the laundry to wash her clothes when the laundry was "closed," as had been the case with Melanie Breidenbach, Wesley's sister.[50]

As 1978 progressed, Jones's tolerance for any behavior that was less than perfect, quiet obedience decreased. Opportunity student Carl's secret Temple girlfriend, Kim Fye, was assigned to Learning Crew because she "talks too much" and was "defensive." And Dorothy's sister, hardworking Loreatha Buckley, whom the Church had trained as a carpenter and was Jones's PR model for women's liberation and civil rights, was put on Learning Crew for a "bad attitude."[51]

Stephan's friend Vincent Lopez was called on the floor for stealing three bananas; Wesley Breidenbach and another young man had reported him.[52] Apparently Wesley was as earnest in Guyana as he had been at Opportunity, whereas Vincent was often in trouble. Author Julia Scheeres reports that Vincent was one of the twenty-two foster children sent to Guyana. He was punished many times in other ways, for stealing, "for sleeping during meetings—even for cracking cynical jokes."[53] Given the number of his punishments, it's clear that discipline did not deter him in the least.

As housing and food were increasingly in short supply, Vincent was not alone in stealing something to eat; a girl was caught eating seed for planting, and another for stealing and eating raw sweet potatoes.[54]

Even Dorothy was called on the floor, Jones having apparently forgotten all about the Shekinah Glory that connected his heart and hers.[55]

The "Shekinah Glory" with Dorothy Buckley to Jones's left

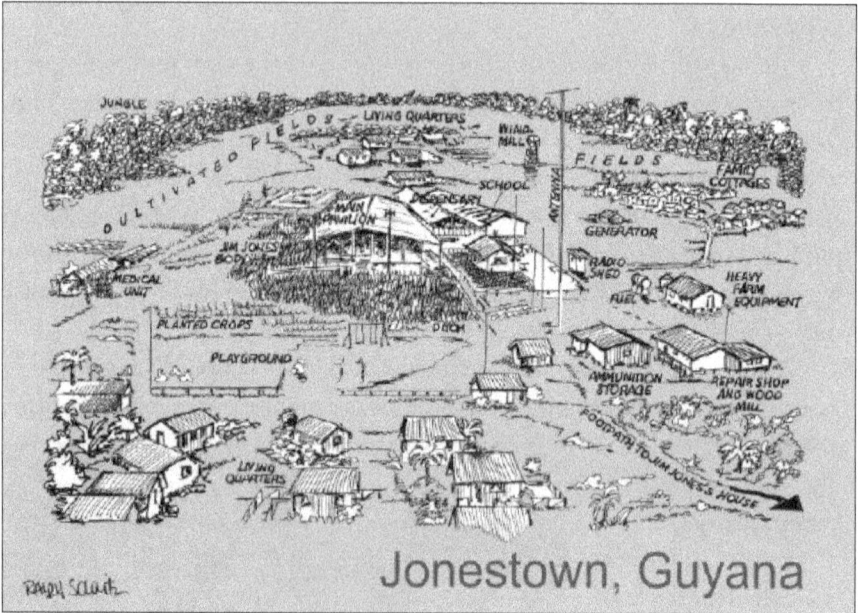

Jonestown map (by Ralph Solonitz)

Chapter 12

"Precious Acts of Treason"

April – October 1978

Small Mercies and Solace

Newcomers to Jonestown quickly learned it was safest to keep their doubts and dreams to themselves—Deborah Layton writes in her book *Seductive Poison* that those who voiced fears or criticism were often reported, even by friends and family:

> *Once you were in, it didn't take long to learn the ropes: keep your head down and don't talk unless it's absolutely necessary. For each person showing weakness by speaking of his or her fears, another would become more trusted for reporting it.[1]*

Jim Jones worked to foster suspicion and fear among the ranks, dividing couples and setting family members and friends against one another. But he could not entirely squelch protest or keep teenagers from being teenagers; neither could he smother camaraderie. Even in this environment, many took risks for friendship or love, or found ways to commit other "precious acts of treason"—as Deborah put it—both small and large.

Deborah describes the first of several such acts she would experience in Jonestown that took place on her very first day. When she and her mother, Lisa Layton, first arrived, their luggage was searched—standard protocol for newcomers by then. Personal items such as letters and medications were always confiscated during such searches—for someone suffering from cancer as her mother was, having medication taken away could be dangerous. But "an elderly black committee member who knew Mama" hid one of Lisa's bottles of liquid medication, a painkiller called Paregoric that she needed, quietly stuffing it back down into her bag.

Much later, Deborah was to see some of her mother's other confiscated medications on a shelf in Jim Jones's cottage.[2]

※

Stephan found a retreat from the deterioration of conditions in Jonestown in the form of the wilderness, just as he had in Redwood Valley. It was a source of solace he was also able to share with both his mother and grandmother, Lynetta Jones, before she died in late 1977.

Wright, in "Orphans of Jonestown," relates the story of Stephan's gift to Lynetta of a trip into the wild. Seventy-eight and suffering from emphysema, she had nearly died from the trip on the roiling Atlantic from Georgetown and then upriver to Jonestown.

Stephan had often visited his grandmother in her cabin, where, too weak to get up, she gazed out at the jungle, "begging Stephan for stories of his adventures in the woods." He made up his mind he had to take her there, "even if it killed her." One day in December he "carried her in his arms" to his haven in the jungle, where Lynetta wept—the only time Stephan ever saw his grandmother in tears. "She died three days later," Stephan told Wright.[3]

One day, Stephan was finally able to show his mother his jungle retreat. Reiterman and Jacobs tell how Stephan took Marceline first to a knoll that had a view of Jonestown. She took it in for some time, in silence. Then she turned to Stephan and told him she had been afraid that moving to Jonestown might stifle his creativity forever, that Jones might crush his spirit. But looking down on the thoughtfully arranged clusters of buildings, from animal shelters, gathering places, cottages—and her beloved nursery—she realized he *had* found an outlet for his creativity. He had helped design and build something important for the people he loved, and she saw that Stephan took pride in what he and others had done. Then he took his mother to his jungle refuge, a green and peaceful spot, water splashing into a small pond. She knew that Stephan had found a place in the wilderness where he could escape periodically from his father's madness.

That day would become a memory both of them would cherish.[4]

Another kind of escape from Jonestown they found on that walk came in an unlikely format. Marceline had to stop from time to time, her back still a painful problem for her. Stephan tells that story.

> Mom sat to rest another time on our walk and when she stood, her rear end was covered with fire ants. I mean COVERED, just solid red roiling. It was a comical but efficient scramble for me to bat them all off her without either of us getting bitten.
>
> It helped that Mom was laughing and quite calm, probably because I was, and she had no idea what a hundred bites from the suckers felt like—and that the ants were such a mass that they came off in clumps.

Laughter too, is a solace and an escape, and in Jonestown, no doubt, more and more a rarity—except in secret places with trusted people or at evening events that included songs with humorous lyrics. Levity might be seen as a refusal to take Jones's dire predictions and crazy newscasts as true. Laughter was yet another "precious act of treason." In the wilderness Stephan and his mother could laugh, even at what might have become a small disaster.[5]

Kids Will Be Kids

As accusations and punishments were meted out by Jones and life in Jonestown became more punishing both physically and mentally, young men and women continued to do what the young do: have fun, flirt, fall in love, and get into trouble.

Some "acts of treason" were small and the perpetrators never caught: There were reports that someone figured out how to unplug the P.A. system so as to escape Jones's monotonous, hours-long harangues. Jones would go on and on into the microphone in his cabin, not knowing he was speaking only to himself and his mistresses. And on one occasion, when Jones required everyone to watch Barbara Walters's interview of Fidel Castro (it was not the first time), Edith Roller wrote that Jones "had been obviously disturbed by the lack of seriousness he had seen" during the screening—almost certainly it had been teenagers unable to contain their laughter.[6]

Finding the comfort of another in the dark in spite of the increasingly grim days was a kind of escape. More than a dozen babies were born to Jonestown parents, according to Stephan.[7] In the midst of a miserable situation—one in which it was nearly impossible to trust anyone—young people nonetheless seemed to find a way to seek out loving human contact. Deborah writes that some cabins "were inhabited by the bold young teenagers who wanted to live with a girlfriend or boyfriend," but Stephan later told Bebelaar that, given the long workdays, the best teenage couples could do to be together was to section off a small space for themselves in a crowded cabin.[8]

In Roller's cottage, where she lived with fourteen others (including Opportunity student Sonje Regina and Tim Jones's older sister Ruth), young people often played music and talked outside the cottage late into the night.[9] They may have considered it a safe spot for private assignations; Roller wasn't one to report wrongdoing, though she wrote once that she threatened to report some students misbehaving in her class. But teenagers know a soft-hearted person when they meet one.

Even the most benign behaviors of young people were criticized or condemned by Jones. Part of the flirting ritual among teenagers at that time involved girls "fixing" boys' hair—combing, braiding, or styling it—which could be seen in cafeterias, courtyards, and the back of high school classrooms. It was no different in Jonestown. At one rally in March, Roller asked Marceline if she approved of young women "curling young men's hair." Jones cut in and said he disapproved.[10] But it's unlikely that the practice was stopped altogether.

At times youthful passions ran high in Jonestown, and one evening in 1978, eighteen-year-old Opportunity student Ricky Johnson discovered his girlfriend, Christine, was sleeping with his friend Thurmond. Heartbroken, Ricky ran off into the jungle and the next night attempted suicide by swallowing gasoline. Overwrought with guilt, Christine tried also, by slitting her wrists; neither succeeded.[11] Jones denounced the two at the rally on October 14, in a rambling, incoherent harangue, complaining he'd "had no peace *two* nights in a row" (another boy, fifteen, had tried to run away three times in one night):

> *I want to hear no shit coming back from you people. No bullshit music. I don't want to be caught up in no goddamned games, sex games or foolishness. . . . You can be in a relationship, but I don't want no goddamned mess like we've seen here in the last few hours of people trying to kill themselves or go running off because somebody's with somebody else.*

Jones goes on:

> *You're upset, you're disturbed. And I understand that. You're disturbed as a whole because you're not getting enough sex and you turn that disturbance towards me so that's why you see yourself threatening me. Hell no, that's as normal as rising of the sun. But you got to get yourself together, and right now you're not together.*[12]

Ricky, known as "Richard" to Jones, responded in stammers. "I guess I'm not. I know I'm not. Uh I . . . I try . . . I've tried to get—pull myself together and get this hostile out of myself and and through—"

Jones cut in, asking if Ricky had ever "had emotional treatment in a mental institution," claiming such treatment would be no more difficult than if Ricky were to get a tonsillectomy or have his appendix out. "I have a strong feeling . . . that people act like this should never even get out," Jones said, suggesting the Extended Care Unit (or ECU), which he calls "the hospital unit," be enlarged so the "two basket cases" could be sent there. He speculated that for Ricky and the other boy it might take "sixteen months" to restore their sanity.[13]

At a rally two days later, Jones warned that any potential runaways would be shot in the legs, or that Guyanese soldiers would kill them outright, adding to the list of deadly dangers to runaways such things as "infiltrators," "mercenaries," and snakes. He was still railing on about Ricky, claiming that Ricky drank "three cups" of gasoline which would have killed the boy, who "shit fire" and vomited flames. Jones bragged that he had miraculously saved Ricky's life, and pronounced that he had acted "loving[ly]" toward Christine, and that she responded by selfishly trying to kill herself. So she too deserved to be drugged in the ECU.[14]

Ricky was apparently ordered to write an apology to Jones.

To Dad

Ever since the incident with Christine and Thurmond I have not really been myself, it has put a deep effect on my feelings. I am fighting it each day but sometimes it gets real hard, because I keep getting flashbacks in my head of what I seen and what she told me about what she and Thurmond did when they suppose to be watching the animals all night and how her best friend knew what was going on and kept on letting it go by. Sure I admit that I have hurt peoples feelings but there is also a time when hurting peoples feelings come to a stop. I guess in one way I had it coming to me things just don't happen[—]they happen just. When I was in New York I use to always wonder why did the man always beat up on the lady. I use to see it almost every day. At least I could say I have never beat up on a girl. I try to beat them up with words. I think about certain films I saw, like The Learning Tree [and] how a young black man[s] girlfriend got fucked by a white guy . . . but the most important thing that comes to my mind is dad when you was sitting in a classroom and how someone drop your girlfriends panties on your desk just because you didn't want to have sex with the girl because you wanted to show respect for her.

Dad, don't worry I'm not going to do anything stupid because eventually my feelings will change. I sure did learn that in a relationship there is a awful big chance of getting hurt and when you do, it hits like a ton of [bricks].

I know its not the end of the world for me it's the beginning believe me when this does fade away I will be [—] damn sure will be stronger. Dad people should understand that life is nothing if [you] don't have a cause to die for. Dad the way I feel now seem like it will never be the same again for as long as I live. I will never forget this incident because it was a part [of] me growing up.

from your Son
Ricky Johnson

A hasty postscript, perhaps dictated, reads, "Without you Dad this would be a cold cruel world."[15]

⤴

Tommy Bogue got into trouble repeatedly: He was whipped for building a still, punished for taking a dish of curry offered to him by an Amerindian boy who knew Tommy was hungry—even though Tommy tried to explain that it would have been rude to refuse. Punishment never deterred him. When he was caught building his own cottage in the bush, a place to get away to—at least temporarily—he was forced to dismantle the cottage and return the lumber, guarded by Stephan. When Tommy dropped a board, Stephan "slugged him behind the ear hard enough to make him stagger," according to Scheeres' book, *A Thousand Lives*. The following day, his punishment continued when he was ordered to dig pits for outhouses in the broiling sun for weeks. Sometimes his punishment included going without food until a certain amount of work had been accomplished.[16]

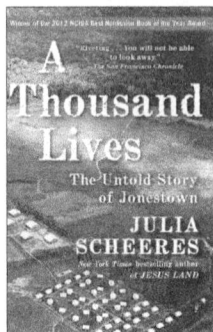

When Tommy's friend Brian Davis was sent to Jonestown, the two were at first uncertain about whether it was safe to trust one another in this new environment, but their old friendship quickly won out. Now both fifteen, they decided to run away together. Having been in Jonestown for ten months already, Tommy knew a good deal about finding his way in the bush. He was fascinated by a full-grown bush cat the size of a kitten, howler monkeys, macaws, and toucans—though he'd been disappointed the toucan didn't look like the one on the cereal box at home. He knew which plants were edible, and he'd learned how to snare small animals from an Amerindian boy he'd befriended.

Tommy and Brian planned to make it all the way to Venezuela. En route, they planned to sell condoms stolen from the Jonestown warehouse and use the money to buy food. Once they reached Venezuela they'd call home. With the condoms stolen and their plan in place, they needed only to await the perfect opportunity. The two found their moment one night when Tommy's latest punishment—for falling asleep while Jones was speaking at a meeting—was to collect still-hot coal from land cleared by burning. When Jones called for someone to supervise Tommy at his chore to make sure he worked hard enough, Brian volunteered. Apparently Jones was too far gone from his intoxicant abuse to remember the boys were longtime buddies and partners in crime.[17]

Tommy and Brian changed their plans and decided to head to Matthews Ridge four or five miles away to try to get help in reaching the American embassy in Georgetown. Their plan was foiled when they were found and captured in Matthews Ridge. Returned to Jonestown, the would-be escapees' heads were shaved and their legs manacled. Fortunately, before too much time passed Stephan discussed the issue with his mother, and Marceline convinced Jones the boys had been punished enough.[18]

⚜

In one of the shipments from San Francisco, a basketball arrived. Stephan, some of the boys from the Opportunity baseball team, and several others began to practice drills, seeking out fields in the settlement where they could play.[19] Stephan describes how basketball began in Jonestown in his essay on the Jonestown Institute website, "Baby Toes."

Stephan Jones executing a slam dunk

We threw together a bootleg basketball court in Jonestown, because I loved hoop, because Mike could weld, and because we'd both had just about enough of Dad's controlling shit. It was a juicy piece of rebellion that ultimately saved many young lives.

We managed to get the floor for a storage and tool room up on stilts before Dad said we had no money for the walls and roof. Without walls and a roof, the floor took up about the same area as two greyhound buses side by side (now there was a measurement the people of Peoples Temple could understand). But for its precipitous—we made them adventurous—edges, it was practically ready made for a basketball court.

I can't remember if Dad had said outright that we couldn't have a court. Everyone in town knew he didn't approve of competitive sport. . . . it seemed like we were always trying to see how far we could get before our drug-whacked leader noticed. . . . it was a lot harder for him to take something away than to snuff it while it was just between our ears.

Once we got the idea, we didn't hesitate. It felt like we were erecting a monument to defiance.

Our ball playing almost immediately became a force to be reckoned with in Jonestown. We needed the release of basketball, of competitive sport, legal

Jonestown's bootleg basketball court

aggression with an undercurrent of communion. And the communion was of our own creation, our own volition, from the bottom up and not the top down. Genuine instead of demanded. The court was birthed in rebellion, and even Dad knew that a larger rebellion lay in trying to stop what Mike and I had started. We were on that court just about every free minute we were given, and some that we took. Much steam was let off there—literally and figuratively.[20]

Lawrence Wright describes how practice was held in the evening, and after the team set up lights for the court, they would play "until all hours," He told how, one night, "Tim walked over to the radio hut and started imitating his father's voice over the P.A. system—slurred speech and all." Amazingly, Tim wasn't punished. "There was a sense of liberation—and also of uncertainty. People began to allow themselves to wonder what life in Jonestown would be like without Jones."[21]

Tim saw a chance when a Guyanese "sports official" came to Jonestown, and convinced the man that the Jonestown team should play in a tournament with the Guyanese national team. As with the Cobras baseball team, Jones somehow went along with the plan. Uniforms were sewn up and practices became serious. "Everyone cheered when the boys ran along the road and through the middle of the settlement on their training drills," Wright reports.[22]

When the team played on the make-shift court, they always had an audience—mostly young and female, some with kids—despite the late hour.[23] At least for a time, the intense physical energy lifted the young men and their loyal fans out of the continuing madness.

The team would come to play an important part in Jonestown's story.

The Diversion of Music

Music provided another form of escape from drudgery and exhaustion, at least for a while. For many of the young people, music and dancing were the preferred respite from the madness. There was still at least *some* fun at the evening rallies. Jones was learning how difficult it was to suppress youthful pluck and spunk.

There was no shortage of performers: Jonestown had the Temple band, several singers, and other musical and dance groups. Roller detailed the program for one particular evening—on the billing were the "stomping" Soul Steppers, a rhythm, marching, and dance group that performed regularly. A woman named Shawanda Jackson danced to the "St. Louis Blues." Diane Wilkinson sang "Summertime" and "Isn't She Lovely," and someone named Patsy Johnson even performed a "snake dance with an emerald green boa constrictor."[24]

Opportunity students Johnny Cobb, Jimmy, and Calvin Douglas plus Bruce Oliver and others formed the lineup for a musical group they called Black Velvet, with a young man named Pancho leading the vocals. Wearing matching suits, they danced in sync and snapped their fingers to the music of Motown groups like the Spinners, the Temptations, and the Dramatics. Despite their having almost no time to practice or to work with the Temple band, Stephan said they "actually sounded pretty good," though a couple of them "were told just to move their lips" and dance.[25]

Other musicians performed Creedence Clearwater Revival's "Proud Mary" (with its refrain, *Rollin' on the river*), and Les McCann's "Compared to What."

Jonestowners wrote original lyrics, sometimes adapting them to favorite songs, often poking fun at their own discomfort: "Diarrhea," "Deworm Me, Please," and "Sittin' on the Toilet Stool," (which *must* have been sung to Otis Redding's "Sittin' on the Dock of the Bay"). Even though the music and performances were often for the benefit of visitors, to demonstrate the "virtues" of the settlement, it was also a form of expression for which one couldn't be punished.

Some of the songs were political, like "I'm Just Another Worker with a Cutlass in My Hand." The Soul Steppers drummed and march-danced to "Guyana Is So Beautiful." And even though Jones dropped most references to religion in favor of teaching socialism, Jonestowners even sang "I'm Going Up to Jonestown Over Jordan."[26]

If Opportunity students weren't participating in the performances, they were surely clapping their hands and dancing in their seats or singing along. Teenagers are for the most part, and under almost any circumstances, irrepressible. Stephan tells the story of one memorable night of youthful musical rebellion, held on the new basketball court:

> *On at least one of Dad's worst drugged-out days, he told Johnny and Tim from his cottage that there would be no meeting but everyone had to occupy themselves in the library or socialism study or some other stupid, contrived control mechanism dressed up like human development . . . and the town had a party instead. I mean it. They somehow got the music going and had a dance on the basketball court. I didn't go and can't say how Tim and Johnny conjured that one up, but it was a street party in the only way Jonestown could've had one.*[27]

Often, though, at the rallies, the music and dancing would precede punishments and humiliation. Eugene Smith describes the rally taking place as he arrived at the settlement in March 1978, in a trailer full of other incoming Temple members:

> *JUMP!! We start jumping off the back and side of this trailer into this mud. Excellent. I have arrived. The pavilion was packed. DAMNNN, this is crazy. I see Ollie, then I see my mom, old friends, folks I thought were gone were here. Ollie was big—8 and a half months pregnant—and she was beautiful. In the group I arrived with, we were 100 strong. We increased the population of Jonestown by 10% overnight. So to say things were not comfortable is an understatement. So we are singing and clapping, looking, listening, making mental notes. This goes on for a while.*
>
> *It's a hyped environment, frenzied. I can see Jones on stage. As the music died down, Jones was calling names. Damn.*[28]

"Calling names" (also "called up" or "called on the floor") meant Jones was ordering people to the stage for criticism and punishment.

≥

While music was often a big part of the rallies, Jones discouraged dancing on at least one occasion, according to Roller, who wrote that "some people," likely young people, "had been disappointed that he wouldn't allow them to dance on the dirt floor which kicks up dirt which is bad for their lungs."[29]

Still, there were some "public relations" activities in Georgetown involving music and dancing that were sanctioned, including free performances featuring some of Jonestown's most musically talented youngsters. These performances were seen as a good way to quell rumors in Georgetown that those who left for Jonestown were never seen again.

On one such trip to the capital, Deborah—who used the trip to conceal her first moves to prepare for her defection—was tasked with accompanying a group of these young people to a week-long, well-publicized series of performances at the Guyanese Cultural Center. The group of Temple kids, "ten adorable girls and five handsome boys, mostly black," would don African costumes, dance, sing "songs of freedom," and recite socialist poems.

The trip was a great escape for the kids: private showers, comfortable beds, good food, no work, no Learning Crew—just practice, which was fun, and a talent show. In her book, Deborah describes the kids pouring excitedly into the Temple's Georgetown house at Lamaha Gardens when they first arrived at the capital. "'Dibs on the upstairs shower!' cried a girl named Joyce," possibly Joyce Polk Brown.[30]

Peoples Temple dancers and drummers

Even if they were also expected to collect money for the Temple on the Georgetown streets, that would still be easy compared to hard labor all day and rallies half the night back in the camp.

Labor as Escape

Another form of escape for some of the young men came in the unlikely form of extra work: Unloading supplies from the *Cudjoe* just in from Georgetown was a job that was really a labor of love for those who formed the team, including Stephan, Mike and Albert Touchette, Phillip Blakey, Ronnie Dennis, Carl Barnett, Mark Cordell, and Emmett Griffith. The young men knew they were feeding the people of Jonestown rather than just following Jones's often-capricious orders. They wouldn't be working alone, but together with a common purpose.

Cudjoe at Port Kaituma

So, though it meant going back to work after a long, sweaty day, the young men looked forward to the bone-banging ride to the dock. It was also an escape from Jonestown; a time to be rowdy, release youthful pent-up energy and laugh; a chance to be themselves, to speak without considering who might be listening. It was an athletic event requiring speed, skill and muscle; a game, a dance they had learned to do together.

The crew ate quickly and set off at about five in the afternoon to unload the new shipment of supplies. Jouncing and banging over the rough road, they headed for Port Kaituma on the tractor trailer.

Two men in tandem would toss—in the near dark—two-hundred-fifty-pound bags of sugar to the next two in line as the goods made their way from the boat to the tractor trailer. Or they could each be carrying hundred-pound bags of flour from the hold, or forming a bucket brigade to pass along heavy boxes of canned goods or nails. "It was all for one and one for all," Stephan said. "And it was so much fun."

At two or three in the morning, or sometimes as the sun was beginning to rise, they'd secure the load and head back, dead tired but still laughing. With a heavy trailer, the trip would take perhaps two hours. They'd take showers, sleep for a couple of hours, and then head off at six to their regular day jobs.[31] The hard work and lack of sleep were a small price to pay for the freedom, fun and sense of purpose the job afforded them.

Even Edith

Open dissent was infrequent—not surprising given the punishments handed down—and sometimes came from surprising ranks. Even Edith Roller, whose journal-keeping Jones encouraged, broke Jones's dictums from time to time, risking a mild complaint about conditions in the settlement, or even expressing doubt or disagreement with Jones. On at least one occasion she retreated to her beloved books and poets when she should have gone to a required film. After monitoring an after-dinner "political enlightenment" test and helping those who couldn't complete theirs, Roller reported: "A required movie on the Nazis was being shown in the pavilion but when I finished the test I didn't stay for it. I went home and read *Identity of Yeats*."[32]

Roller's journals ended abruptly with her August 1978 entries. On September 9, she returned to her cottage to find a significant portion of her journal entries—some originals, some typed copies—gone. She typed a letter to Jones describing the disappearance, but it is not known what happened to the journals, and the possibility that Jones confiscated them cannot be ruled out.[33]

Christine Miller

One of the most notable incidents of Jonestown was enacted by Christine Miller, a sixty-year-old woman who'd arrived in January, just before Joyce and Ollie and Eugene Smith. From her earliest days with the Church, which she had joined in Los Angeles, Christine had repeatedly stood up to Jones; she spoke her mind when she wanted to, and was not prone to intimidation.

Jones sometimes brought a gun to the rallies in Jonestown, which he'd fire into the air when he wanted silence and attention, or to wake dozing attendees. At one meeting, according to an essay by the late Michael Bellefountaine posted on the Jonestown Institute website, when Christine voiced her opposition to something Jones said, he "pointed the gun at her and said he could shoot her, and no one would ever find out." Christine stood her ground, saying, "You can shoot me, but you are going to have to respect me first." Jones threatened her again, but Christine just coolly repeated, "You can do that, but you are going to have to respect me first." Jones then rushed forward and put the gun to her head, "shouting his rage at her defiance." She did not back down. "You can shoot me, but you will respect me." It was then Jones who retreated.[34]

Ruth Tupper

Ruth's Teeth

Ruth Tupper was Tim Jones's older sister, and Stephan was fond of her. Stephan's essay, "Ruth's Teeth," posted on the Jonestown Institute website, paints a picture of youthful camaraderie, of resilience. She was missing two front teeth and used a bridge—two removable porcelain teeth—to fill the gap. She was twenty-two years old:

> *Ronnie Dennis, Vincent Lopez, and I were returning from another day in the bush dropping trees for timber or road access, when someone shouted my name. I turned to see Ruth and a couple of her friends coming toward me. She held her hand in front of her mouth while she scurried over to us, and as she got closer I could see that her neck and face were blushed a bright pink. Her adorably unique seal-bark laugh kept escaping around the hand at her mouth. She walked half-bent and sideways up to me and put her free hand on my shoulder and started rocking to and fro. She continued to guffaw as she turned away from me, then*

turned back, then turned away, while continuing to hold her other hand to her mouth. I was chuckling with her by then, but just as persistently asking what was going on. She might have danced her embarrassment for some time if one of her companions hadn't threatened to tell me herself. At first, all Ruth could muster through her upheld hand was that she needed my help, I answered "Okay," which is how I often respond to a request for help, usually before I know what's required, especially from someone who is as helpful, kind, and unassuming as Ruth was. Mom—and Dad in his way—taught me to be willing to help. Whether or not I actually can help comes out later.

Ruth was finally able to convey that she had been feeling sick—a common occurrence in Jonestown, even among young and healthy people—and had barely made it to the outhouse to throw up. Too late, she realized she had expelled the two porcelain teeth into the smelly sewage.

Jonestown had no dentist, and even in Georgetown dentures would have been difficult to get. The two teeth lying in the depths of the heavily used outhouse "were the only thing keeping young and vibrant Ruth from a six-month-old—or eighty-year-old—grin," Stephan writes.

I told her not to worry, that we would get her teeth back, and I didn't hesitate in telling her I thought the cost was too great for us to fail. I envisioned the teeth perched serenely nine or ten feet down whatever hole Ruth had chosen. I found something very different when Ruth took us to the spot. . . .

I was already thinking about what we could rig up to a string and lower through the hole to scoop up the teeth [with] when Ruth shined the flashlight through the hole. Not straight down, though. At an angle, toward the back. In my imaginings I hadn't taken into consideration the violence of Ruth's purging. The flashlight beam bored in on the red and ivory of the bridge more than six feet to the rear of the toilet hole, and nine feet down. Suddenly things felt more like an expedition than a favor.

After considering several alternatives, Stephan decided that Ronnie and his five-foot-six frame (compared to Stephan's at six-four) was the only solution to the problem:

Ronnie gave an exaggerated look over his shoulder as if to see if I might be looking at someone or something behind him, then angled a glance out of the corner of his eye at me, and with a fought-off smile said, "What?" But he knew what. One of us was going to have to go in and get those teeth. He saw the feasibility of my plan when I explained it, and after a drawn out "Aw, Steve" accompanied by the appropriate body language, agreed that my assignment of roles was the best.

Ronnie Dennis

Stephan sent Vincent to get ropes and a respirator as Ronnie and Stephan collected other tools and went to work removing the boards that served as the "shared throne" over the hole in which Ruth's teeth rested. The work clothes Ronnie was already wearing, designed to thwart bugs and other jungle creatures, would be his protective uniform, providing "a barrier to unspeakable bodily fluids." A set of goggles to guard against the burning methane (at Mike Touchette's strong suggestion) topped off Ronnie's suit of armor.

They secured the rope around a crossbeam and tied it to Ronnie, who put on the respirator and goggles.

> *When we were done, Ronnie looked a bit like a cross between a fly and a pig dressed like a pirate on safari. From that point till we lowered him into the pit, he didn't say a word. . . . I asked Ronnie, whose head was now five feet beneath toilet seat level, if he was okay. He mumbled, "Just beautiful." It took everything I had not to laugh.*

Working together, the group maneuvered and rotated Ronnie until he was head-down, "less than a foot from the six-foot-deep shitmire," then struggled to position him so he was facing Ruth's teeth. After a series of careful, controlled swings to get Ronnie within reach of the teeth, timing would soon be everything.

> *It was a now-or-never moment of breathtaking proportions. Just before the penultimate swing I shouted, "Now, Ronnie!" and on his next swoop for the teeth he bellowed, "Only for yoouuu, Steeeve!," swung out his arm, and plucked them from the muck at the end of his reach. I immediately hit the rope low to prevent a head planting on the swing back, quickly stopped the human pendulum, jumped onto the bench, and heaved upward on the rope. The other two dragged it over the rafter till Ronnie's head cleared seat level and the girls could swing him clear enough for us to lower him to the ground with a blood-rushed head, sweaty body, and a tiny bit of green and brown on the ends of the fingers that were death-gripping Ruth's teeth.*
>
> *This is what I know still: Ronnie was a black kid from East L.A. who, prior to the Temple, had known no one of Ruth's pale complexion and suburban background, and if she, in the very next instant, had somehow dropped those teeth back in, he would not have hesitated to go right back after them.[35]*

Tim's Turning Point

Stephan already had his doubts about his father much earlier on, but Jimmy and Tim had continued to feel loyal to Jones. That began to change as 1978 progressed.

Shanda Oliver

Tim's turning point came when his former girlfriend, Shanda, now married to Bruce Oliver, became Jones's new "object of fascination, easily discarded," as Deborah described Jones's sexual conquests. His purpose, according to Deborah, was to choose young and innocent women and break their spirits. Shanda was a sweet, bright girl, and she and Deborah had become close friends back in San Francisco.[36]

Everyone loved beautiful, vivacious Shanda, with her large dark eyes, sparkling smile, and fluffy Afro. Jones began inviting Shanda, who was just nineteen, to his cottage. Lawrence Wright writes that Jones claimed these visits were arranged so he could "counsel her for 'suicidal tendencies,'" a not uncommon judgment for Jones to make about his followers.[37] Shanda was afraid of Jones, according to Deborah, and didn't want to be with him. Soon, those who happened by Jones's residence, set off from the more humble cottages, when Shanda was there could hear Jones sexually abusing her. Jones would often blame the young women, and men, he chose to have sex with, and shame them in front of the community—especially those who had spirit and charisma. It was part of his cruel strategy to divide his people.[38]

In Georgetown, Deborah had overheard a radio conversation between Jones and Shanda, and could tell that she had been chosen as his latest victim. It made Deborah sick. She knew many would blame Shanda rather than Jones. Although there had been rumors of Jones choosing two black women for liaisons back in San Francisco, Shanda was the first black woman Jones slept with that everyone knew about.[39]

Stephan understood why those who still tried to maintain a belief in Jones refused to see the truth: "My father was capable of doing no wrong, so if something was inconsistent . . . you focused your anger on somebody else."[40]

Still, Shanda was more interested in Al Smart, a black nineteen-year-old who had arrived in Jonestown in July 1978. After Jones called Al on the floor for something trumped up—he'd seen them together—Shanda courageously sent Jones a note, telling him she wanted to date Al instead.

Jones immediately ordered her sent to the ECU, claiming she'd threatened to commit suicide.

Tim Jones read Shanda's note before he handed it to Jones. Tim was now beginning to see his adoptive father clearly. "That's what set me off," he told Wright. "He drugged her and he fucked her whenever he wanted to." Before, Tim had worshipped Jones. Now he understood Marceline's difficult position in Jonestown, and grew close to her. Now, for the first time, he "finally realized what an idiot her husband was." Tim told Wright, "It was hard for her to respect me, because I was always around him, protecting him. I ran his errands. To her, it was as if I were blind to him." Tim also began re-establishing a relationship with his birth mother, and his younger brother and sisters. And now, Stephan and Tim had the same complicated but clear-eyed feelings about their father.[41]

Soon everyone on the basketball team—with the exception of Jimmy, who thus far still believed in his father—was angry with Jones for his retaliation against Shanda, especially when she was seen stumbling out of the ECU in a stupor, unable to walk without assistance. While no one had been surprised that Jones had taken yet another mistress, Shanda was young and innocent. Jones's bragged-about sexual prowess had become obvious sexual predation.

The boys on the team, and others, no doubt—even some of his staunchest supporters—had begun to see Jones's lies, his cruelty, the depths to which he had sunk.

But though his other mistresses apparently still sided with him, Jones had now lost another of his sons, along with the basketball team. Stephan describes his father at his worst: "screwing a teenager in an outhouse and calling others up in front of everyone to say that he couldn't take them on too, publicly proclaiming his desirability and martyrdom, while stumbling about the place and slurring his words half the time and talking insanity and gibberish even more."[42]

Jimmy's Plans

Even as Tim and the rest of the team began to lose faith in Jones, however, Jimmy still remained dedicated to his father. Still, he soon began to make other plans for his life—plans that didn't involve a life in Jonestown. In September Jones sent Jimmy to Georgetown as a sort of Jonestown ambassador, to foster relations with Guyana's important black citizens. Weeks later, in a Georgetown church on October 2, the day after his eighteenth birthday, Jimmy married Yvette Louise Muldrow—his "childhood sweetheart, the first person [he] ever really loved." The couple had already started planning how they'd live their lives. They hoped to attend college in Cuba and then go on to medical school—plus, Yvette was pregnant. Jimmy was "flabbergasted[ly]" happy. For the time being, though, he sent her back to Jonestown on her own, as he was still needed in Georgetown. Though Jimmy felt committed to his duties to the Temple, one foot was nonetheless out the door—the couple had already submitted their visa applications.[43]

"The Center Cannot Hold"

One of Roller's favorite poets was William Butler Yeats, whose poem "The Second Coming" seems fitting for the mood in Jonestown at the time:

> *Things fall apart; the centre cannot hold;*
> *Mere anarchy is loosed upon the world,*
> *The blood-dimmed tide is loosed, and everywhere*
> *The ceremony of innocence is drowned.*

Jones's "center" had always been his family and his closest friends and allies. It was a new experience for him to learn he no longer held a tight grip on his own family.

Tim, now swayed, happened upon Stephan sitting alone in the dark pavilion one night in late October. Reiterman describes this meeting: "Tim Jones still seethed with the anger of betrayal. He felt revulsion for the corruption and cruelty of his adopted father. 'We gotta kill him,' he exploded. 'We gotta kill him. We gotta have a revolution. We gotta throw this son of a bitch out.'"

Stephan answered, "You want a revolution. Let me tell you something. You know what would happen if you killed Jim Jones now? . . . Some of these seniors think he's God and he's their only hope. And you're gonna go up there and kill Jim Jones? That won't work. The only way you can take care of Jim Jones is to hope he dies naturally or gradually phase him out. That's the only way you're gonna do it. I'm sorry."[44]

The next day Stephan came across Jones as he struggled back to his cottage, and complied when Jones asked for an arm. Stephan accused his father of drugging Shanda. When Jones denied it, Stephan called him "a fucking liar." Jones threw back the insult and they parted company, furious.

Since this exchange of insults occurred within earshot of Tim and Johnny in the pavilion, Jones commanded that they put Stephan "under armed surveillance." But not much surveilling took place—the boys went right to Stephan, smiling broadly, and said "We're supposed to be watching you."

Soon thereafter Stephan suffered unusual pain and lethargy, according to Reiterman, and came to believe his father was behind this condition—that he was being drugged too. But Stephan would not give his father the pleasure of his suffering, and went to work as usual. Jones was apparently shocked to see his son up and working. Stephan accused his father of drugging him. Of course, Jones denied the charge, with bluster.

Jones now dealt out accusations and punishments more widely. After accusing Tim of ridiculous offenses at a rally, Tim replied: "'I ain't got nothin' else to say,' refusing to play the penitent son. 'I don't wish to talk about it. Whatever you want to do with me, go ahead on. . . . Three-fourths of it is bullshit.'"[45]

For Stephan, his father's permanent residence in Jonestown had cut especially deep from the beginning. He had long been keenly aware of his father's cruelties and manipulations, but, though he may have longed to escape, leaving Peoples Temple had never seemed an option. He loved his mother dearly, and Marceline, in spite of everything, still seemed to believe in the Church and its mission—and to support her husband. Stephan was just as much a captive in Jonestown as the other residents.

Erik Erikson, developmental psychologist, wrote an essay, "Youth: Fidelity and Diversity," about what he saw as a central task of adolescence. During that time, youth struggle with an existential dilemma. They seek the means to remain true to what they value in their families and communities while simultaneously struggling to break away—to become themselves, to be true to their own developing principles. Erikson points to Hamlet as embodying a particular difficulty of this problem: a young man who finds little in his world he can trust.[46]

Stephan and his brothers shared this dilemma. They loved their parents. But, over time, and as Jones descended into drug-enhanced madness and narcissistic mania, they also saw how wretchedly Jones treated the people—his believers—who had followed him to Guyana. And for Stephan, who had viewed his father with clear eyes for years, watching Jones's slow, dreadful descent was likely excruciating.

The outright rebellion of his sons brought on a significant policy change, as Reiterman describes: Jones demanded that all the firearms in Jonestown be handed over. They were then stashed in a locked building, and only Jones and Joe Wilson had access. Stephan had managed to hide his rifle beforehand.

Not long afterward, Carolyn Layton went to Marceline requesting that she "sign twenty blank sheets of paper." Marceline would not comply, and an argument ensued. Later, Stephan advised his mother to give in to the "lesser" cases, saving whatever sway she had with Jones for the important things. Marceline replied that "she was tired of signing so many blank pieces of paper over the years."

Carolyn was doing Jones's bidding in requesting the signed papers, but even Jones's most trusted mistress could see his rapid deterioration. She wrote to Stephan expressing her full support should "anything ever [happen] to your father."[47] Surely as Jones became more obviously ill and weak—this feeble man who had once been so strong and was now dependent on others, on his drugs—many in Jonestown must have felt he couldn't continue indefinitely. Jones seemed a paper tiger about to catch on fire.

Chapter 13

The Unraveling

February – October 1978

Those who cannot remember the past are condemned to repeat it.
—George Santayana

As Tim Reiterman points out in *Raven*, the words of American philosopher George Santayana "stand as a terrible reminder in the Dachau memorial outside Munich"—and those same words appeared prominently on a banner in the Jonestown pavilion. "Jones had crafted a concentration camp of his own," Reiterman continues, "complete with armed guards, an elaborate system of informants, and special places where people were disciplined or fed powerful drugs to subdue them—a place where punishments seldom fit the crime."[1]

White Nights

As the evening rallies increased in frequency, they were also becoming more exhausting and terrifying under Jones's influence, and more of them were morphing into "White Nights."

Over the years, the term "White Night" had taken on slightly different meanings at various times, but essentially a White Night was a rally occurring during what Jones saw as an emergency state in the Temple that he felt threatened to call for a mass death—a concept Jones had seemed obsessed with for a long time.[2]

White Nights did not begin in Jonestown. Jones's first references to mass suicide dated as far back as 1973, in Redwood Valley, according to Reiterman. Eventually, Jones knew, something would happen to destroy his Church, and the only way to thwart the inevitable would be to "choose the time, place, and manner of the death of his movement." The Peoples Temple "would leave an indelible mark on history. . . . A bunch of common people and a preacher named Jones could take their place alongside . . . the heroes of the Russian and Chinese revolutions, the martyrs of the American civil rights movement, the Jews at Masada." But it was only gradually and "insidiously" that Jones revealed this idea.[3]

One point is striking in this first mention of mass suicide, though: Jones himself would not take his life. Someone needed to speak for the group, he'd claimed, to honor the noble sacrifice, and he felt he should be that person. Jack Beam, a longtime member and minister in the Church, countered that, if things should come to that, it was only right that Jones share their sacrifice. But he was the only one who spoke up.

In any case, the concept took on a more vivid hue the next time the subject arose. During a White Night in 1975 or 1976, Jones presented to his Planning Commission some wine made from Redwood Valley vineyards. Though alcohol was strictly forbidden to Temple members, cups of wine were passed around, with Jones's invitation to drink. Some were reluctant, but all drank the offering. The group was just beginning to feel happily light-headed when Jones announced the wine contained a potent poison and that they would all die within the hour. Only after letting them suffer for a while did he tell them this ruse had just been a test of their faith.[4]

Jones had at first called White Nights "Omegas." He later dubbed them "Alphas," deciding they were a beginning, not an ending. Then he came up with "Black Nights"—but, as race and racism was such a primary concern to Temple members, he finally settled on "White Nights."[5]

The general membership, though, had not experienced a White Night until Jonestown, during the Six-Day Siege—when they were supposedly under threat of annihilation by the Guyanese army and supposed mercenaries and must fight to the death if required.

To some, a White Night was simply a meeting during which people got up to testify to the group that they were ready to die on the spot "for the cause." And during long rallies when Jones kept people up all night to rant about problems and concerns, he would utter the words "White Night" to frighten his exhausted audience awake. By that definition, starting in late 1977 some said there were White Nights almost every week in Jonestown. However one defines the term, there is no mistaking that Jones spoke of death—"his death, the community's death, the death of an enemy and the consequences for Jonestown . . . during nearly every community meeting held in the jungle encampment."[6] Doubtless Jonestowners might also have identified White Nights purely based on their level of fear, exhaustion, or despair at the time.

Stephan believed, and told his friend Mike Touchette, that White Nights were Jones's way of frightening people into obedience, and that he'd never carry one out with real poison. Touchette, who knew from years past how Jones liked to deceive his flock with fake scenarios (not to mention the fact that Stephan told him he'd always suspected the Six-Day Siege "assault" on Jones was a ruse) took advantage of his position as a security guard to break away from the exhausting dramas.[7]

Roller, a trusted servant, spoke up at a rally in February 1978, soon after she arrived in Jonestown. Opposed to the concept of revolutionary suicide, Roller voiced her strong objection to the idea of drinking poison. She may or may not have known that those who opposed the idea of dying were sent to the front of the line to drink the supposed poison. She wrote in her journal the next day:

> I had made several statements from the floor and at one time finding it difficult to speak when my comments seemed pertinent, I sent up a proposal. I thought Jim asked for it to be read aloud but it was not. I suggested that instead of revolutionary suicide . . . we seek to send our young people to some African country where they could be used in a revolutionary cause[,] that the adults support their sons and children in whatever place was most feasible, so that the brains and talents of our little ones would be saved for the future. [She wrote that others made similar suggestions.] At length Jim stated that the political situation showed no signs of clearing up and that we had no alternative but revolutionary suicide. He had already given instructions to make the necessary arrangements. All would be given a potion . . . we would die painlessly in about 45 minutes. . . . The seniors were allowed to be seated and be served first. At the beginning those who had reservations were allowed to express them, but those who did were required to be first. . . . A few questions were asked, such as an inquiry about those in the nursery. Jim said they had already been taken care of.
>
> I find it hard to believe that the threat with which we were faced justified such an extreme action. I would have thought it more in keeping with what we had been taught[—]to go down fighting. . . . I felt that some form of civil disobedience should be tried first, as it could have a profound effect on world opinion and I wondered why we should leave all our buildings and crops to be exploited by the enemy, as Jim had mentioned earlier . . . a scorched earth policy.

These considerations led me in one part of my mind to doubt that Jim was actually giving us a poison. . . . I shuddered. I regretted dying as I feel I have years of work and experience ahead of me, not least of which is the writing I wish to do about this whole remarkable story. It seemed bad luck that just when I had come to Jonestown and had a chance to use my talents as a teacher, I should be cut short. Nevertheless, I am 62 and I think of those who are younger, especially the children, with all their potential. I looked around me. Many had glowing eyes. It was awesome. Even the children were very quiet. I looked at the beautiful sky surrounding us. . . .

Was this movement [Jim Jones] had nurtured to come to naught, to a pile of dead bodies and an abandoned agricultural experiment in the small country of Guyana? . . . Poetry in general was what I most regretted leaving behind. Inevitably, Hamlet came to my mind. And although he was a fictional person, I felt that he most nearly typified the condition we faced: all of us, a sacrifice for the community, dying when he was young and capable of so much achievement.
. . .

I gave some thought to my sisters and Lor. When they heard the news I was afraid they would think Jim Jones was a lunatic and I wasn't much better than one. . . . Everything was very vivid. I was fonder of those around me than I had ever been. . . .

A few people were beginning to collapse. I saw one woman being carried out. . . . It must be about 45 minutes since we have started taking the potion. I was annoyed that I did not have my watch. Then I was amused at myself. When one is about to die, what difference does it make what time it is? I couldn't very well write in my journal: "I died at 5:30 p.m. on the 16th of February 1978."

Just at the moment when Roller gave up her internal protest and was about to take the potion herself, Jones announced they had consumed only "punch with something a little stronger in it."[8] This was likely the Opportunity students' first White Night when they thought they would truly die—most certainly a terrifying experience, when anyone would have felt walled in by the jungle, by fear; forgotten, hopeless, and alone.

Beginning in early 1978, there were as many as two rallies per month that could be called White Nights by one definition or another; these often continued into the early morning hours. On another spring White Night when a supposedly poisoned drink was passed around, ten-year-old Martin Amos begged Jones to relent—he didn't want to die. Some who had drunk the potion started falling over, pretending to die. Though Tommy Bogue laughed at the bad acting in this cruel performance Jones had staged, no doubt some, like little Martin, were terrified, believing people were truly dying. Disgusted with his father, Stephan finally went to Jones and said to him, "You're putting people through unnecessary pain." Jones stopped the sad charade shortly after, citing it as merely another test of their loyalty.[9]

❧

> *The best lack all conviction, while the worst*
> *Are full of passionate intensity.*
>   —W.B. Yeats, "The Second Coming"

Enemies Multiply

In the States, concern about the Peoples Temple and Jonestown did not subside after the barrage of news that had come out during the summer of 1977. The following spring, the Concerned Relatives—a self-named group of fifty-four who had previously defected from the Temple—including Howard and Beverly Oliver, Tim and Grace Stoen, and Steven Katsaris (father of Jones's mistress Maria)—publicly denounced Jones in their "Accusation of Human Rights Violations by Rev. James Warren Jones." The statement, delivered to a Church representative in San Francisco and distributed to the press, accused Jones of the following: violating the human rights of family members; preventing them from leaving and from communicating with people Jones considered "outsiders"; and using "physical intimidation and psychological coercion as part of a mind-programming campaign aimed at destroying family ties, discrediting belief in God, and causing contempt for the United States of America." The signers referenced the U.N. Universal Declaration of Human Rights as well as the U.S. and Guyanese constitutions, and demanded the rights of Jonestown residents be restored. They voiced particular concern over Jones's statement: "I can say without hesitation that we are devoted to a decision that it is better even to die than to be constantly harassed from one continent to the next." To this they added a challenge, "We hereby give you the opportunity now to publicly repudiate our interpretation of your threat."[10]

When he got the news about the Accusation at 3:30 PM on April 12, 1978, Jones screamed over the loudspeaker, "Danger! Security Alert! ... White Night!" Once again, shots rang out in the jungle. Residents dropped their tools and schoolbooks and rushed to the pavilion. It was Deborah Layton's first White Night, and she was told to go sit with Stephan on the wooden railing near the stage. Deborah describes the experience as exhausting and terrifying. Jones was hysterical, yelling, "All is lost. Traitors have betrayed us!"

There were no mercenaries. For each White Night when Jones said they all had to die, Jones assigned different boys into the bush to fire shots; each was unaware of the others; each had been told a different story and warned not to tell others. "No one realized that all of the gunfire was from our guns," Deborah writes. In their weakened, exhausted state, all of them, even the most ready to rebel, had become "feeble, compliant automatons. In madness there is no way to think logically."[11]

Roller reported in her journal the tumultuous White Night, which went on until five the next morning only to start up again the next day at noon. She focused on what she saw, at first, as a positive aspect of the evening. Jones claimed that part of the problem, besides the demonstration in San Francisco, was that Larry Schact's certification as a "doctor" had not been approved by the Guyanese government. Now, Jones claimed, it had been. This entry is a fascinating testament to Jones's talent for manipulating his followers with fantastic, complicated lies and fearmongering. For, though the Concerned Relatives' Accusation was indeed discussed, Jones took the opportunity to elaborate on supposedly more vital concerns:

> *[Guyanese] Prime Minister Burnham . . . has gone to Soviet Russia. . . . Some of Burnham's party, the P.N.C., are disapproving . . . and there is said to be an attempt to adopt a new constitution and policies which would be inimical to our group. . . . There is danger of an attempted take-over by a fascist group which would invade our property.*
>
> *The U.S. is back of this difficulty. The International Monetary Fund, to which Guyana had applied for a loan, under the control of the U.S., had put unacceptable conditions on the giving of the loan in order to secure favorable treatment for capitalist business interests. Guyana had refused. Pressure which resulted in Georgetown's being without power for lights and water had been put on Guyana. . . .*
>
> *We will put up as much resistance as possible to any invasion but we don't have the weapons to prevail in the end.*[12]

Deborah writes that Jones insisted they all had to die rather than succumb to enemy takeover.

> *It was almost dawn . . . I realized that we had been here for at least six hours.*
> *"Hear that sound?" Jim asked us. "The mercenaries are coming. The end has come. Time is up. Children . . . line up into two queues, one on either side of me."*
> *Guards had placed a large aluminum vat in the front of the pavilion near father.*
> *"It tastes like fruit juice, children. It will not be hard to swallow."*

When one young man protested there must be another way, Jones asked for guards to "secure him. He'll have to be given the drink by force." Deborah heard "Stephan muttering something under his breath. He turned to me, his eyes filled with contempt. 'The fucking bastard,' he gasped. 'It's another bloody drill, that's all. Another fucking scare tactic . . .' He shook his head, exhausted."

At first Deborah was surprised to hear him speak like this. Then she remembered that "Jim had sent him here before the other boys because he felt that Stephan was becoming disrespectful and might leave."[13]

When the White Night resumed at noon the next day, Jones announced he had appealed to Cuba to let the settlement move there; Cuba had approved. Jones spoke of purchasing a boat that "would go that far" and "hold all our people." But he also mentioned, in a purely Jonesian twist, that Cuba might not take everyone, especially the seniors who believed in God. Roller wrote that she went up to comment on the matter:

> *I waited for a long time to speak. . . . I was preceded by Carrie Langston. . . . She said she was so grateful to him and she would do anything for him. She believed he was God and didn't want to go anywhere he would not be the leader. He told the members that it was because of such seniors as she that he would not go to Cuba unless they could go, but it was the very answers she gave which might exclude her. He stated that if one [of] his seniors was excluded he would not accept residence in Cuba though others could enter. He and the excluded one would sail on the boat until they died.*
>
> **Realizing that his remarks would be overwhelmingly influential in persuading the crowd not to favor Cuba at all,** *I stated that we should negotiate for admittance of all, but that [I] believed there were certain advantages of going to Cuba. (1) Our leader would have more people for his tremendous talents in the field of international communism; (2) our young people would have more opportunity to serve in some of the struggles for freedom in Africa, as an example* [emphasis added].

But Roller's argument, even her appeal to his ego, did no good.

> *Jim did not hear my complete statement as he was conferring with somebody. . . . Jim took another vote and a very few favored going to Cuba.* **It was not pointed out then that the alternate might be putting to sleep all of our children with concomitant damage to world communism** [emphasis added].[14]

The bolded portions of Roller's statements may have been a serious "act of treason," at least in Jones's eyes. She identifies his manipulation of the crowd, bringing them to vote against going to Cuba in order to show support for the seniors. In talking about the effect of the "alternative" Jones was forcing people toward, the idea of everyone in Jonestown committing revolutionary suicide, she knew that the whole world, communist or not, would be horrified, especially by the death of the children.

Regarding the "demonstration of those purporting to be concerned relatives of Temple members," Roller wrote:

> Jim called all those whose relatives were on the steps (of the San Francisco Temple) to recommend what should be done with them. All said, "Kill them." Usually offering to do it by various colorful means. The only one to arouse any protest was a proposal by Larry Jones (Tupper) that Mr. Tupper and all the others should be put in a big white church and that we burn the church down. One senior objected, seemingly because of concern for the church, not Mr. Tupper.[15]

Stephan later reflected: "If I were forced to offer what I feel most contributed to the ugliness of the Temple ... I would have to say it was peer pressure. Dad played on our concern with what the others in our community thought of us." Stephan recalled the feeling of "sitting in a Temple meeting thinking how crazy it all was, while faking my approval because all around me was an auditorium full of what seemed to be zealous believers, at least half of whom I now believe were doing and thinking the same thing I was, but at the time I could only think there must be something wrong with me, that I was too selfish to see the 'greater good' of it all."[16]

Another Traitor

Deborah decided early on that the trick to self-preservation was to pretend to play by the rules, at least for a while. She worked hard to prove to Jones her self-discipline, her determination to do well at whatever task was assigned her. Eventually, she was moved from the very crowded cabin to which she'd initially been assigned to a much better one that she shared with three of Jones's adopted sons—Jimmy, Tim, and Lew, along with Lew's wife, Terry. Stephan lived in another cabin but visited his brothers often. Being chosen to share such exclusive living quarters was a sign of Jones's trust.[17]

Deborah began to find solace in working hard in the fields, where she thought about what she should do, how she might escape from Jonestown. Her chance finally came in May 1978, after she had earned the trust of Jones. She was chosen to accompany the group of young performers to Georgetown—the kids who would dance, sing, and recite socialist poems at the Guyanese Cultural Center. It was a rare chance to get out of Jonestown, and Deborah used the trip to begin planning her escape. She managed to make a secret call to her sister Annalisa in California. She feared someone was listening in, so she said she couldn't go into detail, and told her sister she and her mother were fine and loved it in Jonestown. But Annalisa could hear in her sister's voice that something was wrong. Deborah promised to send her sister a letter with details, but she never got the chance to leave Lamaha Gardens to mail the letter.

Then, a timely accident at Jonestown—which instigated orders for Deborah to go to the U.S. embassy to make arrangements for an injured child—gave her another opportunity to contact her sister. The two concocted a plan to get Deborah out. Since Deborah would need Jones's permission to leave Temple jurisdiction, they opted for a scenario Jones would likely buy into, using the "good PR" reason for a family trip to South America, as her brother-in-law was on a U.N. mission. Deborah could arrange meetings with prime ministers and other dignitaries, all the while heralding the success of their "agricultural project."

Over the next several days there were many moments when Deborah's true intentions were almost discovered. She worried about causing her friends trouble, or causing another White Night, about being caught and punished, about her mother. [18]

Ultimately, she succeeded in escaping Guyana. At the request of the American vice consul, who had helped her, she had earlier signed a statement for the American embassy stating she feared Jones would "carry out his threats to force all members of the Organization in Guyana to commit suicide if a decision is made in Guyana . . . to have John Stoen returned to his mother." She said there was poison in Jonestown and that plans had been made to kill those unwilling to commit suicide. [19]

Deborah was determined to do all she could to save her fellow Jonestowners. In San Francisco on June 15, 1978, with the assistance of Grace Stoen, Deborah submitted an affidavit—"The Threat and Possibility of Mass Suicide by Members of the Peoples Temple"—to publicize Jones's talk of "revolutionary suicide" and rally support for getting more people out of Jonestown. Details of her defection and her sworn affidavit soon appeared in the *San Francisco Chronicle*, and included references to there having been "mass suicide rehearsals at Jonestown." [20]

⁓

On May 13, 1978—his birthday—Jones learned that Deborah had left Georgetown for the United States. As Roller reported in her journal, at that evening's rally, Jones announced that "one of our people (name and sex not indicated) . . . had defected . . . [and] stolen some official Temple money." Jones repeatedly referred to the defector as if he were male. "He said he was going either to the U.S. or Soviet Russia. . . . A long time member, he knew a great deal about our financial resources and security arrangements and could do more harm than Tim Stoen." Roller continued: "Jim said we take for granted an attack could be launched on us at once. I gathered we had plans to move in on our enemies which the defector could reveal and in the discussion Jim confirmed this. Our radio communications were being interfered with and there may have been no way to conceal the present instructions."

Once again, Jones claimed revolutionary suicide was the only answer to this pending crisis, and thus began another full-fledged White Night.

> *There was continued discussion and votes were taken. At all times those in favor of revolutionary suicide were in the majority, however I felt that these were strongly influenced by his advocacy. Few young people expressed any opinion. The number of those opposed grew as thoughtful statements were made. One by Jann Gurvich was outstanding. . . . Heavy rain came and it was hard to hear. Jim had us rest for a while but I couldn't go to sleep sitting up.*

Roller was again being dangerously honest in her journal. The rally was dismissed at six in the morning. Jones allowed people to sleep until noon.[21]

On May 14 everyone was treated to a chicken dinner, a rare treat by then. Whether Jones was trying to mollify the overworked settlers, afraid of more dissatisfaction, or the special meal had more to do with the fact that the chickens were now infected with a kind of salmonella is not known. Less than two weeks later, Roller reported that "all our chickens died today" of the disease.[22]

On May 15, Jones threatened another White Night, now using code terminology: "Mrs. White drops by and she makes us all equal. Should see Mrs. White now and then. [Marceline] apologized for seeming to disagree with Jim." Among her notes for that night, Roller reported: "USA is going to be in nuclear war. Has no protection for people. . . . 212 million people will die in the first 20 minutes."[23]

Jones Unravels

Roller described Jones that night as growing "more and more exhausted. Finally his head fell and he gasped, 'I cannot go on.'" Roller herself was "afraid he was near death. Marcy and Stephen [*sic*] tended to him. He revived sufficiently to end the meeting, but I was very worried."[24]

Stephan, on the other hand, had seen this kind of act too many times in his life to believe it. But he hoped that maybe this time it wasn't *completely* an act, that Jones's continued drug use would solve the problem for people in Jonestown.

As he told Lawrence Wright, Stephan had had thoughts of killing his father, but as he explained to Bebelaar much later, though he was often "enraged by his father and wanted him to *be* dead," he knew he could never go through with it. Indeed, he felt he was incapable of killing anyone.[25]

It wasn't as if he didn't have opportunities. Once, Stephan was summoned over the loudspeaker by Carolyn Layton ("still Dad's mistress and his most trusted servant") to help her "subdue" Jones, who had slipped into a state of mind in which he seemed to think he was Lenin. It had happened before; he often needed to be calmed down when he was raging in this condition.

Stephan writes, "It quickly became a chance to knock him around a bit." To Stephan, it seemed Carolyn understood Jones's Lenin act was a ruse, but she went along with it, seeing her acceptance of Jones's enacted "past life" as the price for "the power and purpose she believed he gave her." Stephan continues:

> I subdued Dad. He gave me a speech, through gritted teeth, about what a shame it was that a strong, brave, young man like me was a lackey for agents of the Czar—namely Carolyn. I allowed him to escape, knowing he'd run into the bush, because running in the other direction would take him into town. I knew a swamp lay just inside the bush line. As I hoped he would, Dad stumbled into the mire. It wasn't the quicksand of the movies, but acted like it for the first three or four feet. I stood at the edge, happy to watch Vladimir get himself out of this one. After all, I was the enemy. The great Bolshevik would never ask for my assistance. Just as Dad's shorts were about to get all muddy, he started and snapped around, swiveled back and forth as best he could with his calves and feet locked into the earth, and assumed his best befuddled countenance.
>
> "Wha?!" He looked about dramatically, looking very much like a man with very short legs whose feet had been glued to the ground. Then, quickly and quietly, he whispered, "Where am I?"

I swear. That's what he said. I think Dad watched too much Captain Kirk during his many "strategy sessions."

He wrung himself pretty good to get his eyes on me where I was intentionally standing directly behind him. He teetered there, arms splayed like a marionette with torso turned and feet dragging and lagging.

"Stephan, is that you?"

"Yeah, Dad, It's me."

I shifted my eyes off to the left of him and gazed for a moment into the dark, verdant world that terrified him. I wanted to laugh. I wanted to cry, for me and for him. I wanted to grab his fucking head and shove it under the muck that held him. I wanted to hold him. I wanted him to hold me.

"Ya wanna hand?"

In the second episode of Lenin Comes to Jonestown, Dad cocked and leveled a loaded .357 at me. I was enraged by his carelessness. I knew he had no clue how close he was to blowing me away in the interest of keeping his life interesting, which made it more infuriating. I could have tolerated it better if there was intent, but . . . it was all a game rubbed in my face, the fact that my life had been one scene after another just like the one before me. From her place behind Dad, Carolyn could see that I was tweaked, and tried to calm me by pressing the air in front of her waist while giving me her best pleading look.

I barely glanced at her. I growled as I whispered, "You fucker," and moved toward him. He knew that what I had in mind would not be fun, and scrambled into his cabin, slamming and locking the door behind him.

I silently pulled myself up by the outside rafters to his cabin so that I could watch him over the wall. Thinking he was unobserved, Dad quickly unloaded the gun. So that he could brandish it dramatically without wasting his son, I guess. Strange thing for Lenin to do with the enemy so close. [26]

"Things Fall Apart"

As time passed and Jones continued to break down, resistance against him seemed to be more and more possible—at least to Stephan. After Lynetta's death, Jones's mental and physical health plummeted. Lawrence Wright describes how, "between 1977 and 1978, he lost thirty pounds. Taking amphetamines and Percodan alternately, he rocked in and out of reality. . . . (Jimmy believed that his father may also have been injecting heroin during this period.)" Marceline thought she could convince her husband to give up the drugs, but to this Stephan responded, "Mom, you gotta get this in context. You're talking about going to God and telling him he's a drug addict?"

Unlike his mother, Stephan thought of the drugs as his "ally," as they were certain to kill his father "soon enough."[27]

As 1978 wore on, the settlement continued to fall apart in step with Jones. And as Jonestowners grew more and more exhausted, less and less necessary work was being done. Gardens grew weeds, buildings peeled paint, paperwork piled up.

Stephan believes that, because Roller did not hide her journal, she continued to have Jones's approval in keeping it—and that therefore what she says cannot be altogether trusted; that the words of anyone who admired Jones as much as Roller did cannot be trusted.

> *Everything [approved by Jones] was so orchestrated and tainted with people's desire to please and justify that I take everything that came out of JT [Jonestown] with a grain of salt, including the audio tapes because Dad was often monitoring what was recorded and what wasn't.*

Stephan told Bebelaar he remembers differently some of what Roller's journal described, though he acknowledges memories of so long ago can be faulty.[28]

Still, the feelings Roller sometimes shared about small things—like how she broke down in tears one night, or the sympathy she sometimes expressed for those being punished—make Bebelaar believe there is still something to be learned from what she's written. And, as far as anyone knows, hers is the only day-by-day record of life in Jonestown. Sadly, that record was cut short in August 1978, as described in Chapter 12.

The Basketball Team Comes Together

During the unraveling of Jones and the settlement, the basketball team had been preparing, as well as they could, for the upcoming Georgetown tournament with the Guyanese National team. Jones continued to give them at least some support, allowing team members to use thirty minutes of their workday for practice. Reiterman describes the core players: "Emmett Griffith, a big, fast hustling player, bulwarked the defense. [Jimmy], at six-feet-four an inch shorter than Stephan, played center, while Stephan played power forward. Johnny Cobb and Tim Jones started at guard. Mike Touchette, a former high school athlete, became trainer. About sixteen young men tried out, and eleven made the team."[29]

Emmett Griffith was the big brother of Opportunity's Cobra and poet Mondo. Stephan listed the other players as Preston Wade, Mark Cordell

(Cindy and Candy's cousin), Cleveland Newell, Burrell Wilson, Carl Barnett, Walter Williams, and Opportunity student Calvin Douglas Williams. Stephan elaborated on the team picks for the Georgetown event:

> *Wesley Breidenbach, Albert Touchette, and Emmett Griffith practiced with the team in Jonestown, but were not selected to go to Georgetown because we could only take twelve players. Emmett would definitely have been one of the twelve, but he was the only bulldozer operator other than Mike Touchette and me. . . . Emmett was just an incredible athlete—very little specific hoop skills, but no one wanted him to guard them; he could jump through the roof, and would give his body up in a second, frequently skidding off the edge of our makeshift, raised basketball floor. He was also the ultimate team player and truly inspirational to all of us.*[30]

The young men on the team represented hope for the beleaguered community, a fragment of life—or at least the way it used to be—that could be experienced, vicariously, by everyone.

Basketball at Jonestown. Tim Jones at right.

Chapter 14

The Last Days

October – November 1978

The Breakdown

ecause Edith Roller's journal disappeared in September and ends with her August entries, there is no internal written record of the last months, weeks, and days of Jonestown. The audiotapes recorded in the pavilion are not necessarily reliable—Stephan has said that Jones "monitor[ed] what was recorded and what wasn't, his finger always at the ready on the recording button."[1]

Much of what we do know about this period in Jonestown derives from the scholarship of Tim Reiterman and John Jacobs, as well as from the reports of Charles Krause and Ron Javers, who, along with Reiterman, were in Guyana on those last days. What *is* clear is that Jones and the conditions in Jonestown were deteriorating even more rapidly.

Jones's drug use was by this time extreme, both in quantity and variety. But while he was clearly no longer of sane mind, Jonestowners must have struggled with remaining clear-headed themselves, considering their state of fatigue caused by excessive work, lack of sleep, inadequate diet, and harsh punishments, as well as illness and infections.

A welcome break from the police state Jonestown had become came with the visit of Soviet Consul Feodor Timofeyev on October 2. A surprisingly lucid Jones made a ringing speech for their honored guest, and led his followers in singing socialist songs, gospel-style. The applause for Timofeyev was long and thunderous, as was usual in the Temple, but this time people may have clapped with real fervor, clinging to a crazy hope Jones had instilled: that Russia would accept nine hundred socialist immigrants from Guyana.[2]

But the next day Jones resumed his usual slurred and rapid-fire loudspeaker ranting, insisting people must study for tests based on his rambling, confusing, sometimes terrifying, and often fabricated "newscasts." They must also learn to speak Russian, he demanded, and men must cut long hair and shave beards "immediately," because "socialist nations have made an issue of hair." More Soviet visitors would be coming, and the people of Jonestown must prepare to pass muster by getting themselves and Jonestown "apple pie order." Jones claimed the Russians planned a huge "entertainment center" for Jonestown residents while warning of an imminent nuclear attack on America.[3]

It was hot. The sky darkened. No doubt, as was usual this time of year, hard rain fell.

Another Betrayal

On October 28, Jones announced at a rally, "I'm *very* emotionally disturbed with another traitor." As with Deborah's defection, Jones did not identify the "traitor," but Teri Buford, another young woman who had been a trusted aide, had been given permission for a trip to San Francisco, and had gone missing. Jones claimed to have suffered a heart attack as a result, indeed was "three minutes dead." He said the traitor would be killed along with all the others. "Every last damn one of them will *die*." Jones repeatedly warned that "there's to be no more talk about who the traitor is."[4]

Marceline, who had been visiting her parents, Walter and Charlotte Baldwin, in Indiana, returned to Jonestown with them two days later, on October 30. Jones greeted them, "badly swollen with edema," weak and confused. Marceline soon discovered that while she was away Jones had sedated "almost twenty people on tranquilizers for causing unrest."[5] As was often the case when Marceline returned to the compound, she did what she could to ease the suffering of those so badly treated by their leader in her absence.

At the next evening's rally Mr. and Mrs. Baldwin were welcomed and entertained by residents singing Jonestown versions of Joe Cocker's "You Are So Beautiful to Me," (changing the lyrics to *Jonestown is so beautiful*), and Nina Simone's "To Be Young, Gifted and Black" (substituting *strong* for *young*). Marceline apologized to the crowd for Jones's absence:

> Before we go, I would like to say that uh, Jim Jones is very sorry that he could not be up here tonight, but as he said over the microphone, he had a very high uh, fever today. He had a heart attack a couple of days ago too, and uh, uh, he's had to have medication but we know that he's going to be all right.[6]

One can only imagine how the Baldwins viewed this strange reality in which their daughter now lived.

Enter the Congressman

In a rally on November 5, Jones addressed residents, railing at "the god-damn treasonous defector back there. . . . Everything was dying, till that started. And they've got a congressman [Leo Ryan] they want to come in [visit the settlement] who's close to the member of the John Birch Society [a conservative anti-communist group], just to drop on—drop in, and my opinion is, to tell them to stick it." He announces that some in the audience have betrayed him, that there is "an element in here trying to kill me. And you know who you are now. I've down—I've got you singled down." With an angry, crazy "logic," he swings from supposed conspirators to statues of Stalin "being pulled down. . . . and moving [Stalin's body] to a common grave," when "nobody in God's half acre, I told the ambassador, could ever've brought the Soviet people together and resisted the fascists as well as they did. . . . The city named after Stalin, that's where the turning point came."

Jones goes on to compare himself to Stalin and references his own Six-Day Siege: "Because I had six days of it. It wasn't as long as Stalin, but I know what it is to agonize over your people, and to be tortured to death over whether your people are going to be killed or not killed. I have at least—(Angry) And I know some of you fuckers want to kill me. Goddamn you . . . "

He then turns his anger onto a child, who apparently found a bug on the ground more interesting than another of Jones's tirades. "I saw you step your foot on that bug," Jones accuses the child. "The little one," he says to the adult holding the child. "The one in your lap." He declares that he "deplore[s] violence," And asks the crowd, "Don't you . . . have any counseling set up for these kids?"

His attention turns next to his son Tim. "I'm talking to you. I know one thing, Tim. I'm talking to you, you got an arrogant ass—asshole, a lot of time. You're arrogant. You can't say nothing to you."

Then he seems to be addressing the basketball team, especially his sons, saying their behavior in the upcoming tournament "can make or break Jonestown." Abruptly, he begins to praise Tim, saying he's seen "*tremendous growth*" in his adopted son. Then he advises the team to applaud the opposing team whenever they make a basket, demonstrating several times how they can clap briefly and then get back to the game. He says if he were taller and had hands like those of his sons, he would have been a "pro." However, he quit the game because he "saw them treat one black man wrong." Later he focuses on Calvin Douglas, another Opportunity student on the team, whose "attitude's not the hottest" at times, according to Jones, and he asks Teddy McMurry "What is it you want to say?" A tape edit cuts out whatever Teddy may have said in reply.

Jones then returns to the expected visit from Ryan, telling the crowd to reply to any questions they may get about food with a predetermined list of the healthy meals they should falsely report they have eaten that day, adding that they should also say "And a piece of pie."[7]

And thus was introduced the figure who, despite his good intentions, would mark the beginning of the end for Jonestown and its people: Jones announced an impending visit to their hard-earned socialist paradise by Congressman Leo Ryan. The man, Jones claimed, was yet another enemy of their righteous mission.

Leo J. Ryan was a Democratic member of the U.S. Congress, representing California's eleventh congressional district—part of the San Francisco Bay Area. The congressman paid particular attention to Peoples Temple after he read a *San Francisco Examiner* article by Tim Reiterman, dated November 13, 1977, that concerned a friend of his (and of Reiterman's as well),

Cong. Leo J. Ryan   Sam Houston. Headlined "People's Temple and a father's grief," the story recounts the mysterious death of Houston's son Bob "beneath the wheels of a freight train" on October 5, 1976, one day after Bob had announced his decision to leave the People's Temple.[8] Teenagers Judy and Patty Houston, who were sent to Jonestown the following August, were Bob Houston's daughters.

A number of subsequent reports by Reiterman and others maintained Ryan's interest in Jones's Church. One was the *San Francisco Chronicle*'s account in June 1978 of Deborah Layton's defection and her claims of abuses against members of Ryan's own constituency. The congressman also received letters from members of the Concerned Relatives, authors of the "Accusation of Human Rights Violations by Rev. James Warren Jones." After collecting extensive information about the Peoples Temple, Ryan ultimately decided he needed to investigate Jonestown for himself. In a letter to the House Foreign Affairs Committee Chairman, Ryan wrote:

> *It has come to my attention that a community of some 1,400 Americans are presently living in Guyana under somewhat bizarre conditions. There is conflicting information regarding whether or not the U.S. citizens are being held there*

against their will. If you agree, I would like to travel to Guyana during the week of November 12–18 to review the situation first-hand.[9]

The title of an Agatha Christie novel, *Towards Zero*, conveys a concept that was at work in this last month of Jonestown: that a particular combination of acts, decisions, and trajectories, once put in motion, could proceed toward an unavoidable collision of catastrophic effect. What were the elements of Jonestown's particular "zero"? The settlement housed over nine hundred exhausted, undernourished, overworked, and overwrought Temple members, who had probably waffled between sustained dedication to their Church and its cause and an escalating sense that the figure at the helm was both dangerous and unsympathetic to their suffering. The people had been continually ravaged by Jones's particular reign of terror, scared too many times into thinking their lives, their land, their work were on the verge of assault and destruction at the hands of sworn enemies. And Jones—after the long string of defections, the long-standing efforts of the Concerned Relatives, and the long-lasting effects of his drug abuse—was on the verge of self-destruction, his frazzled brain practically a frayed wire connected to a bomb detonator. As long as Jones viewed the impending arrival of Congressman Ryan as the ultimate assault, Jonestown crept closer and closer toward zero.

The Team Heads to Georgetown

On the morning after the November 5 rally, the Jonestown basketball team set off for the tournament in Georgetown, and only Jim Jones himself was not there to wish them well. Mike Touchette said he "never had seen such a spontaneous outpouring of emotion." Worried that Jones might reverse his consent, Marceline, happy for the boys but still anxious, urged them to get on their way. When they were all in the truck, Marceline gave Mike a tearful hug, telling him, "No matter what happens . . . please take care of my sons for me." Mike particularly noticed that his mother, Joyce, was crying too; he could remember only one other time when he'd seen her cry. Many in the crowd were in tears.[10] It was surely a bewildering mixture of emotions they would have felt: happiness for the boys, regret that they too were not leaving, dread of returning to what had become their daily lives; homesickness, fear, and hope mixed with despair.

Another Jonestowner in Georgetown at the time was Eugene Smith, husband of Opportunity student Ollie Smith. Eugene was in charge of relaying shipments of supplies from San Francisco to Jonestown. He valued this post, as he too saw how the settlement was falling apart, and sought an escape for his little family, Ollie and their baby Martin Luther. But despite Eugene's familiarity with both Georgetown government officials and their methods, no embassy official would help him.[11]

Jimmy's Turning Point

Though most of the team members no longer saw Jones as a leader, Jimmy still felt considerable loyalty to his father at that time, especially as Jones had told him he was the only son he still trusted. While stationed in Georgetown, he had missed the recent drama with Jones and the emotional team send-off in Jonestown. He nonetheless sensed something was off when he wasn't permitted to speak to Yvette when he radioed Jonestown.

On November 7, the day after the team arrived in Georgetown, Jones ordered Jimmy to escort the new American consul, Douglas Ellice Jr., for his first visit to Jonestown the following day. Eager to see Yvette, Jimmy welcomed the assignment. But when he arrived, he discovered his father was punishing Yvette—having blamed her for "mechanical problems on the boat ride back to Jonestown," on account of the "negativity" she brought on board. Jimmy said, "That was when my eyes started opening, because it directly affected me." And it didn't help that, when he went to get Jones ready to meet the consul, his father was so heavily drugged that Jimmy had to drag him from bed and "h[o]ld his dick so he could go pee." Jones blamed his intensely green urine on Marceline, claiming she was poisoning him.

Later Jimmy escorted the diplomat back to Georgetown. Jimmy would never see his wife again.[12]

Back in Jonestown

Jim Jones, in the meantime, his paranoia intensified, continued his fantastical harangues. When he delivered his news report at a November 9 rally, he warned:

> By the way, we may have a—a group of bad relatives who are working with the conspiracy of which you refuse to speak to . . . if one of them come with this right-winged Birchite bla—anti-blacks, uh congressman, you are uh, to refuse to speak to him. Tell him you will not see them and refuse to see them. . . . His name is Congressman Ryan.[13]

He continues his report, saying that "in New York City a young black youth was castrated and ha—tied to a tree, left to die." He instructs Marceline to get Jonestowners to sign a paper, that night, stating that they will refuse to allow their family members to visit them and refuse to be taken prisoner or return to the States—he wanted to test his people to see who would agree to sign such a statement. He calls for attention and directs "peoples helpers" to go find those who hadn't come to the rally and get them to the pavilion right away. He says Ryan's group of forty may come by night, and by sea. He claims that they are "planning some kind of violent action" and are bringing along "some astrologer" who will help them determine when a surprise visit to the settlement should occur. [14]

That night Jonestowners signed a petition indicating they did not want the Ryan party to come, and Jonestown leaders alerted the media as to the resolution passed by the settlement's board of directors in opposition to the congressman's visit. Almost every adult in Jonestown did sign and no doubt would have suffered greatly if they had refused. [15]

Escape Plans

Despite Jones's vivid exhortations and descriptions of the supposed consequences in store for anyone who might try to escape Jonestown, some nonetheless plotted to flee. According to Scheeres' *A Thousand Lives,* Jim Bogue, Marilee's father, was growing increasingly fearful and anxious to find a way to get himself and his family out of Jonestown. Although it had been Bogue who had convinced his family to follow Jones in the early California days of the Temple—at the time dismissing Jones's exaggerated rhetoric about being "willing to die for the cause"—Bogue now feared that Jones would make good on this repeated threat of "revolutionary suicide," as he had with others. As Scheeres writes, Bogue "got [his family] into the church, and now he had to get them out."

Bogue came up with an idea: He'd tell Jones he had a plan for how to prospect for gold—he'd seen "wildcat miners in rubber boots trudging up the road to Port Kaituma" with their findings, and he thought Jones might fall for it since it would be a potential source of income for the settlement. Then Bogue could cut a trail through the jungle to use for an escape.

Bogue's scheme worked: Jones approved the "project." Bogue chose Al Simon, a Pomo Indian from California whom he trusted, as his partner. Like Bogue, Simon was a quiet, thoughtful man who worried about his children and whose wife remained committed to Jones, just as Edith Bogue was. The two discussed how many of their family members and friends they could safely include in their escape plans. It was an agonizing decision, but in the end they decided to stick to trying to save only themselves and their children. The constant efforts in Jonestown to break up families and weave together new ones meant that it would be too great of a risk to include in their plans others whom they cared about, including a sister, a niece, and the Bogue girls' boyfriends. If just one person revealed the plan, all was lost. The work the undernourished men set out to do was punishing, requiring that they fight with the thick jungle every day to get to the theoretical gold—in reality to get to Matthews Ridge, where they hoped to get aboard a train somehow. Simon and Bogue's daughter Juanita had to sneak protein—eggs and cured pork—to Bogue, who had shed one-third of his body weight since arriving in Jonestown and "weighed less than one hundred" pounds. Bogue knew that Marilee, who worked in the nursery and on the medical staff and lived with her security guard husband, was, like his estranged wife, totally dedicated to Jones; he could not tell her. But he would bring her along too, when the time came, even if he had to steal her away, "kicking and screaming if need be . . . dragging her to freedom; she'd thank him someday."[16]

Opportunity student Monica Bagby, who had arrived that summer when conditions in Jonestown were worsening dramatically, had never wanted to be in Jonestown in the first place, and her hatred had only intensified. Shortly after she arrived, Vern Gosney writes that she introduced herself to him by approaching him out of the blue and saying "Let's get the fuck out of here!" In Vern's essay, "Remembering Monica," on the Jonestown Institute website, he says Monica's mother had sent her to Jonestown to get off drugs, and that Monica, Vern, and another young man named Keith were all gay and had quickly become friends.

Monica had taken an enormous risk by making such a bold statement to someone she didn't even know, but Vern had long wanted to escape too, and they started to make their plans. (Keith was too afraid—previously he had tried to run away and had been "caught, beaten and physically thrown down, landing on his head.") They thought they saw a chance when Richard Dwyer, the U.S. Consul in Georgetown, visited Jonestown after Deborah Layton's mother's death in late October 1978. They hung around during the visit, hoping to approach Dwyer with a plea to take them away, but in the end they couldn't go through with it. It turned out that they would have made a terrible mistake: The man they had thought was Dwyer was actually the pilot of the plane Dwyer had arrived on. There was no telling what might have happened to them if the pilot had reported them to Jones. But Monica and Vern were ready to try again during the congressman's visit, and would be the first to ask the Ryan party to help them get out of Jonestown.[17]

~

Harold Cordell, Cindy and Candy's father, worked on the *Cudjoe*, which was scheduled to ferry Marceline's parents to Georgetown on November 13 so they could return to the States. But with Ryan and the delegation due to arrive in Georgetown on November 14, Jones abruptly cancelled the *Cudjoe*'s trip to the capital. Marceline arranged for the Baldwins to fly out instead. After the Baldwins left, Jones reversed himself and allowed the boat to go after all. When the *Cudjoe* returned from Georgetown, Cordell noticed a large paper-wrapped drum that was not on the shipping manifest. He soon discovered it contained an extremely toxic cyanide compound. Having also learned earlier that Jones had ordered research on explosives, Harold was certain Jones was ready to kill his own people, and was thus truly mad. He too began to think of ways to get out of Jonestown.[18]

Convergence in Georgetown

November 13

The Jonestown basketball team played their first tournament game against the Guyanese national team on Monday, November 13. Gary Smith describes the game in a *Sports Illustrated* profile of Jimmy that was published years later:

> *[The] first game against Guyana was a calamity. Out of sync and out of shape to play a full-court game, Jonestown's 12-man team was devoured by 30 points. Jim, a long-armed 6'4" center whose specialty was rebounding and shot-blocking, seemed as lost as his teammates against taller foes who'd been training and competing for years.[19]*

After this humiliating rout, the boys, determined to do better, practiced as much as they could, especially glad to have access to a real court.[20] Jones, however, had other plans for the boys. Anxious about the approaching Ryan visit, he ordered the team to return to Jonestown.

Stephan says, in an essay he wrote that appears on the Jonestown Institute website entitled "Death's Night":

Almost since we'd arrived in Georgetown, we'd been bucking the Temple system—if there truly was such a thing—and ignoring or blatantly countermanding orders. We were still in town only because I had represented the team in flatly refusing Dad's direct order to return to Jonestown to avoid any incident with Congressman Ryan and the Concerned Relatives. . . . At the time, I didn't think much about the reasoning behind Dad's imploring voice, dissembled by the ham radio in Jonestown . . . and reconstructed by the radio in the Temple house in Georgetown. I figured that any plans he had for us back in Jonestown had to be worse than what we were doing. Even when Mom came on and half-heartedly asked us to listen to Dad and return to our jungle home, I responded by saying, "You don't have to talk for him." (I learned years later from Mike Carter, the radio operator on that end—who escaped Jonestown on a mission for my father—that I was right on the money with that one. My comment left Dad in a rage similar in appearance to a grand mal seizure. I relished that knowledge for years.) [21]

Jones's about-face regarding the tournament only added to the boys' new view of him as an erratic, unworthy "leader." Having witnessed the eye-opening experience of Jones's treatment of Shanda, many on the team now found Jones repulsive, ridiculous. They were relieved to have this break from the oppression of life in Jonestown.

But there were other reasons that Stephan held firm to their plan: The games were important to the boys, and they were having a good time. With money Stephan had taken from his father's cottage—just as he'd done in San Francisco—the team ate well and were enjoying some long-earned R & R. Plus, it was always possible they'd return victorious to those who had given them such a heartfelt farewell. That victory could offer Jonestowners a much-needed sense of hope, a sense that brighter days were just around the corner.[22]

November 14

The next day saw the arrival to Georgetown of the Ryan party. The journalists were determined to learn more about the experience of living in Jonestown; the relatives hoped to bring their family members home. Making up the largest contingent of the group were thirteen Concerned Relatives, among them Sam Houston's wife, Nadyne, mother of the late Bob Houston, and Sam and Nadyne's daughter Carol Houston Boyd. They wanted to bring back Bob's daughters (the couple's granddaughters), Judy, 14, and Patty Houston, 15, who had been in Jonestown for a year.

Also traveling with the group were Jim Cobb, Johnny's brother, along with Wayne Pietila and Mickey Touchette, all from the "Gang of Eight." All three hoped they could convince some of their Jonestown relatives to leave.

For Howard and Beverly Oliver, whom Jones labeled "the two *sinister* Olivers" at a rally several days prior, this would be yet another trip to try to retrieve their boys, Bruce and Billy. Howard Oliver had suffered a stroke and, according to Reiterman in the *San Francisco Examiner-Chronicle* Sunday issue, had together with his wife taken out loans from relatives and burned through over $11,000 in travel costs and efforts to get their sons back. Even with all these efforts, though, they had only "met resistance from the temple, its attorneys and the Guyanese government." As Oliver told Reiterman, "They were good boys and they came from a close home." The boys' parents had to try one more time.

Accompanying them were Clare Bouquet, worried about her son Brian, and Sherwin Harris, father of Liane, who'd been living with her mother, Sharon Amos, in the Lamaha Gardens house. Also in the group were Steve Katsaris, who had been to Guyana twice before, though, like the Olivers, he'd not succeeded in seeing his daughter, Maria. Steve's son, Anthony, and Tim and Grace Stoen, whose son, Jon Jon, Jones claimed as his own, were also part of the group of relatives.[23]

Personnel from no fewer than five media outlets accompanied the Ryan delegation: Charles Krause was from the *Washington Post*; Gordon Lindsay from the *National Enquirer;* Don Harris, Steve Sung, and Bob Brown of NBC; and from San Francisco's two major newspapers, Ron Javers of the *Chronicle* and Reiterman along with cameraman Greg Robinson of the *Examiner*. The Ryan party also included Reverend Edward Malmin and his daughter Bonnie Thielman, who had known the Joneses from their days in Brazil. Thielman had stayed in close touch with Marceline and thought she'd have a good chance of entering Jonestown.

Congressman Leo Ryan and his aides Jim Schollaert and Jackie Speier, who made up the formal congressional delegation, brought the total number

Lamaha Gardens

traveling in the party to twenty-seven. The group landed in Georgetown's Timehri Airport on Tuesday, November 14.[24]

November 15

On his first full day in Guyana, November 15, Congressman Ryan went to the Lamaha Gardens house, where he was told that Jones was "very ill." It seemed the group would not be able to continue on to Jonestown. Both Ryan and the relatives continued to seek permission to make their visit in spite of being discouraged at the Temple house and the embassy.[25]

Also happening on that day was the second tournament basketball game.

Suddenly, from all their years together, they remembered the music. Point guard Johnny Cobb began running the pick-and-roll and hitting the open man. Rail-thin Stephan's sweet outside shot bloomed again, Tim found his old ferocity and his running one-hander, and Jim did the dirty work on the boards and in the lane. The Guyanese coach, his players trailing in the first half, called a timeout to rant at them.

Late in the game Guyana's conditioning and depth wore down the Americans, and it won by [20 points]. But the Jones boys walked off the court knowing it was only a matter of time, lung and legwork: they were going to take that team down.[26]

Stephan's memory of the game is less glowing. The court had "no scoreboard, no clock you could see, no audience," he writes in an email many years later. "We played them tough enough to frustrate them at times, and have their coach riled up at timeouts . . . but . . . well . . . they actually had plays and training . . . you know, like *real* teams."[27]

All the same, the Jonestown team had bested their previous score by 10 points.

November 16

Meanwhile, the Concerned Relatives, who had also gone to Lamaha Gardens in an effort to talk to Temple members, were turned away and told, "None of you are welcome. Go see the American ambassador." Their meeting with the ambassador on the sixteenth was a "shouting, angry and tearful" one, according to reporter Ron Javers, and just "the same old embassy runaround," as Oliver said to Javers. At the same time, Ryan was told that he could come to Jonestown the next day—just him, no press or relatives. The relatives toggled between frustration and despair. "If Jonestown is so free,"

Jim Cobb protested to Javers, "why won't he [Jones] let us and the press talk to these people?"[28]

That evening, Congressman Ryan, no doubt hoping to bolster spirits, arranged for a banquet dinner for the entire group. Some of the relatives reported that earlier they had talked with Stephan and other members of the basketball team—who were defying another one of Jones's orders to "stay as far away as possible" from Ryan and the relatives—outside, not far from the hotel. The talk was friendly; indeed, hugs were even exchanged.[29]

November 17

Finally, the word came that the group could enter Jonestown. But this good news had a catch: The small plane that would transport the visitors from Georgetown to Port Kaituma could not accommodate everyone. The relatives decided it was more important that the newsmen go, so they could report to the world about the situation in Jonestown. Nine family members had to stay behind, as well as the Rev. Malmin and Bonnie Thielman—all very disappointed. The four who were chosen to go were Carol Boyd, Sam Houston's daughter; Jim Cobb, Johnny's brother; Beverly Oliver, Billy's mother; and Anthony, Steve Katsaris's son and Maria's brother. Ron Javers reported that the party also included "two of America's most colorful lawyers—Charles Garry of San Francisco and Mark Lane of Kennedy assassination theory fame—who had flown to Guyana to help protect the interests of Jones and his followers." At last, sometime after two in the afternoon, the twin-engine Otter took off from Timehri airport near Georgetown for the hour's flight "over dense, almost uninhabited rain forest."[30]

The Delegation Heads to Jonestown

Port Kaituma: November 17, Late Afternoon

Charles Krause, in *Guyana Massacre: The Eyewitness Account*, published shortly after he returned from Guyana in 1978, tells of the delegation's journey to Jonestown. When the little plane and its twenty passengers landed at Port Kaituma, the group was told by Temple members who had come to meet them that that they would drive only Ryan, his aide Jackie Speier, the two Temple lawyers, and U.S. Consul Dwyer to Jonestown, but that the rest of the group must stay with the plane, "under guard." As the newsmen and relatives waited, the guard told them about "badly injured Americans" from Jonestown who were taken away by plane on a fairly regular basis. Officially, their injuries were said to stem from "working with machetes or machinery," but the guard seemed dubious, and he went on to warn Krause, "When you go there, keep your eyes open."

Finally, more than two hours later, the Jonestown dump truck arrived to take the rest of the group to the settlement. After a bumpy ride up the muddy road, Krause writes, the truck emerged from the pitch-dark jungle and approached the settlement. They could see "electric lights blazing," and, as they drew closer, a flurry of activity that was also "peaceful" and "orderly": black people, and some white, "baking bread in the bakery . . . washing clothes in the laundry." Krause writes that "children were chasing each other in the little park," while many people stood in line for dinner. He noted that "nobody seemed to be starving. Indeed, everyone seemed quite healthy."[31]

Jonestown: Early Evening

Entering the pavilion with the other newsmen, Krause saw a large table in the center set up for the visitors. Lane and Garry were seated there, speaking with "a man in his forties, who wore a red sports shirt and [the usual dark] glasses and had jet black hair." It was Jim Jones.

"Everything seemed to be going well," Krause reports, family members talking to each other, the reporters speaking with residents, the photographers taking pictures, and Ryan interviewing the people he had asked to speak with. Krause writes that "the buildings were impressive," and "the people seemed healthy, rational and friendly." Coffee was served, then a dinner of "pork sandwiches, greens, and potato-like roots."

As the group ate, more Jonestowners (who had apparently already eaten) began filing in to the pavilion, and soon the entertainment began, with singers "good enough to be professional" performing a rendition of Guyana's national anthem and "America the Beautiful." "Ryan was very impressed," Krause writes, and took the stage to proclaim, "I can tell you right now that by the few conversations I've had with some of the folks here already this evening that . . . there are some people here who believe this is the best thing that happened in their whole lives." The audience went wild, according to Krause, applauding "for nearly twenty minutes."[32]

Based on the tape recording of the gathering found on the Jonestown Institute website, the evening was civil, joyous even, and the crowd seemingly adoring of Ryan. When he declared his regret that the crowd couldn't vote for him, a man rose to his feet and said they could, "by proxy." Ryan laughed.

"By proxy. Okay. We'll do that if we can," then thanked the crowd and told them what a pleasure it was to be in Jonestown, which triggered another eruption of applause.[33]

As the performance continued, Krause describes, Jones "rambled as he talked" with the visitors, his temperament shifting before their eyes as he jumped from one topic to another. He "might have cancer," he claimed, and told them "he had lost 31 pounds in recent months [and] . . . his temperature had just reached 103 degrees" hours earlier. "In many ways I feel like I'm dying," he told the newsmen. "Who the hell knows what stress can do to you." When questioned about Jon Jon Stoen, Jones said the child was his but denied that anything had happened with Grace Stoen. "I never had an affair with anyone but my wife," he maintained. Producing his own "evidence" for the cameras that the boy was his, Jones called Jon Jon over and asked the six-year-old to show his teeth and turn his head to the side for the reporters. "The bewildered, dark-haired child" complied as Jones exclaimed, "See, he looks exactly like me." He went on to say he couldn't give up the boy. "Oh, God, it's so painful, it's so painful. I feel so guilty about it."

※

Krause, having heard that Jones had forbidden couples to have sex, asked him if residents could "have normal sexual lives." Sarah Tropp, one of Jones's close aides, chimed in, "Bullshit," while Jones claimed that "thirty babies had been born . . . since the summer of 1977." Stephan believes his father was exaggerating the number, that it was perhaps more than a dozen, but it was not as many as thirty babies born over the entire existence of Jonestown.

When Krause asked whether Jones was a socialist, Jones said, "Call me a socialist. I've been called worse," then began another "tirade." He claimed to hate "violence," "power," and "money," saying, "What kind of power do I have walking down the path talking to my little old seniors. . . . The only thing I wish now is that I was never born."[34]

Ron Javers, for his part, marveled at the way Jones attempted to paint the picture of a settlement that was "blissful, productive and above all, peaceful," even while contradicting his own responses. "If one answer didn't seem to convince his hearers," Javers writes, "Jones was ready to offer another." At first Jones claimed that "there wasn't a weapon in the place," then, following another man's comment that there were bows and arrows for hunting, Jones admitted that there were some weapons, "but only rifles and hunting guns." When asked about beatings, Jones said there had been none for some time and claimed that he himself had received beatings. Javers writes that "it appeared [the beatings] were psychological. He was asking us to understand how much he suffered when somebody else was enduring physical pain." When asked about The Box, Jones said it was all "lies . . . nothing but lies."[35]

At one point that evening Stephan radioed in from Georgetown. He later writes of the exchange:

> *I nearly swooned in release when we heard that Ryan was pleased with what he had seen in Jonestown. . . . We elatedly responded with our own good news: We had played against the Guyanese National Team with our aggressive, play-ground style of basketball and had lost by only ten points. We'd pawed, grabbed, bumped, and confused them with our own confusion, while going at the basket with a zeal that they seemed to both enjoy and disdain. . . . We walked away from our . . . game with the Guyanese Nationals feeling a little more like men.*
>
> *The news was passed on to Dad. In his mind we became ten-point winners, which he announced dramatically over the loudspeaker. You could hear it over the radio as Dad pumped it up and poured it on, followed by the lusty cheers of a crowd in desperate need of their own release. They needed it to be true and Dad knew it. And the instant we heard their rejoicing, we needed it to be true.*[36]

Jonestowners may have been—understandably—pulled into a desperate kind of magical thinking, seeing this victory as a good omen. Perhaps many, particularly the teenagers, were coming to hope, even believe, the situation would soon be better: Jones was diminishing and deteriorating with each passing day, and a Jonestown with Marceline and Stephan in charge would be a completely different place. Some might have felt that the visit marked a new era for the community, that with someone like Ryan paying attention it could only change their lives for the better.

To the newsmen, it was an ambiguous picture so far: so many smiling faces, but so much that seemed suspect or, worse, ominous. As the evening in Jonestown had come to a close, Javers heard Marceline tell Jones that she could find beds for the relatives and the newsmen, but Jones snapped that they were all to leave. At the last minute, Krause was told he could stay—apparently a chat he had just had with Sarah Tropp and her brother Richard had earned their trust—but he decided to avoid possible conflict with the other newsmen and leave the settlement in the dump truck with them. And so those who had come to report what they had observed and the relatives who had come to see their loved ones clambered back into the dump truck for the long and bumpy ride back to Port Kaituma for the night.[37]

It wasn't until the next morning that one important development was made known to Reiterman and Javers: Monica and Vern had slipped a note to reporter Don Harris the previous evening: "Vernon Gosney, Monica Bagby. Help us get out of Jonestown." They had proceeded with their plan to take a second chance to try to make it out. They were the first.[38]

Port Kaituma: Late Night

The guard told them Jonestown had "at least one automatic rifle," and confirmed that he had seen one Jonestowner who had been badly beaten and managed to flee.[39]

The three reporters returned to the disco at 3:00 AM and slept on the floor with the rest of the news crew. Other arrangements had been made for the relatives. As for three of the newsmen—Don Harris, Bob Brown, and Greg Robinson—"It was to be their last night on earth," Krause writes.[40]

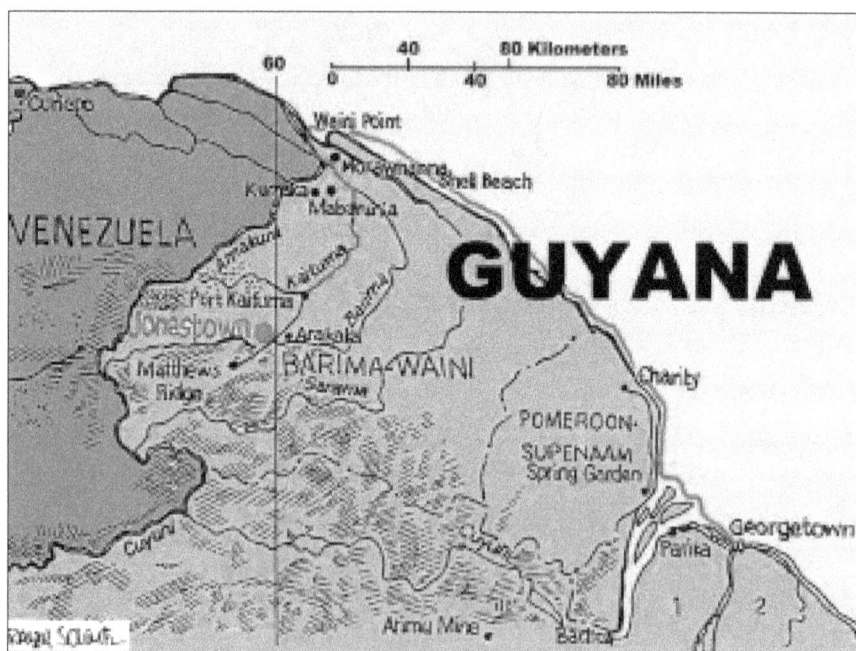

Guyana from Georgetown to Jonestown map (by Ralph Solonitz)

Chapter 15

The Last Day

November 18, 1978

Port Kaituma

Morning

The Peoples Temple truck, which was supposed to arrive early the next morning to transport the press and relatives back to Jonestown, finally rumbled into Port Kaituma at ten o'clock. On the journey to the settlement, *Washington Post* reporter Charles Krause describes in *Guyana Massacre* the dump truck first getting stuck in the mud, then nearly rolling over on the rutted road.

In Jonestown, the visitors were greeted by Marceline, the Temple lawyers, and some others, and were told a breakfast of pancakes and coffee was waiting for them. But the newsmen, tired of delays, wanted to jump right in to their work and opted for only coffee.[1]

They headed to the pavilion, where, under the sheltering rooftop, the visitors encountered a group of children engrossed in watching *Willie Wonka and the Chocolate Factory*.[2] In the movie, Willie Wonka tells the children in the candy world that paradise is all around them, that imagination can make anyone free. In another area of the pavilion Ryan was continuing the interviews he had begun the previous evening. Jones had not yet made his appearance and, the reporters were told, might not come at all that day, as he was ill. Don Harris insisted they be allowed to interview Jones at least briefly, and appealed to Lane to intercede.[3]

Jonestown

Late Morning

The first stop on the tour was the nursery, Marceline Jones's "special project," according to Krause, that gave her great pleasure to show off. It was "spotless," Krause writes, with "an incubator, a respirator, a bright playroom, a nurse's office, cribs, and other modern equipment."[4] It was clear that children were cared about and well cared for here. Although Mrs. Jones was in charge, most likely the Opportunity students who worked there—Marilee Bogue, Cindy Cordell, perhaps also nurse's aides Willie Thomas and Ollie Smith—had also contributed to the pleasant atmosphere.

Next, the group visited "a classroom building for children with learning disabilities," where a teacher spoke to them about the care these children received—"individual attention," she said, that she hadn't been able to give as a special education teacher back in California.[5] Since there is no mention of such a building or special education class in Edith Roller's journal, and Roller instead describes the difficulties of conducting class in the school tent, this structure was likely part of the planned school that had never come to be.

It was at this point that the tour began to break down. The reporters were tiring of what seemed to be a carefully scripted introduction to Jonestown, and they all had different priorities in terms of which parts of the settlement they wanted to investigate. Along the tour, Reiterman noticed what seemed to be phony, set-up scenes—kids clumsily and halfheartedly playing catch, people walking down paths while appearing to have no particular destination—and apprehension thickening in the air as rumors circulated that some residents were trying to leave. Indeed, Reiterman reports, someone approached Marceline with a quiet message that obviously caused her great worry. One by one, the newsmen wandered away from Marceline's carefully planned tour to learn more about living conditions and who might be asking to leave.[6]

Krause, spotting a building called Jane Pittman Gardens that was completely shuttered, went to investigate. The sun was high, and it was hot. He could hear people inside, but no one answered when he knocked. He tried to pry open one of the shutters back so he could peer inside, but, he says, "someone inside was holding on to it." A woman came by to inquire why he was there, and told him that those in the building were probably resting but that she'd go around to the back to ask whether he could be allowed in. "It was no surprise to me when she came back and said the people inside didn't want visitors," Krause writes. He returned to the pavilion and alerted the other reporters about the building, telling them his theory that it was some kind of "warehouse for people," perhaps victims of beatings or worse.

Upon seeing Jane Pittman Gardens closed and shuttered, the newsmen, convinced, pushed to be allowed in. Garry and Lane arrived on the scene and promptly gave them permission to enter, later explaining that the reason for the reluctance to admit reporters into the building was that the Temple was "embarrassed" about overcrowding.

It was a dormitory, Krause reports, packed with "at least 100 bunk beds in long rows," with most of the residents older black women. Though the place seemed quite clean, there was barely room to walk between the bunks.

Javers and Reiterman spoke with several of the women, asking them how they felt about their living arrangements. They all claimed that they were perfectly content. "I'm happy as can be," one woman insisted to Reiterman, even after he managed to ask her the question away from prying Temple ears.[7]

The journalists headed back to the pavilion. Near the school tent, just outside the pavilion, Reiterman saw Ryan posing for pictures with Carol Houston Boyd and her nieces, Judy and Patty, along with their mother, Phyllis Houston. When the reporter introduced himself to them, Judy and Patty "smiled courteously," but were guarded when they answered his questions in a manner that sounded prepackaged and rehearsed.[8] Many of the letters written by Opportunity students and other Jonestowners that can be found in files at the California Historical Society had had the same "ring" to them.

Not far away, Johnny Cobb's family extolled the "wonders" of Jonestown to Don Harris, with Johnny Cobb's mother repeating what Judy had said about having no bad feelings about America. Also nearby, Bruce and Billy Oliver, sitting with their mother, in turn recited the party line on camera for NBC. Beverly Oliver smiled a "confident, knowing smile," likely imagining they'd soon be home in San Francisco.[9]

Afternoon Storm Clouds

Threatening clouds roiled overhead as NBC set up cameras for the official interview with Jones. It was here, at the end of the visit, that the reporters would have their chance to ask the tough questions. Krause joined the group just as Don Harris asked Jones about the automatic weapon that the guard in Port Kaituma had alerted the reporters about. "Jones went into a rage: 'A bold-faced lie,' he declared."[10]

According to Marshall Kilduff and Ron Javers, in their book, *The Suicide Cult: The Inside Story of the Peoples Temple Sect and Massacre in Guyana*, the journalists had been told of so many beatings that they weren't able to accept Jones's assurances there were none. Questioning Jones again about the beatings, referring to the clear evidence in photographs that Linda Mertle had been badly whipped back in California with "the board of education," Jones answered, "We don't use physical punishment anymore. . . . We stopped it a few months ago—maybe a year." He claimed that it was Deanna Mertle (now Jeannie Mills), Linda's stepmother, who had demanded that her daughter be punished. "The girl was a kleptomaniac," Jones claimed. Jones went on to declare, "I live for the people I'm trying to save. . . . But people lie and play games."[11]

Jones said that it was unusual weather that was responsible for most of Jonestown's food being imported from the States despite the fact that around 10,000 acres had been freed of jungle overgrowth for planting. Though the visitors had been served meat, the reporters had discovered that the people of Jonestown often had only rice and gravy, for breakfast, lunch, and dinner.

Jones returned again to his many physical afflictions and the "conspiracy" against him that he claimed existed. Javers asked who was responsible, and Jones responded with his own question. "Who conspired to kill Martin Luther King, John F. Kennedy, and Malcolm X?"[12]

"Suddenly," Krause writes, "the word came [to the newsmen] that several families had decided to leave with Ryan. . . . Tension, for the first time, was so apparent that it could be felt."

Families were split, with some members wanting to leave while others preferred to stay. Krause writes that Patricia Parks was one who was pressured to leave with her family; leaving Jonestown was not her choice. Al Simon, Jim Bogue's partner in the gold prospecting ruse and whom Stephan had trusted to tell him the truth during the Six-Day Siege, was ready to defect with his three children. Simon's wife, though, was adamant that the children stay with her and, shrieking, came running after her husband, who had the children with him. Unwilling to leave without his children, Simon would stay behind.[13]

As the clouds grew darker, the people who had declared their intention to defect were beginning to gather in a corner of the pavilion. Vern Gosney writes that Ryan had taken Vern and Monica aside the previous night (presumably, Harris had shown Ryan the note before the newsmen left for Port Kaituma) to tell them that they'd been the first to ask to leave and thus "would have the first seats on the plane." Now, the congressman spoke with them again.[14]

According to Javers, it was at this point that it seemed to sink in for Jones that so many were choosing to go. "Excuse me," the preacher said to the reporters. "I want to hug them all before they leave." A strong wind swirled through the pavilion and rain poured down, clattering on the corrugated tin roof.[15]

Jones set off to speak to those who had decided to defect. "Are you lovers?" he asked Vern and Monica. They replied that they were not, and when Monica started to tell Jones about the problems she saw in Jonestown, Vern reports that he "stomped on her foot to get her to shut up." He knew that anything they told Jones "would be used against us," Vern writes.

"Don't talk to reporters! They are all liars!" Jones said to them. Then, turning to Vern, who Jones knew had a young son whom he'd hoped to get out later, Jones "spoke the most diabolical statement of all: 'You can come back and visit your son any time you want.'"[16]

Having been given leave, the defectors went to their cottages and dorms down the now-slippery wooden walkways to retrieve their belongings. Harold Cordell, who was among those leaving, was embraced by his old friend Jack Beam. Cordell, who had long since separated from Candy and Cindy's mother, would leave with his Jonestown partner, Edith Bogue, Jim Bogue's estranged wife. The rest of the Cordells, fourteen in all, would remain. Jim Bogue, with Tommy, Juanita, and Teena, were also among the departing group. Marilee remained.[17]

Dwyer, from the embassy, along with Ryan, Jackie Speier, and Mark Lane, saw that the Simon family's dispute over custody of the children needed resolution, and the men went back to help settle the problem. The rest of those planning to leave were headed to the yellow dump truck.[18]

Jonestown

2:45 pm

A few minutes later, those on the truck saw some sort of struggle back in the pavilion. Krause, Harris, Reiterman, and Javers hurried over to see what was happening, but guards intercepted and blocked them from proceeding, though Harris was allowed to go. He returned to tell them someone (later found to be Mark Sly's father Don) had tried to attack Ryan with a knife. "Ryan soon appeared, walking with Dwyer toward the truck. Ryan's shirt and trousers were badly stained with blood, but he was unhurt." It turned out that when Ryan approached the Simons, who were speaking with Jones,

Sly came from behind with a knife and moved to slit the congressman's throat. When Lane wrestled the knife away, Sly was cut in the process. The blood on Ryan's shirt was Sly's. Ryan still wanted to remain to help solve the custody dispute, but the lawyers convinced him he must leave, indicating that Garry and Dwyer would take care of it. Ryan agreed and headed for the truck.

As it began to roll forward, Larry Layton came to join those heading for the airstrip. The other defectors were worried: They didn't buy the fact that he was actually defecting from Jonestown; they said they believed the young man was going to "cause trouble." But he was allowed onto the truck, and shortly after, Ryan was helped into the cab.[19]

When the truck stalled several times on its way out of the settlement, Vern Gosney writes that he "was sure it was intentional."[20]

Many of those who stayed in Jonestown, no doubt, were paralyzed—with fear, like Vern and Monica's friend Keith, or indecision. Had Candy and Cindy Cordell wanted to go? Had they seen their father off? Perhaps they had been required to keep their distance, tending to the children or to the ill in the infirmary. Why hadn't Mark joined the defectors? He'd hated Jonestown as much as Monica had. Mondo, Teddy, Ricky, Wesley, and Billy were probably on guard duty. Surely Edith Roller had been there to witness this significant departure. If her journal hadn't disappeared, would she have recorded this scene before she died?

Reiterman reports that Wesley Breidenbach was in the truck as a "Temple escort," stationed near Layton at the back of the truck bed. Noting a bulge at Wesley's back under his rain slicker, the journalist engaged him in conversation, all the time keeping an eye on Layton. Wesley seemed to convey unease, and Reiterman feared neither of the men were there for the reasons they claimed to be.

At first Wesley seemed sad when he repeated the familiar mantra that all those leaving Jonestown could have gone whenever they wanted. But when the journalist began to praise the gorgeous open country around them, Wesley responded with enthusiasm, relaxing a little as he described the sunsets and abundant tropical plants and animals. Upon hearing this, Reiterman wondered briefly if he was being overly suspicious of the "likable" young man—until he noticed Wesley was not impervious to Reiterman's wary eye on Layton—who had not said a word, and whose hand appeared to be inching slowly toward the back of his slicker.[21]

Port Kaituma Airstrip

Afternoon: 4:30 pm

Krause writes that the trip out of Jonestown was even more difficult than the one coming in—the road was muddier and the load heavier with sixteen more passengers than before. In an apparent gesture of good will—or perhaps as a cover-up for his intentions—Jones had given each of the defectors their passports and five thousand Guyanese dollars to buy tickets back to the States. At that point, Krause still wasn't sure that Jonestown was a prison. En route to Port Kaituma, Edith Parks had even said she thought she'd likely come back to Jonestown after a visit with her relatives back in California.[22]

Arriving at the airstrip, they saw the two small aircraft, together capable of carrying twenty-four passengers. There were more than twenty-four people who were trying to fly out, but the defectors took precedence. They made their way toward the two planes, with Speier working out who would go on the smaller plane, which seated only five, and who on the larger craft, while keeping family members together. When she excluded Layton from the small plane, which would be the first to take off, he demanded that he be seated there, insisting that Ryan had told him he could be on the first plane. Ryan told Speier to let him on. The reporters helped Ryan in an effort to search the passengers for weapons, finding none—not even on Layton, who then boarded the small plane, with Vern next to him and Monica in the front near the pilot. The aircraft was ready to go.[23]

It was at this point, Javers writes, that he saw the same dump truck that had brought them, "with a red tractor and trailer partially shielded behind it," approaching the planes. A handful of men dropped from the truck.

"And then the shooting started," Javers reports. He was hit in the shoulder and fell, creeping close to the ground to shelter behind one of the plane's wheels. Then Harris was hit, "at close range." Bob Brown, the cameraman, in the line of fire, courageously kept filming—until he was shot point blank in the face.

After taking cover in the swamp and crawling back to the high grass beside the airstrip, Javers peeked out at the runway to see what was happening and noticed the smaller plane was gone—somehow it had managed to take off, saving at least a few from the group (it turned out that Monica, who was alive but had been shot twice in the back, was among those on board; Vern, who had also been seriously injured, was not). Javers spotted Reiterman on the runway and ran out to help. Reiterman's left arm had been hit, and Javers could see that Ryan had been killed. Don Harris, Bob Brown, Patricia Parks, and Greg Robinson were all down, and still.

Those who could, aided the others with nothing but a small first-aid kit, napkins, and their own clothing for bandages. The Guyanese soldiers, stationed at the airstrip, who said they had not fired for fear of sending the death toll even higher, agreed to allow the critically injured use their army tent. In spite of massive wounds in her thigh, arm and chest, Speier managed to somehow record a tape, a message for her parents. Though she insisted to Javers, who says she'd been "tremendously brave," that she believed that she'd make it, she asked him to take the tape to her parents in the event she didn't.

Those who could walk were invited to take shelter in the rum shop.[24]

Port Kaituma

After the Ambush

The sun had just begun its descent into the jungle when the first shots had rung out. After a long, terrifying night, Guyanese soldiers would finally arrive from Georgetown at 8:30 AM to assist.

Javers reported that "somehow Jackie Speier still was smiling whenever anyone looked at her." Two rescue planes landed about two hours later. It took the others half an hour to convince the relatives to board. They were worried about those who had taken cover in the bush, like Tommy Bogue, and had still not appeared. It turned out Tommy had led four other young people through the jungle to safety. The survivors, besides being concerned about their loved ones, were also frightened to fly to Georgetown, sure a trap was waiting for them there as well.[25]

In the end, Congressman Ryan, Patty Parks, Bob Brown, Don Harris, and Greg Robinson had all been shot dead. Ten others were seriously injured, including Monica and Vern, Anthony Katsaris, Jackie Speier, Tim Reiterman, and Steve Sung. Inside the Cessna, Larry Layton had shot at his fellow passengers, wounding Monica and Vern badly, before he was disarmed and later taken into Guyanese custody.[26]

Georgetown

Same Day

That morning of the eighteenth in Georgetown, the basketball team, still riding the wave of both their tournament and the good news from the night before about Ryan's visit, continued to enjoy their respite from Jonestown.

Given this latest development—that things had gone well with Ryan's visit—Stephan imagined the time was ripe for facilitating a change at the helm. As he later wrote in his essay, "Death's Night":

> *We were getting exhausted. Dad had pushed us all to the edge one too many times. It was time to stop playing the waiting game—waiting for the right reason, the right moment to rise against him; waiting for his key supporters to see the light; waiting for him to get too sick, too strung out to lead; waiting for him to die. We had to do something about Dad and his leadership circle.*
>
> *Soon we would retrace our three-day journey across hellish ocean, heavenly river, and dusty, tortured road. I told myself that when my new allies and I got back to Jonestown, my father's days were numbered.*[27]

Lamaha Gardens

Afternoon

When the boys returned to Lamaha Gardens that afternoon, they discovered that Sherwin Harris was there to see Liane, his daughter with Sharon Amos. With a mind to leaving them to visit in peace, Stephan suggested the boys go to a movie.[28]

Jimmy had stayed behind at the house and was there when news began to come in around 4:30 PM about the growing number of defectors and the need for an additional plane. Jones said he'd ordered his "avenging angels" to go after Ryan and his delegation, and instructed Jimmy to send for the other boys at once.[29]

Lamaha Gardens

Early Evening

A Temple messenger relayed the news in the dark theater, passed in whispers across the group of boys until it reached Stephan: "We've been ordered to get revenge." Stephan knew that "something horrible, perhaps irreversible" had happened. He worried about the Concerned Relatives who were still in Georgetown at the Pegasus Hotel. His thoughts naturally turned also to his mother, his girlfriend, his friends.

During the ride back to the house his mind churned with possibilities. "I sure wasn't going to help my father kill anyone; I was going to stop him." But he would have to be careful not to enflame his father or those dedicated to him. "Dad was on the precipice," and Stephan was "terrified of doing anything to push him over the edge." At nineteen, he writes, he had felt at the time that he "didn't know shit," even as he believed the other boys trusted him, looked to him to be a leader.

When Stephan and Tim entered the radio room back at Lamaha Gardens, they found Amos bent over the receiver, translating from the code to detail the weapons those in Georgetown were being instructed to use. Jimmy, according to Wright's *New Yorker* article, had joined them in the radio room and was equally stunned. "Is this real? Is this real?" Stalling for time and pretending to be calm, Stephan said they really couldn't do anything until they had "a plan." He announced that he would go with Tim and Johnny to the Pegasus Hotel where the relatives were. Before leaving, Stephan quietly instructed Lee Ingram, the basketball team's coach, to find a way to call the Temple in San Francisco and tell them to take no action until Stephan contacted them. As the two spoke in low tones, Stephan looked past Ingram to Amos at the radio, then back to his coach. "In few words," Stephan writes, "we agreed that [Ingram] could not let Sharon out of his sight."[30]

It felt to the boys as if it had taken forever to get to the hotel. Stephan spoke with Tim Stoen, "who seemed shocked" when Stephan told him his father might call a final White Night. Stoen, like Stephan, and many others, had heard Jones's "cries of wolf" too many times.

"Beneath all my denial and delusion, at my soul," Stephan said, "I knew that Jim Jones's worst was upon us." The boys went on to the embassy, where they were told after they had identified themselves through a locked door that Ryan "and others" had been shot at Port Kaituma. Stephan blurted out "I know," then began to try to explain what he meant, that he was beginning to realize what might happen, that the boys were not at the embassy to kill but to seek help, when Tim quickly silenced him and pulled his brother away and steered the group back to Lamaha Gardens.

As they approached the house, Stephan heard a plane overhead, silently "pleading to who-knows-what to let everything be okay" and spoke to the others his hope that Ryan was aboard, alive.

Just outside Lamaha Gardens, a Temple woman ran out to tell the boys, "Sharon killed herself and her children." The police had gone to the Temple house directly on hearing the report of the shootings. Stephan knew Sharon had believed what Jones had said would happen to her children under "fascism," and had followed the terrible orders.

Stephan, in a state of numbed shock, went upstairs to the master bathroom and started to push open the door. As he struggled to take in the scene, he writes, "a tiny flash of white" glinted at the periphery of his view: It was an open eye—Martin, Amos's young son, his gaze directed at the ceiling. "That face," Stephan writes. "Little Martin staring at the ceiling, lips parted, his expression unbelieving, shocked. And below that dumbfounded face, the rift from which his life had poured. . . . I had to push his tiny body clear with the door; the thought of touching him was unbearable."

Then Stephan saw Martin's sister Christa lying nearby with the same startled expression, and, finally, he saw his childhood friend Liane. He called her name as she tried to lift her head then fell back into the blood. Her only response, Stephan writes, was "a slow, unnatural sigh as she died."[31]

Timehri Airport and Georgetown

Later that Day

All afternoon at the Timehri Airport in Georgetown, Howard Oliver had waited patiently with a Ryan staffer to greet his wife and, he hoped, Billy and Bruce, on their successful return with the Ryan delegation from Jonestown. Once word of the shootings reached the embassy and congressional staffers, Oliver was sent back to the hotel, though because of his fragile health no one told him what by then they all knew had happened. After waiting all night with no news, Oliver suffered a stroke the next morning, and died in Guyana.[32]

Empty houses in Jonestown

Chapter 16

The Last White Night

Saturday, November 18, 1978

Jonestown

Early Evening

n Jonestown, Marceline had sent everyone back to the dorms and cottages to rest in the late afternoon. The sun set at about 5:30 PM, although it would not be fully dark for another hour. A little before six, an urgent call crackled over the public address system: Everyone was to report to the pavilion.[1]

As people collected from all parts of the compound in the now deepening twilight, the young were no doubt helping the seniors down the rain-slippery paths. Sometime after six, Jones took the microphone, his hand at the ready with the tape recorder. The last White Night was about to begin.

Voices from the Last White Night

The infamous "death tape" chronicles the last hour of Jonestown as its leader addresses the community, goading them to come up and receive the poison that would end their lives. A transcription of the "death tape" can be found on the Jonestown Institute website, which also includes MP3 files of the recording of the death tape as well as three hundred other tapes that had been made in Jonestown.

Jones opens his last address to his followers with: "How very much I have loved you. How very much I've tried my best to give you the good life." The assembly, as they are accustomed to doing, respond with affirmations: this time a somewhat weary-sounding chorus of "right," and "yes," with various noises in the background: children's voices, general talking, a baby quietly fussing. The group of vocal adults sounds small. Perhaps many are sitting in silence.

Jones's voice—always the most prominent on the rally tapes—sounds worn, and though it sometimes rises with indignation, it does so weakly, his lisp and slur clearly evident.

Jones's voice, and the voices of others, ebb sometimes into silence, some-times surge into anger—at the "enemies" Jones offers up as scapegoats. Always the maestro, always conducting, Jones will pause the recording thir-ty-one times that evening: an orchestration of what history will and will not hear.

JONES: But in spite of all that I have tried, a handful of our people, with their lies, have made our life impossible. There's no way to detach ourself from what's happened today. Not only are we in a compound situation, not only are there those who have left and committed the betrayal of the century, some have stolen children from others, and they are in pursuit right now to kill them, because they stole their children. And we—we are sitting here wait-ing on a powder keg. I don't think it is what we want to do with our babies. . . . It was said by the greatest of prophets from time immemorial: "No man may take my life from me; I lay my life down."

A SMALL, RAGGED RESPONSE: Right!

JONES: So to—to sit here and wait for the catastrophe that's going to happen on that airplane—it's going to be a catastrophe, it almost happened here . . . the congressman was nearly killed here. But you . . . can't take off with people's children without expecting a violent reaction. . . . The world—the kingdom suffereth violence and the violent shall take it by force. If we can't live in peace, then let's die in peace.

CLAPPING, A FEW MORE VOICES PEPPER JONES'S WORDS: Right!

JONES: [WEARY] We've been so betrayed. We have been so terribly betrayed. But we've tried and as Jack Beam often said: . . . if this only works one day, it was worthwhile.

CLAPPING, AND A FEW CALLS: Right!

[TAPE EDIT]

JONES: Thank you. [TAPE EDIT] Now what's going to happen here in a matter of a few minutes is that one of those people on that plane is gonna—gonna shoot the pilot. I know that. I didn't plan it, but I know it's going to happen. They're gonna shoot that pilot, and down comes that plane into the jungle. And we had better not have any of our children left when it's over, because they'll parachute in here on us. . . . I've never lied to you. [MORE EMPHATIC] I never have lied to you. I know that's what's gonna happen. That's what he intends to do, and he will do it. He'll do it. [Un]fortunately, being so bewildered with many, many—pressures on my brain, seeing all these peo-ple behave so treasonous—it was just too much for me to put together, but uh, I—I now know what he was telling me. And it'll happen. If the plane gets in the air even. So my opinion is that we be kind to children and be kind to seniors and take the portion like they used to take in ancient

Greece, and step over quietly, because we are not committing suicide. It's a revolutionary act. We can't go back. They won't leave us alone. They're now going back to tell more lies, which means more congressmen. And there's no way, no way we can survive. Hmm?

SILENCE, THEN A FEW QUIET MURMURS. [TAPE EDIT]

JONES: Anybody. Anyone that has any dissenting opinion, please speak.[2]

Christine Miller, the woman from the Los Angeles Temple who had previously faced off bravely and successfully with Jones, most notably the time he had put a gun to her head, is one of the first to take the microphone, asking if it would be possible to go to Russia rather than die. Jones quickly quashes her idea.

JONES: Here's why it's too late for Russia. They killed. They started to kill. . . . Otherwise I'd said, Russia, you bet your life. But it's too late. . . . They've gone with the guns. . . .And once we kill anybody . . . If one of my people do something, it's me. And they say I don't have to take the blame for this, but I can't . . . I don't live that way. They said deliver up Ujara [Don Sly], who tried to get the man back here. . . . You think I'm going to deliver them Ujara? Not on your life. No.

A STRONGER CHORUS OF MEN AND WOMEN SHOUT: No! No!

And so, as Jones refuses to sacrifice Don Sly to "them," the whole community must die in an act of solidarity. Sly offers to give himself up, his voice sincere and strong:

SLY/UJARA: Is there any way that if I go that it'll help us?

JONES [WITH BRAVADO]: No. You're not going. You're not going.

MANY VOICES CALL OUT: No! NO!

Jones insists he won't sacrifice Sly and instead "will die for all." But this does not satisfy Christine, who presses that all hope is not lost, that Russia is their answer—adding that she thought Jones had an understanding with them. To this Jones replies she is mistaken, offering: "We can check with Russia and see if they'll take us in immediately. Otherwise we die. . . . But to me, . . . death is not a fearful thing. It's living that's treacherous. . . ."

SPIRITED CLAPPING: Yeah, right!

Jones insists that things have gone too far, that the children will be killed, that it is "not worth living like this." Undeterred, Christine continues to debate with him, pointing out that there were "too few who left for twelve hundred people to give . . . their lives"—that all those in Jonestown needn't make amends for the "twenty-odd" who decided to leave. Jones again refers to his vision that the plane will go down, that there is "one man," referring to Larry Layton, on that plane "who blames, and rightfully so, Debbie [Layton] for the murder . . . of his mother, and he'll stop that pilot by any means necessary." Christine refuses to be taken off track, and speaks again of their leaving for Russia.

AGITATED VOICES FROM THE CROWD

JONES [SPOUTING, EXASPERATED]: To Russia. Do you think Russia's gonna want us with all this stigma? [PAUSE] We had—we had some value, but now we don't have any value.

Christine counters with Jones's own words, quoted verbatim from a previous rally: "Well, I don't see it like that. I mean, I feel like that—as long as there's life, there's hope. That's my faith."

Jones twists her meaning, then speaks of death, as well as his untarnished dedication to his people, and asserts, "Without me, life has no meaning," before returning to the topic of revolutionary suicide. He declares he's a prophet and knows what the Russians will say, yet he orders someone to "call the Russians."

CHRISTINE: [Not] that I'm afraid to die—by no means—

JONES [INTERRUPTING]: I don't think you are. I don't think you are.

CHRISTINE: But, I look at our babies and I think they deserve to live . . .

JONES: I agree, but also they deserve much more, they deserve peace.

CLAPPING AND ASSENT FROM THE CROWD

CHRISTINE [HER VOICE STRONG AND SURE]: We all came here for peace.

JONES: And have we had it?

A FEW CALL FROM THE CROWD: No!

Jones continues, saying he's "practically died every day" to give them peace. To another speaker's inaudible comments Jones invokes Tim Stoen, stating, "He has done the thing he wanted to do: to have us destroyed." To this Christine rebuts: "When you—when we destroy ourselves, we're defeated. We let them, the enemies, defeat us." Again Jones deftly manipulates the discussion. Further exchange ensues, including support for Jones from Jim McElvane, who declares, "It's over, sister. It's over. . . . We've made . . . a beautiful day, and let's make it a *beautiful* day." But Christine won't back down. "I have a right to what I think, what I feel. And I think we all have a right to our own destiny as individuals."

Jones responds, "You can't separate yourself. We've walked way too long together." But he also seems to agree about her rights, says that he's listening to her. A woman praises Jones. After a tape edit, the same woman calls out, "You must be scared to die." Miller insists on being heard and Jones responds, "How can you tell your leader what to do if you live?" The crowd stirs and McElvane tries to quiet people. Jones returns to consideration of the children, that they should not be killed by the Temple's enemies. The crowd responds with a chorus of "no"s. Out of the confused exchange, a woman is heard to say, "You mean you want John to die?" referring to Jon Jon Stoen. Jones declares the boy is not "above others."

[TAPE EDIT]

JONES: Some months I've tried to keep this thing from happening. But I now see it's the will . . . of Sovereign Being that this happen to us. That we lay down our lives in protest against what's being done. . . . The criminality of people. The cruelty of people. Who walked out of here today? Did you notice who walked out? Mostly white people.

SOME IN THE CROWD: Yeah! Right! White!

JONES: Mostly white people walked. [PAUSE] I just know that there . . . there's no point to this. . . . . They won't accept us. And I don't think we should sit here and take any more time. . . . Because if they come after our children, and we give them our children, then our children will suffer forever.

A while later, Christine finally gives up the microphone. "That's all I've got to say."

It must have been at this point when, for the young people in particular—many of whom had surely been clinging to the thought that they might make it through this White Night as they had the others—all hope drains.

Another stretch of discussion winds down to its inevitable end when guards from the airstrip step in and report to Jones what has happened.

JONES: It's all over. The congressman has been murdered.

SILENCE

A WOMAN DECLARES: It's all over.

JONES: It's all over, all over.[3]

Jones speaks of "legacy." He calls for "justice." He requests "some medication . . . before it's too late." The "medication" is potassium cyanide, administered at a makeshift dispensary of sorts: a table set up just outside the pavilion complete with vials of liquid Valium and of cyanide, hypodermic needles, syringes, squeeze bottles, and paper cups.[4] Around the pavilion stand security guards holding crossbows; they are in turn encircled by more men, more guns. "About twenty-five armed guards . . . their weapons . . . trained on the residents, not on the jungle."[5]

JONES [MORE EXCITED]: Don't be afraid to die. You'll see, there'll be a few people land out here. They'll . . . torture some of our children here. . . . Are you going to separate yourself from whoever shot the congressman?
VOICES: No. No. No. Hell no.
[TAPE EDIT]

A woman speaks after a confused exchange between Jones and others: "I appreciate you for everything. You are the only—You are the only. . . . And I appreciate you," followed by applause and another tape edit.

JONES [URGENTLY]: Please, can we hasten? Can we hasten with that medication? You don't know what you've done—and I tried.

A man speaks about Wesley warning of two GDF soldiers.

[TAPE EDIT]
JONES: You've got to move. Marceline? You got forty minutes.[6]

Marceline's voice is nowhere on the tape.

❧

The children are brought up first. Many had the cyanide injected to the backs of their throats so that they would reflexively swallow. Later, Stephan was told that his mother had to be "physically restrained" when the poisoning of the youngest children commenced, and that a nineteen-year-old known as Poncho had attempted to help Marceline. Not one to be overruled, Jones had then commanded Poncho to take the poison himself.[7] The whole of this part of the story will never be known, but it is important to Stephan, because it means Marceline resisted. And he admires Poncho, both for joining Marceline in resisting and also for following Jones's final command. Many years later Stephan recollected:

> *What happened to Pancho [sic] is a wonderful example, no matter how misguided it was. He took the poison because my father told him to take it, O.K.? What a brave and devoted and wonderful act it was, in retrospect. If you set aside the loss, and the tragedy, and even the ridiculousness of what happened in that moment, and you just step inside the shoes of a young man with years and years ahead of him, who, on the one hand, is fighting against my father's orders out of devotion to someone he loves very much, and who, on the other hand, has the bravery to throw his shoulders back on the order of his leader and step*

up and take the poison—when you look at everything that went into that, my
God! What a brave human being! I can't hold a candle to that!

As Stephan told Wright, "I . . . knew the respect people had for my mother, and I know that my mother did not sit blindly by and say, 'Yeah, let's take the poison.'" And even though he also said at that time, "We were young and we were strong and we knew where the weapons were, and we knew who was holding them," he later told Bebelaar that he'd "had no grandiose ideas" about what he might have done, that "better people than me, who didn't like Dad, died there that night." But he also said that if the team had been in Jonestown, "what happened at the airstrip might never have happened."[8]

❧

Wesley Breidenbach was apparently with the group returning from the ambush at the airstrip. It's also likely that among those guarding the perimeter were the strong young men assigned to security (especially needed now since the basketball team was in Georgetown), including Teddy McMurry, Mondo Griffith, his big brother Emmett, and Bruce Oliver; Billy Oliver and Lew Jones were patrolling the perimeter, according to Reiterman—they were the last two guards still carrying guns, since the others had been told to trade in their guns for crossbows.[9]

[CHILDREN CRYING]

JONES: Somebody give them a little rest, a little rest. . . . It's hard, it's hard, but only at first . . . Living—when you're looking at death, . . . living is much, much more difficult. Raising up every morning and not knowing what's going to be the night's bringing. It's much more difficult. It's much more difficult.

[CRYING AND TALKING]

One of the faithful protests that people should stop crying and rejoice. "I'm looking at so many people crying," she said. "I wish you would not cry. And just thank Father."

JONES [PLEADING]: For God's sake, let's get on with it. . . . We've had as much of this world as you're gonna get. Let's just be done with it. Let's be done with the agony of it.

[TAPE EDIT]

JONES: They'll pay for it. This is a revolutionary suicide. This is not a self-destructive suicide. So they'll pay for this. They brought this upon us. . . . I leave that destiny to them.

[VOICES]

[TAPE EDIT]

JONES: Who wants to go with their child has a right to go with their child. . . . I want to go—I want to see you go, though. I—they can take me and do what they want . . . I want to see you go. I don't want to see you go through this hell no more. . . .

MAN: And the way the children are laying there now, I'd rather see them lay like that than to see them have to die like the Jews did, which was pitiful anyhow. And I'd just like to—to thank Dad for giving us life and also death.

JONES [PLEADING]: Lay down your life with dignity. Don't lay down with tears and agony. . . . Don't be this way. Stop this hysterics. . . . We must die with some dignity. . . . Look children, it's just something to put you to rest.

[TAPE EDIT]

[DESPAIRING TONE] Oh, God.

[CHILDREN CRYING]

JONES: Mother, Mother, Mother, Mother, Mother, please. Mother, please, please, please. Don't—don't do this. Don't do this. Lay down your life with your child. But don't do this.

WOMAN: We're doing all of this for you.

JONES: Free at last. Peace. . . . Keep your emotions down. . . . Children, it will not hurt. If you'll be—if you'll be quiet. If you'll be quiet.

JONES: Be patient. Death is—I tell you, I don't care how many screams you hear, I don't care how many anguished cries, death is a million times preferable to ten more days of this life. If you knew what was ahead of you—if you knew what was ahead of you, you'd be glad to be stepping over tonight. . . . [REPRIMANDS] If you'll quit tell[ing] them they're dying . . . Adults, adults . . . I call on you to stop this nonsense. I call on you to quit exciting your children, when all they're doing is going to a quiet rest. . . .

[TAPE EDIT]

Hurry, hurry, my children. Hurry. All I think [UNINTELLIGIBLE] from the hands of the enemy. Hurry, my children. Hurry. . . . quickly, quickly.

[TAPE EDIT]

❧

JONES [CLAPPING IN REPRIMAND]: Stop this, stop this, stop this [UNINTELLIGIBLE]. Stop this crying, all of you.

❧

JONES: All they're doing is . . . taking a drink. They take it to go to sleep. That's what death is, sleep.

[TAPE EDIT]

—of it. I'm tired of it all.

❧

Where's the vat, the vat, the vat? Where's the vat with the Green C on it? . . . Bring it here so the adults can begin.

❧

JONES: . . . Take some.

[TAPE EDIT]

Take our life from us. We laid it down. We got tired.

[TAPE EDIT]

We didn't commit suicide, we committed an act of revolutionary suicide protesting the conditions of an inhumane world.[10]

True to form, Jones gave himself the last word. His declaration, presuming to speak for everyone, marks the end of the tape.

❧

Where are the "screams," the "hysterics" Jones speaks of? Were there sounds of struggle? Where is Poncho's voice? Where is Marceline's? All that is known is that she died of cyanide poisoning with the others, and that Stephan is sure she would have spoken up. Did Edith Roller try to speak again as she had at her first White Night?

The recorded voices seem to be those of grown men and women, and the cries of the very young. Where are the voices of the adolescent and young adults? What were the teenagers thinking as twilight deepened into night? Were they silent, every one of them?

How many spoke up or wordlessly rallied behind Christine Miller's brave and determined effort to explore another option? How many endorsed Don Sly's offer to give himself up for them? What had been cut out by the thirty-one tape edits? Stephen speaks of "the constant emotional roller coaster" people experienced because of Jones. The humid and wet weather, now headed toward another season of heavy rains, took its toll too, as did illness and lack of adequate food. How many were exhausted and in despair at this point, and believed what Jones said—that Jonestown would be attacked, the children taken, tortured? How many could not bear to live after seeing the babies and toddlers dying painful deaths?

No one will ever know, and there is no way to know how many tried to resist, or how many ingested the poison against their will or were forcibly injected.

As for Christine Miller, who had debated so long with Jones, it's unclear whether she had to be forcibly injected:

Eyewitnesses confirm that Christine and her friends were sitting in the second row toward the front. Some authors have written that her body was discovered with injection marks on her upper arm, but do not provide sources or proof for their claims, so it is not clear where the line between truth and speculation begins and ends.[11]

First the babies and the children, then the young adults.

As twilight fell into darkness, the human voices—the last goodbyes, the sounds of pain and of dying—were gradually obscured by the sound of the rain drumming on the tin roof. Bodies filled the pavilion. The rain fell on those lying near the boardwalk outside, on those scattered in groups in the fields. Otherwise, all was still.

Echoes of Poems: In Small Dreams

San Francisco, 1976

Wanting my brother to come home,
But he won't never come back.
Empty and dark like a cave,
I'm afraid to face reality.
Just like I can't go in that cave,
My heart grasps me
I bite my tongue in pain
I miss you my brother.
You did it for something meaningless,
I still love you my brother.
        — *Dorothy Buckley*

I was sitting in the dark
not waiting for the dark
the dark is like no sound around
it's quiet
very quiet
        — *Mondo Griffith*

They're laying down a little black child …
Who killed that little boy?
Somebody tell me
Who killed him?
        — *Willie Thomas*

…As the rain tingles on the roof of the
tropic island,
Birds fly to the nest in the tropic trees,
Little creatures hiding from
The small rain.
        —*Joyce Polk Brown*

Chapter 17

Aftermath

November 18 and Beyond

The Toll

On Sunday, November 19, 1978, the Guyanese Army, the first to arrive at the scene in Jonestown, reported 408 dead. On Wednesday, November 22, U.S. military forces arrived, after which the count increased with each new day.[1]

In all, 918 people died, the vast majority in Jonestown. Five were killed at the airstrip: Congressman Leo Ryan, NBC correspondent Don Harris, NBC sound man Bob Brown, *Examiner* photographer Greg Robinson, and defector Patty Parks. Another four died in the Lamaha Gardens house in Georgetown: Sharon Amos, and her three children: Liane, Christa, and Martin.

One-third of the dead—304—were under eighteen; more than half were in their twenties or younger.

In Jonestown, two died from gunshot wounds: Jim Jones, and Ann Moore, sister of Carolyn Layton and Rebecca Moore. According to one report, Jones's injury was self-inflicted, but Ann's was murder; a subsequent report claimed the opposite. The remaining population were said to have died of "acute cyanide poisoning."[2]

Only a small fraction of the dead received any post-mortem examination, and most of these were cursory. The first autopsies were performed by Guyana's chief pathologist, Dr. Leslie Mootoo, who examined less than a quarter of the population; these he began on November 20, after two days of heat and rain. Though Dr. Mootoo's efforts were cut short when U.S. military forces stepped in on November 22, he nonetheless stated he believed that seven hundred "had died unwillingly." The reason: He had discovered small holes in the shoulders of many of the dead that were consistent with needle marks, and he also found syringes "indicating that poison had been squirted into people's mouths."[3] But Dr. Mootoo's findings were necessarily incomplete, and later embalming of the dead additionally distorted any potential findings.[4]

At Guyana's inquest held on December 22, 1978, the coroner's jury in the end found that Jones and "persons unknown" were "criminally responsible" for the deaths of 910 out of the 914 who died in Jonestown.[5] And, indeed, in his sworn statement, survivor Stanley Clayton said, "Jim Jones was the big boss of the settlement, he ran everything. He had power of life and death over all inmates of Jonestown." [6] Unfortunately, numerous media reports spoke of the tragedy as one that all went to willingly.

All we really know is that some went willingly, some did not; probably most felt they had no choice. "Murder-suicide" is the term that seems most apt, since we will never know how many people, trapped in such dire circumstances, took the poison of their own free will. They had been through this routine before, or so they thought. But after the first among them—a young mother named Ruletta Paul, holding her baby—approached the table with its poison vat, the syringes and the cups, gave her baby the cyanide mixture, then took it herself, everyone would have quickly realized this was the real thing. Stephan Jones knows Paul had her own reasons, besides heeding Jones's order, for wanting to die.[7] How many others were exhausted and hopeless? How many felt this was their last act of loyalty to the Temple community? And how many resisted? We'll never know.

As for those who lived, we know that about eighty-seven Temple members who were in or near Guyana survived, including fifteen of the sixteen defectors who had left with the Ryan party. Some of the survivors, the basketball team and Eugene Smith, had been in Georgetown. A few were on the Temple boat or away on Temple business.[8] Eleven had escaped the morning of the tragedy, leaving on a "picnic" to Matthew's Ridge—really an escape that had been planned for months.[9] Three others—Tim Carter, his brother Michael, and Mike Prokes, the Temple spokesman (who would commit suicide four months later)—had been dispatched by Maria Katsaris just as the White Night was beginning to take a suitcase with a large sum of Temple money to the Soviet embassy in Georgetown. Before they left, Tim ventured to the pavilion to see what was happening, just in time to see his child dead, hear his wife's last words. Not knowing what else to do, he went on the embassy mission with the others, thus escaping.[10] One elderly woman had slept through the deaths. Thirty-six-year-old Odell Rhodes, who'd gone to get a stethoscope that Larry Schacht had requested, sneaked out the back of the nurse's office and found a hiding spot under a senior residence. Later, under the shield of darkness, he made his way to the main road to Port Kaituma.[11]

Stanley Clayton, who was twenty-five at the time, described his escape at the inquest:

> When I realized it was the real thing, I began to move backwards from side to side looking for a way to escape. The crowd was getting less and less as persons were dying. . . . Between 100 to 200 persons were still alive. I heard over the public address system that persons with weapons [were] to report to the radio room. . . . I started walking away from the pavilion and one of the security guards [Mondo] Griffith asked me where I was going.

Stanley told Mondo he was heading toward a friend to say goodbye—"to tell him I was going—I was going to take a portion." Mondo told him the friend was not in that direction. When Stanley claimed otherwise and continued on his way, Mondo followed him, so Stanley turned, seemingly heading back to the pavilion, until he eventually found his moment and ran into the bushes, where he hid for several hours.[12]

Stephan

When Stephan had found Sharon Amos and her children, including his friend Liane, in the bathroom at Lamaha Gardens, he didn't push his way in very far, partly because the door was blocked by the bodies, and partly because he was afraid. Though he writes in "Death's Night" that saving Liane at that point was no doubt impossible, that he didn't try "has been a great source of shame" for him. But he later saw "it was a realistic enough fear," after the treatment he was to receive by the police and in court. "Imagine the Guyanese authorities coming upon Jim Jones's son, smeared with blood, his fingerprints all over the victims. What a tidy scapegoat I would have made."

Someone told Stephan that the person who had first discovered the bodies of Amos and her children had found Temple member Chuck Beikman standing there in the blood, and that Stephan's nine-year-old adopted niece Stephanie had also been found on the floor among the bodies, alive but "covered in blood, some of it her own." Stephanie had been carried downstairs, away from the bloody bathroom. When Stephan went to see her, he observed that her superficial cuts appeared "haphazard and feeble," in contrast to the deep wounds on the throats of the other children.

No one, Stephan included, considered Beikman to be a murderer. He surmised Beikman had tried to follow Amos's orders, but that the man had no will to kill the girl. Looking at Stephanie, now being comforted by a woman from the Temple as the girl sat quietly, staring into space, Stephan could see she was, perhaps irreparably, traumatized.

Soon, the police and the Guyanese Defense Force "were crawling all over" Lamaha Gardens. Stephan's memory of what followed is foggy. He knows the police questioned him, but can't remember what they asked, or his responses.

Later that night, he and a few others chose to retreat to a downstairs room just under the bathroom where the bodies had been found. At last giving in to exhaustion, Stephan watched as the blood from the bathroom upstairs, which had obviously not yet been attended to, seeped through, darkening the ceiling.[13]

Because that first report cited only around 400 dead, Stephan, as well as his brothers, at first believed—or held some hope—that the remainder had escaped into the jungle and lived.[14] The Guyanese authorities held Stephan, Tim, and Jimmy at Lamaha Gardens under house arrest, despite their pleas to go to Jonestown to help find the people they thought had surely survived in the bush. Stephan writes in "Death's Night" that he tried to talk the authorities into allowing him and his brothers to help in Jonestown, where they could perhaps prevent more deaths from happening, claiming that the officials "couldn't reason with the survivors—or holdouts" the way he and his brothers could. "I told them that I knew the bush well, and could help them find anyone who might be hiding." The police said everything was being handled. Stephan didn't tell them he thought he might be "the *last* person who could reason with" his father; still, he wanted to do everything he could to "block [Jones's] murderous reach." He had told Ingram to make the call to prevent those in San Francisco from following Jones's orders, and he told the others under house arrest in Georgetown "not to do anything stupid," to "talk to someone if it gets to be too much."[15]

The police arrested Chuck Beikman for wounding Stephanie Jones and murdering Sharon Amos and her children. Stephan tried to intervene, defending him even without knowing what had actually taken place.

Stephan considered Beikman, who could neither read nor write, "a simple man," a mere "victim of circumstance." And Stephan, like the others, felt "Chuck was one of our own. He had to be protected."[16] It wasn't right for

Beikman to be punished for the murders that Amos had committed, and for which Jones was ultimately responsible.

The police alternately assured those at the house that there were "hundreds of survivors" in Jonestown (possibly to extract more information from them) and frightened them, returning to take one and then another off to the station to be questioned. To his surprise, Stephan received permission to accompany Temple members who were summoned, but he later understood this was likely a "strategic" kindness, an effort to distract them from requesting legal representation or assistance from the U.S. embassy. Everyone was grieving, hoping, not sleeping much; their nerves were raw.[17]

Released from their five-day house arrest, Tim and Johnny Cobb were taken to help identify the dead, now counted at nine hundred as reported by Guyana's deputy prime minister. A photograph of Tim, a rag held over his nose to ward off the stench of death, was widely circulated. Tim and Johnny were unable to utter words when they came back to Georgetown.

Not long after, Wright indicates in his *New Yorker* piece, Stephan watched as someone wrote down the names of the known dead as they were recited by phone from the States: Vincent Lopez, Shanda James, Agnes Jones, Lew Jones, John Victor Stoen. Almost all the people Stephan knew—his mother, his girlfriend Michelle, nearly all of those most dear to him—were gone.[18]

His life was about to get more complicated: Stephan was brought in, ostensibly to take Beikman's statement. Beikman had been put in isolation and interrogated by four detectives with no legal counsel present, so Stephan—who later said he "probably knew less than [the] interrogators about the deaths of Sharon" and her children—suspected Beikman had been bullied into talking.

Stephan began to write down Beikman's testimony: He'd gone into the bathroom as ordered by Amos, thinking he was to help hide the children. Instead, he watched her kill the children and herself. He'd been immobilized by the horrific scene. Stephan can't remember if Beikman spoke about Stephanie. But the fact that Chuck had done nothing to stop the killings was enough for the detectives.

Stephan was told that if he testified that Beikman had not been pressured into making his statement, Stephan "could go home tomorrow." If he didn't testify, he might be held indefinitely. He did testify, but he said Beikman had been bullied into saying what he did, although he lied about when he was bullied—indicating it was while Beikman's statement was being taken, not before. Stephan said he himself had been pressured as well.

The prosecutor—a man named Singh—incensed, called a recess and the next day proceeded with a line of questioning that implied Stephan himself was guilty of the murders. When Stephan said he had not been at Lamaha Gardens at the time of the murders—knowing many could bear witness to this fact—Singh shot out sarcastically, "Ah, that's right. You weren't there." Singh's accusatory manner, his insinuations, touched a nerve. "On a raw level," Stephan writes in an email to Bebelaar many years later, "I felt responsible for what had happened to the children while I was running around." And, even more deeply, Stephan "believed we all knew that those responsible, those truly deserving of prosecution, were already dead." Finally, exasperated and hopeless, Stephan replied to Singh in a sarcastic tone of his own, "Yeah, I did it and I'm trying to put it off on Chuck."

The magistrate asked him to confirm what he'd just said. Instantly, Stephan knew he'd done something irreversible. He was seized with fear as a recess was called and the shocked audience filed out of the courtroom, "openly staring" at Jim Jones's son.

That was enough for Singh. The next day he formally charged both Stephan and Chuck Beikman with murder.

They were transported to the prison. Beikman felt he'd let Stephan down; Stephan felt his own "temper and arrogance" was the reason both of them were locked up. "A part of me took up the role of the prosecutor and blamed me for what was happening. Not because I'd shot my mouth off, but because I'd been a part of the sickness that had led to so much destruction. It was more what I had *not* done than what I had."

Beikman had already been in jail for some time, still in solitary. Stephan was sent to the Murder Remand Dormitory, a long room holding fifteen bunks. He and Beikman "were the only two white men in the entire prison," he writes, "and the most widely read Guyanese newspaper was saying that we were part of a group of white crazies who'd taken the property, then the freedom, then the lives of hundreds of black Americans." Some of his fellow prisoners, from a safe distance, took to shouting "Jim Jones!" at him. "I fucking hated that," Stephan says. Only two men refused to participate in the staring and mocking—one whom Stephan called "One-Eye," who constantly worked on his exercise regimen, and one known as "Cornbread," who later saved his life, Stephan says, "and—as a bonus—my sanity."

Every night Stephan was taken to a vermin-infested cell, with a peephole in the iron door, a bare bulb burning all night, a straw mattress, no sheet or blanket—all by design "to protect me from death by my hand or another's." Although he says he considered suicide only briefly, he punished himself with thoughts of what more he might have done in that bloody bathroom, and in Jonestown. "Now all that was left of those I'd failed was hundreds of faces, rising from the darkness, one after the other."[19] He would remain in jail for three months, until the magistrate decided to release him.[20]

Jimmy

Having lost his beloved Yvette in Jonestown, Jimmy came back to San Francisco, with his brother Tim, while Stephan was in prison. On the plane from Guyana, sky marshals guarded Tim and Jimmy until they landed at Kennedy Airport. There, as Wright reports in the *New Yorker*, they were each "grilled, separately, for about ten hours by representatives of the Customs Service, the F.B.I., and the Secret Service; then . . . given lie-detector tests and, eventually, allowed to go. It was [Jimmy's] first experience with what he calls being 'leper-tized.'" People in the Bay Area had seen pictures of the brothers, and wherever the young Jones men went, people would stare and point "in horrified recognition." Police tailed them "for months" after they returned.[21]

When Jimmy got back to San Francisco, he knew some survivors and relatives of those who died in Jonestown felt resentment against Jones's sons—who had been, in a way, part of the Jonestown "elite," and who had survived. Nonetheless, reports Gary Smith in his *Sports Illustrated* piece:

> [Jimmy]'d swallowed his fears and shown up at a half-dozen funerals for Temple members whose bodies had been shipped back to the Bay Area. Then the mother of one of the dead, at a post-funeral gathering, put a gun to his head and hissed, "Why should you be alive when my daughter's dead?"
>
> "I don't want to be alive," Jim replied, "Kill me now."
>
> Mourners grabbed the gun and gave him some advice: Stay away from the survivors; they'll blame you. Hell, he blamed himself, mostly for having sent Yvette, the pregnant bride who had wanted to stay at his side, back to Jonestown a few weeks after their wedding in Georgetown while he remained in the Guyanese capital to do public relations and liaison work for Jonestown's economic and outreach projects, including the basketball games against the host country's Olympic team.[22]

Jimmy got a job as an orderly in a hospital in San Francisco—a kind of full circle since his father had once worked as a hospital orderly. Lawrence

Wright observed, when he interviewed the brothers in 1993, that it was as if Jimmy were "beginning to re-create his father's life and try to make it turn out right this time." While working, sometimes for twenty-four-hour shifts, Jimmy also studied to be a respiratory therapist.

Jimmy soon met Erin, a neonatal nurse, another repeat of history: It was when working as an orderly that his father had met Marceline. On one of their first dates, Jimmy and Erin went for a walk on the beach and afterward sat in his car, talking. When Jimmy told Erin who he was, she opened the car door and ran.

But Jimmy's shocking revelation didn't scare her off for good. Erin had more in common with Marceline than just being a nurse; she too was "stubborn, white, and liberal." Two years later, in 1987, Erin and Jimmy were married, and now have three sons, Rob, Ryan, and Ross. Wright points out that Jimmy didn't "think it particularly significant that he named his second child Ryan." Jimmy and Erin are Catholics, and are bringing up their sons in the Catholic Church. Their elder boy, Rob, grew up loving basketball, and was a star player on the Saint Mary's College team. Ryan was drawn to football and played as an offensive lineman for San Jose State University.

Jimmy named Rob after Yvette's father. When Rob was three, Jimmy took him and his one-year-old brother to the mausoleum in Colma, near San Francisco, where Yvette's ashes are interred. While the boys played, Wright reports, Jimmy sat there thinking "how unfair it was that his life was still going on, while Yvette's had ended." At the same time, Jimmy believed Yvette would be pleased for him, at "the way his life had turned out."[23]

In April 1993, a situation tragically reminiscent of what had happened in Jonestown fifteen years earlier took place. Agents of the Bureau of Alcohol, Tobacco, Firearms (ATF), accompanied by members of the media, served a search warrant to the Branch Davidian cult in Waco, Texas, and six cult members and four agents were killed in a gun battle. After a second siege, seventy-six cult members—including twenty children—died in a fire apparently set by the cult's leader.[24]

After these events surfaced in news reports, Jimmy's friends and colleagues expressed concern about him, but Jimmy brushed them off. And though Erin noted his heavy drinking, which began soon afterward, he wouldn't talk to her about it.

Then she told him that their son Rob, while watching a television report about Waco, had seen footage of Jonestown, including images of bodies around the pavilion. After that the boys had asked her if they could go visit the town that was "named after us." In that moment the awful similarity of the two situations broke through in Jimmy.

As Wright reports, when a childhood memory would come to Jimmy, it would always culminate in "that person dying in Jonestown." He had dreams, too, of course, often about Yvette. But in his dreams he could never catch up to her—until finally, in one dream, he did. "She was sitting on a park bench in [San Francisco's] Japantown, where they used to go together," Wright indicates. "He walked up to her. She looked up at him and said, 'Goodbye, Jimmy,' and he said, 'Goodbye, honey.' That was the last time he dreamed about Yvette."

When interviewing the brothers, Lawrence Wright told them that "each of the sons had a unique and in some ways unbearable legacy from his father: Stephan was left the blood relation, Jim was left the name, and Tim was left the stench of Jonestown." To this Jimmy said, "You know what the scariest part is? If you take all of us together, we make Jim Jones." He continued, "You know, he *was* a monster! He became a monster. Maybe it was the drugs. Maybe it was the paranoia. Whatever it was, that's what he became. That's what he was. That's what he was when he died. And that's his legacy."[25]

The Jones brothers: Amy Arbus ©1993: Tim, Jimmy and Stephan

Tim

Tim, like Jimmy, lost most of his adoptive family. He also lost the mother who bore him, twenty-three other relatives, his wife, Sandy, and their daughter, Monyell, not yet a year old, whom Tim and Sandy had adopted, and whom Tim had adored.

Stephan and Jimmy told Wright at the time that that their adopted brother "hasn't been the same" ever since coming back from the grim task in Jonestown just after the tragedy. In the fifteen years leading up to the *New Yorker* interview in 1993, Stephan said he had "virtually never heard Tim talk about Jonestown." And as of that time, Tim hadn't told his wife Lorna much either—he had asked her to go with him to New York to do the interview with Wright, so he wouldn't have to repeat his story to her. The couple met Wright at a restaurant; when they sat down to begin, Tim "immediately burst into tears."

As they began to talk and Tim ran into occasional blanks in his memory, he said, "When someone asks me about someone I can't remember, and they died there, that just pisses me off beyond all means! It really pisses me off!"

Unlike Stephan, who wasn't sure he would have prevented the deaths if they hadn't been away at the tournament instead of in Jonestown, Tim believed he could have stopped it. When Wright asked Tim what he would have done, he said he "would have killed the bastard!" He went on to say that at that time, in 1993, he didn't "have the balls anymore," but back in 1978, he said, things would have been different. "I would have done it," he said. "I swear on my life. Do you think I would have let a girl, with cyanide being made with Kool-Aid . . . ? The jokes I hear! Would I have let people walk up and take that? Stephan wouldn't have. I wouldn't have. I'd have talked to Jimmy and he wouldn't have."

Wright pointed out that Tim's adoptive brother Lew had not stopped the tragedy, that he was even the one who told people to go to the pavilion that night. Wright also reminded Tim that, after what Tim calls "the catastrophe" was over, Lew went through Jonestown with a gun, to be certain no one was still alive.

Tim responded, "I don't want to hear about that. . . . See, that wouldn't have happened if there had been someone there to say, 'Lew, come on!' Tim clapped his hands loudly in front of [Wright's] face, as if he were talking to his dead brother. 'Lew! Jesus!'"

Tim's painful memory lapses about Jonestown even included momentarily losing his daughter's name. Tim "stared desperately into space" until it came to him. Once he'd said Monyell's name, Lorna asked, "Is that whose baby clothes you still have?"

But Tim clearly remembers going to see his father's body. "He shot himself or he had someone do it—he didn't drink Kool-Aid, that son of a bitch!"

Tim too has dreams, and images that come to him from time to time—like the face of his sister Mary, seventeen when she died—but the faces come and then go, "like any other thought."[26]

It wasn't until 1992, the year before they met with Wright, that Tim and Stephan decided, independently, to go to the annual Jonestown memorial service for the first time. Tim said he hadn't "paid much attention" to the services before then. As Tim left that day, he rolled down the window of his car and called out to the trauma specialist, Chris Hatcher, who had headed a team to help Jonestown survivors adjust to their lives after returning from Guyana. "I told you I was going to turn out all right!" Tim cried. It took Hatcher a moment to realize the stocky, balding man was Tim—whom he'd last seen as a thin boy with a full head of curls.[27]

Tim apparently still finds it hard to talk about Jonestown. Bebelaar has tried to reach him and get permission to include two of his poems from Opportunity days—one about Nat Turner, and one that may be about Sandy. He has never responded.

Stephan: Years Later

Stephan's response to the tragedy can be seen most vividly and hauntingly by comparing his two passport photos, one taken before he entered Jonestown at age sixteen, and the other taken after the tragedy. In the first he looks young. He gazes straight into the camera with a mixture of sadness and defiance, and something like apprehension masked by boyish bravado. In the second photo he looks many years older, his eyes deep pools of loss and shock.

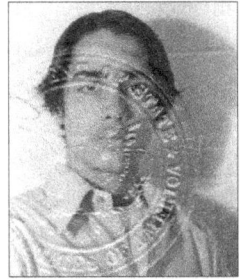

Stephan's entrance passport

When he finally returned to the United States, Stephan said, "For years, I was content sitting, facing a wall, just in my head. Completely isolated and comfortable with that." Except, that, is when something—a face, a gesture, a scent—would trigger a memory. "When I would smell somebody that smelled like my mom, then I would lose it," he said. He "spent

Stephan's exit passport

years dreaming every night, searching for dead people"; in his dreams he'd get "glimpses" of those he'd known in Jonestown, who would "stare at me with anger and then disappear from view. I'd run to the corner where I'd seen them and turn . . . and they were no longer there."

Then he began having dreams in which he learned that people he loved who had died were alive—"my mother, for example." In these dreams he found himself "really believing that, finally being convinced of that, only to awaken and mourn all over again."

But he never found his mother in his dreams, however much he looked for her.[28] Instead, in his waking hours he would search in an unlikely place—his own eyes. His girlfriend at the time wondered why she found him so often staring into the mirror. Believing that Lawrence Wright got it wrong in the 1993 *New Yorker* piece when he claimed Stephan had "his father's fiery eyes," Stephan felt that, when he gazed into the mirror, he was looking into his mother's green eyes.[29]

Among those in his dreams was Michelle Touchette, Stephan's first love. He straightforwardly describes her death in Jonestown as a murder.[30] He never had the chance to say goodbye to her when the basketball team had left Jonestown, headed for the big tournament—she hadn't been able to bring herself to join the crowd of well-wishers. As Stephan writes in his essay "Reunion," he had "wondered where she was, but [he] didn't wonder much," his mind on the game and another girl in Georgetown.

A few days later a letter from Michelle was delivered to Stephan in Georgetown, in which she apologized for not being there to see him off and said she was hoping the two of them could "try us again, once more." Stephan recalls, "There was more weariness and sorrow than longing in that letter. A resolve. Once more meant once more."

He adds, "I thought that might be nice. I wanted to do right by her. But first there was this girl . . . " He never saw Michelle again, except in occasional "dreams of yearning." Then, after a long while of not dreaming of her, he had one in which he touched her and she smiled, as if she'd been expecting him. He breathed her in, "each time deeper than the last. Then I drop my arms, stand and turn and walk away. Time to go."[31]

Some time after his return to California, Stephan began using cocaine. Now he says he's actually "grateful" for that, because seeking to end his dependence led him to a more spiritual path which in turn helped him come to terms with his many losses.[32]

Surely, writing about his experiences in Jonestown and his life afterward has also been part of the process of regaining his life (his reflections can be found on the Jonestown Institute's website (www.jonestown.sdsu.edu).

~

A peaceful slope in Evergreen Cemetery in Oakland, California, marks the final resting place of 410 of those who died in Jonestown. Most of those interred there are among the ones, many of them children, whose bodies were never claimed—there was no one left to do so. In some cases entire families perished in the tragedy. Previously a small headstone and two rose-bushes marked the graves; now the site bears four memorial plaques, listing all the names of those who died, including Jim Jones's.

Fielding McGehee III, head of the Jonestown Institute at San Diego State University, explains to those who might wonder why Jones's name was included in an article in the *San Francisco Chronicle*: "Let's recognize his culpability, but let's also recognize his death." He explains that Jones was not the only one to blame. Someone ordered the poison; someone shot Ryan on the tarmac. "It's really hard to draw a line if we're trying to define responsibility," he said. "Where does it stop?"[33]

Stephan, too, has long contemplated the complexity of what happened on November 18, 1978, and the question of the responsibility of others. He told Lawrence Wright in 1993 that he believed "loyalty to the community played a large part in the decision

Jonestown Memorial, Evergreen Cemetery

of the people to kill themselves." He continued, "There was fatigue. I think everybody was defeated and tired. They wanted relief from the constant emotional roller coaster that my father put [us] through. . . . Not only did all these things contribute but the weather cooperated! It clouded over. The wind picked up. It was gray and black. It threatened rain. Everything contributed to set the scene for what happened."[34]

Much later, he told Bebelaar in an email:

If I were forced to offer what I feel most contributed to the ugliness of the Temple . . . I would have to say it was peer pressure. Dad played on our concern with what the others in our community thought of us . . . [something that is] largely missing from anything [else] . . . I've seen. There's lots about us and Jim Jones, us and the United States, us and the world—our grand dream that could never be realized in such a cold world, but not much about us and us. Why is no one willing to hold us responsible for what happened? I'm pretty sure we can take it and there were many amazing people that died in JT that would've welcomed an opportunity to tell their story in a way that was approachable and most beneficial to the young, impressionable, and vulnerable.

When I shared my experience and enjoyed some discussion with some classes at Stanford [University] and Cal [University of California, Berkeley], what had them flood the stage afterward was my description of what it was like to be sitting in a Temple meeting thinking how crazy it all was, while faking my approval because all around me was an auditorium full of what seemed to be zealous believers, at least half of whom I now believe were doing and thinking the same thing I was, but at the time I could only think there must be something wrong with me, that I was too selfish to see the "greater good" of it all.

Those college students excitedly likened it to being in a classroom with a godlike person at the front saying how it is, and they don't get it or they don't agree, but everyone else seems to, so they act like they do . . . they compared it to the social pressure within their respective schools, the implied and dictated norms and expectations.[35]

For Bebelaar's part, she wondered whether any of the young could be held accountable for what happened when they had almost no choice about going to Jonestown. They and everyone were, in effect, imprisoned there, with no passports, the jungle all around, and faced terrible punishments for even suggesting "this is wrong." After Bebelaar relayed this to Stephan, he replied:

I'm not talking about blame. I'm talking about what was my part, what might I have done better—even better, what do I hope I would do differently in similar circumstances? Most of us did the best we could with what we had and I believe that some of us had the means to stop the terrible things that happened, but we didn't get it done. In fact, some of us fed and participated in the madness, even as we railed against it . . . and, as I see it, everything happened just the way it was supposed to. So, what can we learn/gain from what has happened? So, what do we do now with that knowledge and growth?

So what? Now what?

To me, this view and approach are the best way to honor my loved ones. It tends to turn tragedy into triumph (oh, that's almost too corny to leave in but I can't help myself).[36]

Not long after the deaths in Jonestown, at a memorial service at Evergreen Cemetery, Stephan spoke to Congressman Ryan's daughter Patricia, who had sought him out. When he told her how sorry he was for "what my father did to your father," she told him no apology was necessary, that it was his father who had done it, not Stephan. Seeing how much Stephan looked like his father, Ryan noted the much more difficult position Stephan was in. "Horrible as what happened to my father is," she said, "at least I have the benefit of having him revered and respected. You don't have that. You lost your friends and your family, and you have to live in shame." Later, at a lunch for survivors and family, the two talked "for several hours," and afterward Patricia said, "It was one of the strangest and most moving experiences I've ever had. . . . I remember his telling me how absolutely horrible it was at times being Jim Jones's son, but he kept saying that he's fine now, he's just fine—that life goes on." [37]

Stephan wrote another piece for the Jonestown Institute website, titled "The Man They Loved." What follows is an excerpt:

> *In his prime, Dad dripped charisma. At his best he engaged and charmed and enthralled. He could be so playful and could appear courageous. I don't think even he knew if he truly cared or was really good at looking like he cared, or both. Whatever it was—and I suspect it ran the range—in the time when his eyes were clear and unshielded and his smile bright and warm, he seemed to care deeply.*
>
> *He had a strong sense of justice, with his scope deftly trained on others at all times. He could be beautifully eloquent in a down-home country sort of way, or in a manner befitting an aristocratic dinner party . . .whatever got it done.*
>
> *And he was a sick man who wanted everyone to adore him and so would mold himself constantly to that end. But . . . when I gnash my teeth slightly as my heart swells while I play with a child or animal, I'm reminded of Dad. Right up to the last time I saw him, he could lovingly and playfully engage babies and animals . . . probably because he didn't need their adulation and so could enjoy them more genuinely . . . and of course others were watching, so . . .*
>
> *When my eyes twinkle just enough to let my daughters know that I'm pulling their leg, he's in there.*
>
> *When I rise up with eyes flashing, ready to verbally lash someone I deem ignorant and intolerant—how ironic—I know where that came from.*
>
> *When my heart aches for the world, I know his did too . . . occasionally.* [38]

When Bebelaar saw Stephen again in 2015 to discuss sections of the manuscript for this book, he had just come from coaching his youngest daughter's basketball team after work. His oldest daughter, he'd told her earlier, is a "hoopster" too. He rose to greet his former teacher, smiling, and once again, his expressive eyes, full of life and joy now, were the first thing she noticed—that and his six-foot-four height. At 56 he still looks like a basketball player, strong, carrying himself with an athlete's ease. He says he plays whenever he can fit a game into his busy schedule. Stephan's second-oldest daughter sat at a nearby table in the café, working on the résumé Stephan was going to help her with after the meeting. He introduced her, his eyes bright with pride.

In Stephan's essay "Reunion," he describes one aspect of his healing, in the form of a dream—the last dream he ever had of Michelle. In it, he kneels to embrace her, and he can't figure out why; he wasn't that much taller than her in life. Then he understands:

> *I am healing.*
>
> *The Michelle of my subconscious, of my conscience, was ready to see me. My daughter, who was six at the time of the dream, is the reason I kneel to love Michelle . . . Low is a familiar place for love.*
>
> *Michelle and I have reserved a piece of our hearts for each other because that is as it should be in love. Michelle loves me. She has forgiven me.*
>
> *I have forgiven me.*[39]

Afterword

ews of the deaths in Jonestown came to the outside world in pieces. First came the report that Congressman Ryan and others had been killed at the airstrip. Then came the successive reports revising the total death toll, each higher than the last.

On Monday, November 27, as people in San Francisco were still reeling from the Jonestown news, Mayor George Moscone and Supervisor Harvey Milk were shot and killed by Dan White, a former supervisor who had been a city policeman. Though it was supposed to be the holiday season, celebration seemed irrelevant.

Only some names of the dead were published soon after the events. It was not until December 17, after the majority of family members had been notified of their loved ones' deaths, that the *San Francisco Examiner– Chronicle* Sunday issue released the longest list of names of the dead—850. It was a month after the fall of Jonestown that San Franciscans could finally learn whether a neighbor, a friend, a fellow student, or a pupil had lived or died in Guyana.

What follows is a sampling of reactions—of people who appear in this book—to the deaths in Guyana.

Carl Ross

Opportunity student Carl Ross says he will never forget November 18, 1978; the only other day that comes close for him is September 11, 2001.

When he first heard the news, the faces of those he knew from the Temple flashed through his mind: Which of them had gone to Jonestown? Who had died? He prayed that Kim had survived. It wasn't until many years later, when he learned about the *Alternative Considerations* website that listed those who had died, that he realized what her fate had been.

> *I cried and prayed for them all and thanked God that my family had not fallen into that trap. . . . [T]o this day, I still don't understand it. I remember think- ing that these were all good kids and most of them came from families that cared about them, not like my crazy family. I felt that these kids were stolen from us by the devil himself and maybe [God] had not let my family go there because we were already living in hell with my parents.*[1]

267

Linda Mertle

At the time of the Jonestown tragedy, Linda Mertle was working at the rest home her father operated on Regent Street in Berkeley. The home also became the base for the Human Freedom Center that Al Mills and his wife had established to support people who wanted to leave the Temple and others escaping cults. Linda liked the job; she'd always enjoyed working with seniors in the Church. But she'd told her father, "Don't try to be nice to me." She hadn't forgiven him and her stepmother for leaving her in the Church.

Linda remembers how she first heard about the deaths in Jonestown: Everyone at the Center was gathered around the television set when local news anchor Dennis Richmond announced the story. They were all "devastated," she said. She felt as if her "world had just collapsed." Watching with them was Linda's good friend Mickey Touchette, who had also left the Church before Jonestown. Mickey's younger sister was Stephan's girlfriend Michelle. Linda and Mickey drank so much that night they felt "poisoned."

She remembers seeing Cynthia's name on one of the first lists a few days later; she left the room to vomit in the bathroom. Michelle also appeared on the earlier lists. So did Tiffany, the toddler Linda had cared for in San Francisco.

For years, Linda never slept through the night, awakened by nightmares and her own screaming. She pretended to be "normal," trying to fool herself and others, doing her job. But she couldn't forget Cynthia, and couldn't forgive herself knowing Cynthia had gone to Jonestown when Linda hadn't.

Other names on the lists haunted her too: Melanie Breidenbach, Wesley's sister, who had been her best friend; Bertha Ford, her roommate in San Francisco.

Sometime later, Linda drove to the ocean beach near Fort Cronkhite, not far from Point Richmond where she lived with her mother. She wanted to die. She thought she could make her drowning appear to be an accident. She swam far out, but in the end couldn't go through with it. She knew her death would devastate her mother, her family, her friends. She made her way back, against the current, in the dark, at about 1:00 AM. It was perhaps on that night when she first realized that the deaths in Jonestown affected the world in the way a suicide affects a loved one. She said of people like herself, and those in Guyana who survived: "Some survivors have learned to be in this life; some are still [over] there," in the other life.

Linda says about her life in the Temple, "When I think back, I loved the experience. I loved the camaraderie." She says she wouldn't change anything in her life except, of course, "the outcome at Jonestown." But she still feels ambivalence about any organized religion. When her now-adult son had as a child asked to be taken to church, Linda told him she couldn't: "I believe in humanity; I believe in the cycle of life. I believe in the universe. But I can't enter a so-called 'house of God.'"

She has her own guidelines for life: "Walk gently. Be as peaceful as you can."[2]

Ron Cabral: Silver Terrace Park, Spring 1979

Cabral left Opportunity when most of the Temple students had; when the next school year started in September 1978, he began teaching at Wilson High, where he also coached the varsity baseball team. The Wilson team practiced at Silver Terrace Park, an old San Francisco baseball field. One late afternoon on a blue-skied, windy day in the spring of 1979, Cabral was just about to start batting practice with the team when he spotted two tall men walking slowly toward him across the outfield. When they came into view, he was startled to see they were none other than Stephan and Tim. Stephan's dark hair was long now, and he wore a headband; Tim's blond hair was ruffled by the wind, and he looked pale. Cabral could hardly believe his eyes. He hadn't seen them since they had left Opportunity two years before. He had seen two photos of Tim in a *Newsweek* story and on a television report; both showed Tim identifying the bodies of his friends and family, pointing at corpses with one hand while holding a rag to his nose and mouth with the other.

Both boys looked thinner, taller, older. Though Cabral was used to seeing how quickly sixteen- and seventeen-year-olds can mature in a year or two, there was a difference in the way these boys were now men. Cabral approached them and shook their hands. He didn't really know what to say but managed to blurt out a greeting. "Glad to see you, Tim, Stephan. How's it going?" Tim seemed at a loss for words too, but Stephan said, "We happened to be in the neighborhood and thought we would drop by and say hello."

Tim had been glancing out at the pitching mound, and said, a little shyly, Cabral thought, "Hey, Ron, mind if I throw a little batting practice? I haven't even held a baseball since that last Lincoln game in 1977."

Cabral responded, "Of course. Take a bucket of balls out there and go for it." He told current players that Tim had played ball at Opportunity, and that he was going to pitch for them for a while. Stephan went up in the stands right off first base to watch his brother. None of the Wilson boys seemed to recognize Tim—or Stephan—as Jonestown survivors, but they did seem impressed as they watched Tim pitch. Cabral thought he looked a bit out of shape, and seemed not his old self at all, but he did throw twenty pitches, and got most of them over the plate. When the bucket was empty, Tim came off the mound to thank his former coach. They talked a little, about the San Francisco Giants and baseball as an entertainment business. Tim asked if Cabral might know of any semi-pro teams that needed players; Cabral gave him a name or two. Then the young men said goodbye and walked back across the outfield, disappearing onto Silver Avenue.

Ron Cabral with Stephan Jones behind him.
(Woodrow Wilson High School Yearbook, 1979).

Epilogue

Opportunity teacher **Hal Abercrombie** (social studies and karate), transferred in 1978 to Lowell High, later became a speaker on the American West and today writes music and plays piano at a restaurant in Florida.

Robert Alioto (radio interviewee) was superintendent of the San Francisco Unified School District from 1975 to 1985. In 1988, at age fifty-four, he died in a car accident.

Opportunity student **Cindy Allen** graduated from Opportunity II. She lives in the Bay Area.

Opportunity student **Monica Bagby** defected from Jonestown, was wounded, and escaped in the Cessna plane that had brought Congressman Ryan and others. She was later employed for a short time by the San Francisco Unified School District as a classroom assistant at Galileo High. Monica died in Oregon in 2009.

Opportunity student **Rory Bargeman** died in Jonestown at age eighteen, along with his sister Terri Bargeman and his mother, Dorothy Williams Macon.

John Bebelaar, the first husband of Judy Bebelaar, was a high school teacher who later became a psychotherapist for children and teenagers, known affectionately by the children as Dr. Treetop. Though diagnosed with lymphoma in 1984, he maintained an active life, working, surfing, and running until three months before his death, at age forty-nine in 1991. His memorial was held at Año Nuevo Beach, one of his favorite surf sites.

Judy Bebelaar, a cofounding teacher of Opportunity High, transferred from Opportunity II to Galileo High, and later to International Studies Academy. Her students won many national awards for their writing, including eight from Scholastic: in 2002, Scholastic honored her with a Whitehouse Women's Leadership Teacher award. Her poems have appeared in many magazines and anthologies. Her first book of poetry, *Walking Across the Pacific*, was published in 2014.

Opportunity student **Raymond Berrios** worked in the family construction company for many years and then for the San Francisco Department of

Building Inspection. Sadly, Raymond passed away before this book's publication, but he was proud to know his poem was included.

Opportunity student **Manny Blackwell** graduated from Opportunity II and became a park director with the San Francisco Department of Recreation and Parks.

Opportunity student **Marilee Bogue** died in Jonestown at age nineteen along with her husband, Cordell Neal. Her parents and siblings Tommy, Teena, and Juanita escaped from Jonestown. Today **Thom (Tommy) Bogue** is a small business owner and City Council member in Solano County, California, and will be running for mayor in the next election. He and Stephan have become friends, "having gone through the same hell."

Opportunity student **Wesley Breidenbach** died in Jonestown at age nineteen along with his wife, Avis, sister, Melanie, and mother, Lois.

Opportunity student **Dorothy Buckley** died in Jonestown at age seventeen along with her brother, Christopher, sisters Francis, Loreatha, and Odesta, and their mother, Minnie.

Opportunity teacher **Ron Cabral** transferred to Woodrow Wilson High in 1978, where he taught World History and English and coached the varsity baseball team. He became a middle school principal, retiring after thirty-five years with the school district. In 2003 he published his book *Country Joe and Me* about himself and rock-folk icon Country Joe McDonald.

Temple member and counselor **Tim Carter** survived, but his wife and child died in Jonestown. He lives in Oregon.

Opportunity student **Johnny Cobb** survived along with the other basketball team members, and returned to the San Francisco Bay Area, where he currently works in the furniture business and is writing a memoir.

Opportunity student **Cindy Cordell** died in Jonestown along with her sister Candy, both eighteen; their mother, Loretta Mae; their sister, Mabel; their brothers, James and Chris; aunts Edith Cordell and Barbara Jeanne Cordell; and five Cordell cousins, including Mark.

Opportunity teacher **Colin Covey** taught at Washington, Opportunity II, and Alamo Park High Schools. Retired from the San Francisco Unified School district, he died in 1998.

Opportunity student and school photographer **Mary Delema** graduated from Opportunity High. She is a mother and grandmother and lives and works as a nurse in Oregon.

Opportunity student **Hugh Dinneen** graduated from Opportunity II. He has been happily married for over twenty-five years and has four children. He lives in Berkeley and is involved with Little League Baseball in Albany, California.

Opportunity student **Bruce Dixon** graduated from Opportunity II. He owns a painting company in Berkeley and is an active member of the Native American community.

Opportunity teacher **Kent Dondero** left Opportunity II in early 1976.

Opportunity student **Sonje Regina Duncan** died in Jonestown at age fourteen along with her mother, Verdalla Duncan.

Opportunity student **Kevin Eddy** graduated from Opportunity II and lives in the San Francisco Bay Area.

Opportunity student **Marty Emmons's** whereabouts are unknown.

Opportunity student **Henry Flood** graduated from Opportunity II and became a professional musician.

Opportunity student **Kimberly Fye** died in Jonestown at age seventeen.

Opportunity student **Cleveland Garcia** died in Jonestown at age eighteen along with his wife, Tanya, and their child, Tiffany Latrika.

Opportunity principal **Yvonne Golden** remained at Opportunity II as principal. In 1978 the school became Alamo Park High, then, Ida B. Wells High. Golden later retired and moved back to her home town of Daytona Beach, Florida, where she ran for supervisor; she was elected mayor and died in office in 2006 at age eighty.

Opportunity student **Mondo Griffith** died in Jonestown at age eighteen along with his mother, Mary Magdalene, his father, Emmett Sr., his brother, Emmett Jr., and his two sisters, Marian Louise Griffith and Cornella Truss.

Opportunity teacher **Fong Ha** transferred to Mission High. He continues to teach Tai-Chi, both in the San Francisco Bay Area and around the world.

Opportunity teacher **Danny Hallinan** left public education in 1979, but returned to teaching in Berkeley, California. Now retired, he is the coauthor of *Take Your Kids to Europe*.

Opportunity's visiting poet **Victor Hernández Cruz** has published several books of poetry and has received many honors, including an NEA grant and a Guggenheim fellowship.

Opportunity student **Judy Houston,** age fourteen, and **Patty Houston,** age fifteen, died in Jonestown. Their grandmother, Nadyne Houston, was among those Concerned Relatives who traveled to Guyana with the congressional delegation. Their aunt, Carol Boyd, was one of the Concerned Relatives to visit Jonestown.

John Jacobs was Tim Reiterman's coauthor of *Raven: The Untold Story of the Rev. Jim Jones and His People*. Jacobs worked as a political reporter for the *San Francisco Examiner* for fifteen years, then he was political editor and a respected political columnist for the *Sacramento Bee*. He also penned an award-winning biography of Phillip Burton entitled *A Rage for Justice: The Passion and Politics of Phillip Burton*, which inspired Consumer Watchdog's annual Rage for Justice Awards. After a valiant battle with cancer, Jacobs died in 2000 at age 49. It was Jacobs, Reiterman is quoted as saying in an article about Jacobs's death in the *Los Angeles Times*, who had persuaded Stephan Jones to talk to the authors, a feat Reiterman attributed to Jacobs's remarkable "ability to connect with people." Stephan "gave many hours and days" to the two reporters, Reiterman says, and those interviews as well as others Jacobs conducted, are a valuable part of the story *Raven* tells.

Opportunity student **Ricky Johnson** died in Jonestown at age twenty.

Jim Jones [Sr.] died in Jonestown of a gunshot wound. His ashes were scattered in the Atlantic.

Opportunity student and Cobra **Jimmy Jones [Jr.]** survived and returned to San Francisco. He is married with three boys. His son, Rob, was a star performer for the St. Mary's basketball team in 2011 and 2012.

Marceline Jones, wife of Jim Jones, Sr., died in Jonestown and was buried in Richmond, Indiana, by her surviving family.

Opportunity student **Stephan Jones,** in his own words, "is being raised by his three daughters." A survivor and member of the Jonestown basketball team, he has lived in the San Francisco Bay Area since his return from Guyana. Today he runs operations for a successful office furniture business. He continues to write and speak about Jonestown and Peoples Temple.

Opportunity student **Tim Tupper Jones** survived. He has four children and works in the office furniture business in Southern California.

Opportunity teacher **Tina (Kollias) Johns,** one of the first teachers at Opportunity I, left Opportunity II in 1977 to move to Clovis, California, where she taught for many years. She later returned to San Francisco, where she volunteers at the Museum of Modern Art and serves as a national educational consultant.

Carolyn Layton died in Jonestown at age thirty-three.

Deborah Layton escaped from Jonestown. Her book, *Seductive Poison,* describes her experiences in Peoples Temple and her life in Jonestown.

Opportunity student **Lisa Lewis** died in Jonestown at age sixteen with her mother, Doris Lewis, and siblings Adrienne, Alecha, Barry, Casandra, Freddie Jr., and Karen. Her father, Freddie Lewis, now deceased, requested that he be buried with his family at Evergreen Cemetery.

Opportunity student **Cobra Debbie Liatos,** the first female to play on a junior varsity San Francisco AAA baseball team, graduated from Opportunity II. She later ran for Supervisor in San Francisco, and in 2010 for the U.S. Senate in Florida (she did not win either seat). In 2013 she ran for Public Advocate in New York City.

John Liu-Klein, Opportunity teacher and the school's head counselor, left the San Francisco Unified School District, teaching computer classes at Berkeley High and then at Heald College and in Hawaii. He moved to Southern California to be near his son Jared and Jared's wife, two grandsons, and a granddaughter. John passed away in 2016. He is much missed.

Opportunity student **Michelle DiQuattro MacClellan** graduated from Opportunity II. She is married and has a daughter, and works for a San Francisco Bay Area water agency.

Opportunity student **Dean Marcic** graduated from Opportunity II and is now a sergeant in the San Francisco Police Department. He requested that we add: "I would not be where I am today if it weren't for Opportunity turning my life around. . . . There is something to be said for patience and communication." Dean is "happily married to his lovely wife Carmen" and has two grown children, Lilia and Dean Jr.

Opportunity student **Donald Marshall** graduated from Opportunity II and became a driver for the San Francisco Municipal Transportation Agency. His current whereabouts are unknown.

Opportunity teacher **Mary McCrohan** transferred to Woodrow Wilson High and became a mainstay of the Physical Education Department. Later she taught at Washington, Mission, and Lincoln high schools. Retired, she is now an artist.

Opportunity student **Cynthia McGraw** graduated from Opportunity II and attended City College of San Francisco. She died January 4, 2013.

Opportunity student and Cobra **Cary (Maki) McLellan**, the first female to play on a varsity San Francisco AAA baseball team, graduated from Opportunity II. She works with children in Astoria, Oregon.

Opportunity student and Cobra **Teddy McMurry** died in Jonestown at age twenty along with his wife, Eileen McCann, their child, Takiya Channe McMurry, his brother Sebastian, and his sister Renee.

Opportunity student **Linda Mertle** lives in the East Bay and has worked as a truck driver for a national mail delivery service for over twenty years. Linda cares for her mother and is a proud mother herself. She has written for the San Diego State University *Alternative Considerations of Jonestown and Peoples Temple* website.

Opportunity teacher **Bob Morrow** died of cancer in the early 1980s.

Opportunity student **Christopher Newell** died in Jonestown at age seventeen along with his mother, Hazel Newell, sisters Shirley, Jennifer, and Hattie, and brother Karl.

Opportunity student **Billy Oliver** died in Jonestown at age eighteen along with his brother, Bruce Oliver, and sister-in-law, Shanda Oliver. Bruce's and Billy's parents Howard and Beverly Oliver were among the Concerned Relatives who traveled to Guyana with the congressional delegation. Howard died in Guyana, where he suffered a stroke; Beverly, one of the Concerned Relatives, died in 2002.

Opportunity founder **Marcia Perlstein** left the school in 1976 to become a full-time therapist, a career which she had begun to study in parallel to her teaching career. In 1978 she ran for the Alameda County Superintendent of Schools; though she lost, she received 82,000 votes. She eventually relocated to Washington State where she has a small psychotherapy practice in Port Townsend and Sequim.

Opportunity poet **Joyce Polk Brown** died in Jonestown at age eighteen.

After Opportunity student **Terry Preston** graduated from Opportunity II, attended San Francisco State University and U.C. Berkeley Law School. Today, married with one son, he works for Walk Sacramento, which promotes and helps develop "Walkable Communities and Communities of Walkers."

Tim Reiterman was a longtime reporter and editor for the *San Francisco Examiner* before he worked for the *Los Angeles Times,* where he helped supervise Pulitzer Prize–winning coverage of both the Los Angeles riots and the 1994 Northridge earthquake. A lecturer at the U.C. Berkeley Graduate School of Journalism for ten years, he later worked as Northern California news editor for the Associated Press (AP) and is now AP's global environmental beat team editor. His book, *Raven: The Untold Story of the Rev. Jim Jones and His People,* coauthored with John Jacobs and published by E.P. Dutton in 1982, was reissued in a paperback second edition in 2008 by Jeremy P. Tarcher/Penguin. *Raven* was recognized in 1983 with the Thomas Thompson PEN Award for nonfiction.

Opportunity student **Scott Roberts** graduated from Opportunity and became an accomplished musician. He lives in the Santa Cruz area.

Edith Roller died in Jonestown at age sixty-two.

Opportunity student **Carl Ross** graduated from Opportunity II and is the proud father of two. He became the business officer at Folsom State Prison. Carl won a "Mr. Universe" title as a bodybuilder. In 2011 he took an early retirement to start an antique business.

Opportunity student **Ronnie Ross** graduated from Opportunity II. Today he restores and sells automobiles.

Opportunity student and Cobra **Junior Siufanua** lives with his wife and two daughters in Washington State, where he has worked for his city government for over thirty years.

Opportunity student **Mark Sly** died in Jonestown at age seventeen, along with his father, Don. Mark's mother, Neva Sly, was an early defector. For his parents, Mark was "the light of our lives," his mother says. Following her escape, Neva spent several years as a volunteer counselor for children and adults who had been abused. She is now a minister who teaches healing techniques. Her writings can be found on the Jonestown Institute website, *Alternative Considerations of Jonestown and Peoples Temple.*

Eugene Smith survived and returned to live and work in the San Francisco Bay Area. He was portrayed in Leigh Fondakowski's play, *The People's Temple*, and participated in Stanley Nelson's documentary, *Jonestown: The Life and Death of Peoples Temple.*

Opportunity student **Ollie Smith,** beloved wife of **Eugene Smith,** died in Jonestown at age nineteen along with their baby, Martin Luther Smith.

John Victor (Jon Jon) Stoen died in Jonestown at age six. His mother, Grace Stoen, was among the Concerned Relatives who traveled to Guyana with the congressional delegation. She later remarried and lives in the San Francisco Bay Area.

Opportunity student **Willieater Thomas** died in Jonestown at age eighteen.

Opportunity student **Cornelius Truss** died in Jonestown at age eighteen.

Ruth Tupper died in Jonestown at age twenty-two along with her mother, Rita, and siblings Janet, Larry, and Mary.

Opportunity teacher **Norman Vogel** (social studies and assistant Cobra baseball coach) became a physical education teacher and department head at Philip and Sala Burton High. He served the San Francisco Unified School District for over thirty-seven years until he died, shortly before publication of this book.

Opportunity student **Calvin Douglas Williams** survived and returned to California. His whereabouts are unknown.

Opportunity teacher **Anna Wong** left Opportunity and became an elementary school teacher in Berkeley. An award-winning artist, she lives in the East Bay with her husband and children.

Notes

All the student poems and excerpts originally appeared in Opportunity publications *In Small Dreams* or *Fire*. All the newspaper articles written by students are from *The Natural High Express*. Both publications are in the Peoples Temple Miscellany collection, MS4126, at the California Historical Society in San Francisco. All poems by living students appear by permission of the authors.

Introduction:

[1] Laurence Urdang, ed., *The Timetables of American History* (New York: Simon & Schuster, 1996), 390.

[2] National Center for Education Statistics, Institute of Education Sciences, *Digest of Education Statistics*, Table 219.76: Population 16 through 24 years old and number of 16- to 24-year-old high school dropouts (status dropouts), by income level, labor force status, and years of school completed: 1970 through 2012, accessed December 26, 2015, https://nces.ed.gov/programs/digest/d13/tables/dt13_219.76.asp.

[3] The description of the school board meeting where a group of thirteen Nazis protested busing derives from an email from San Francisco Unified School District administrator Jim Dierke to Ron Cabral, July 29, 2009; from "Nazis, crowd, in melee at school board," Stephen Cook, *San Francisco Examiner*, January 9, 1974; and from an obituary of Yvonne Golden in the *San Francisco Chronicle* by Nanette Azimov, December 9, 2006.

Chapter 1: Peoples Temple Comes to Opportunity

Information about Tim Carter's participation in and subsequent protest of the Vietnam War derives from hearing him speak at a panel discussion of former Temple members and Jonestown survivors. Although Carter doesn't remember much about his time at Opportunity, we remember him and his clipboard.

[1] California Historical Society Library, MS4124, Box 2, Folder 1, The People's Forum 2, page 1, September, 1976.

Chapter 2: Of Poetry and Baseball

Information about Dean Marcic's experience in other schools derives from a phone interview with Dean conducted by Judy Bebelaar, May 27, 2009.

Chapter 3: In Small Dreams

Information regarding Carl and Ronnie's views of the other Temple students, Carl's relationship with Kimberly Fye, and Ronnie's request that Jones take off his glasses derive from phone interviews with Carl Ross and Ronnie Ross conducted by Judy Bebelaar, August 23, 2009.

[1] John G. Neihardt, *Black Elk Speaks: Being the Life Story of a Holy Man of the Oglala Sioux* (Lincoln: University of Nebraska Press, 1988), 67.

[2] *Ibid.*, 76.

[3] *Ibid.*, 271.

[4] *Ibid.*, 273.

Chapter 4: Freedom of Expression

Information about the field trip derives from two interviews: Norman Vogel, in discussion with Judy Bebelaar and Ron Cabral, Berkeley, CA, October 27, 2009; and Tina Kollias and Mary McCrohan, in discussion with Judy Bebelaar and Ron Cabral, Oakland, CA, February 21, 2009.

[1] Edith Roller journals, September 15 and 17, 1976, transcribed from her handwritten and typed journal notes by Don Beck, The Jonestown Institute, accessed January 24,

2014, http://jonestown.sdsu.edu/?page_id=35682; and Tim Reiterman with John Jacobs, *Raven: The Untold Story of the Rev. Jim Jones and His People* (New York: E. P. Dutton, 1982), 166.

[2] Roller journals, September 17, 1976, http://jonestown.sdsu.edu/?page_id=35682.

[3] "A Testimonial for Founder of Peoples Temple" September 6, 1976, *San Francisco Chronicle*; Reiterman and Jacobs, *Raven*, 306; and "Why We Marched," *Peoples Forum*, 1st October issue, 1976. California Historical Society, Peoples Temple ephemera and publications, MS4124, Box 2, Folder 1.

[4] Cabral did many radio shows with Opportunity students from his Radio Production class; Bebelaar did a few poetry radio shows with her Creative Writing students. As all the tapes of those shows have since been destroyed, the radio transcripts in this book are reconstructed from memory. In her question posed to Superintendent Robert Alioto, Debbie Liatos likely referenced this article: "Education: Here Come the Mr. Fixits," *Time*, July 28, 1975.

Chapter 5: The Cobras Practice and the Temple Pays a Visit

Information about Linda Mertle derives from an interview with her conducted by Judy Bebelaar, Berkeley, CA, February 28, 2009.

[1] "Q735 Transcript," prepared by Gay Marie Powell-Cabral, The Jonestown Institute, accessed January 24, 2014, http://jonestown.sdsu.edu/?page_id=27568; and Edith Roller, journal entry, October 20, 1976, transcribed from her handwritten and typed journal notes by Don Beck, accessed January 24, 2014, http://jonestown.sdsu.edu/?page_id=35683.

[2] The details of the entertainment derive both from memory and from what the authors later learned about the young Jonestown performers from Stephan Jones.

[3] Ron Cabral, California Historical Society Peoples Temple files MS3800/16.

Chapter 6: The Cobras Play

Information about Michelle DiQuattro and Mark Sly derives from a phone conversation with Michelle conducted by Judy Bebelaar, February 27, 2009.

[1] Leo Pierini, "Opportunity Knocks, AAA Officials Listen," *San Francisco Progress*, March 23, 1977.

Chapter 7: More Departures

Dorothy Buckley's article, "Message from Dorothy," and Cindy Cordell's article, "What Is Peoples Temple?" first appeared in the May–June 1977 issue of *The Natural High Express*.

[1] Mareta Siufanua, note to Judy Bebelaar, dated approximately May 1977.

Chapter 8: Temblors

Information about the 1977–78 school year at Opportunity derives in part from an interview with students Cindy Allen, Bruce Dixon, Cary McClellan, Cynthia McGraw, and Hugh Dinneen conducted by Judy Bebelaar and Ron Cabral, September 1, 2007.

Information about Lisa Lewis, Sonje Regina Duncan, and Manny Blackwell derives in part from conversations and communications with Danny Hallinan in discussion with Judy Bebelaar, January 30, 2009, and February 16, 2009; and emails to Judy Bebelaar, February 4, 2009, and February 6, 2009.

[1] Faaluga "Junior" Siufanua, personal letter, June 14, 1977.

[2] George Draper, "Strange S.F. Break-In at Magazine," *San Francisco Chronicle*, June 18, 1977.

[3] Raul Ramirez, "Magazine Attacks Peoples Temple," *San Francisco Sunday Examiner-Chronicle Magazine*, July 17, 1977.

[4] *Ibid.*

[5] Marshall Kilduff and Phil Tracy, "Inside Peoples Temple," *New West*, August 1, 1977.

[6] *Ibid.*

[7] *Ibid.*

[8] "Mayor Won't Investigate Rev. Jones," *San Francisco Chronicle*, July 27, 1977.

[9] Jeannie Mills, *Six Years with God: Life Inside Rev. Jim Jones's Peoples Temple* (New York: A. & W. Publishers, 1979), 68.

[10] E. Cahill Maloney, "Temple dominated city school," *San Francisco Progress*, August 3, 1977. Cahill Maloney interviewed Ron Cabral by phone for this article. Soon after this Ron also met with Dr. Cleveland of the San Francisco Unified School District in early August 1977.

[11] Marshall Kilduff, "A Peoples Temple 'Bloc' at S. F. School," *San Francisco Chronicle*, August 4, 1977.

[12] Tim Reiterman and Don Canter, "Jones quits housing board: Churchman sends message from Guyana," *San Francisco Examiner*, August 4, 1977.

[13] Tim Reiterman and Nancy Dooley, "Rev. Jones: The Power Broker," *San Francisco Examiner*, August 7, 1977.

[14] Marshall Kilduff, "Peoples Temple—Families Complain," *San Francisco Chronicle*, August 11, 1977.

[15] Marshall Kilduff, "Rev. Jones and Disciples May Be Leaving," *San Francisco Chronicle*, August 12, 1977. Kenneth L. Woodward, Marc Whitaker, and Stephan Gayle, "Temple Trouble," *Newsweek*, August 15, 1977.

[16] Tim Reiterman and Nancy Dooley, "The temple—a nightmare world," *San Francisco Examiner*, August 14, 1977.

[17] Kenneth L. Woodward, Marc Whitaker, and Stephan Gayle, "Temple Trouble," *Newsweek*, August 15, 1977.

[18] Herb Caen, "The Morning Line," *San Francisco Chronicle*, August 18, 1977.

[19] "Jones and Peoples Temple Under Investigation," *San Francisco Chronicle Sunday Magazine*, August 28, 1977.

[20] Marshall Kilduff, "$1.1 Million Suit Against Rev. Jones," *San Francisco Chronicle*, August 31, 1977.

[21] "Entry to Guyana," The Jonestown Institute, accessed January 25, 2014, http://jonestown.sdsu.edu/?page_id=35655.

[22] "Peoples Temple Radio Codebook," The Jonestown Institute, accessed January 25, 2014, http://jonestown.sdsu.edu/?page_id=13221.

Chapter 9: Behind the Scenes

[1] John R. Hall, *Gone from the Promised Land: Jonestown in American Cultural History*. 2nd ed. (Piscataway, NJ: Transaction Publishers, 2004), 132–133.

[2] Reiterman and Jacobs, 246.

[3] Deborah Layton, *Seductive Poison: A Jonestown Survivor's Story of Life and Death in the Peoples Temple* (New York: Doubleday, 1998), 137.

[4] Reiterman and Jacobs, 248.

[5] "Housing in Jonestown," The Jonestown Institute, accessed January 25, 2014, http://jonestown.sdsu.edu/?page_id=35658.

[6] Reiterman and Jacobs, 276.

[7] Stephan Jones, email to Judy Bebelaar, August 5, 2011.

[8] "Entry to Guyana," The Jonestown Institute, accessed January 25, 2014, http://jonestown.sdsu.edu/?page_id=35655.

[9] Reiterman and Jacobs, 52-57.

[10] Reiterman and Jacobs, 52-54, 71-72.

[11] Catherine Wessinger, *How the Millennium Comes Violently: From Jonestown to Heaven's Gate* (New York: Seven Bridges Press, 2000), 38.

[12] Wessinger, 34; and Reiterman and Jacobs, 98.

[13] Reiterman and Jacobs, 164.

[14] Marcia Smith, *Jonestown: The Life and Death of Peoples Temple*, directed by Stanley Nelson (New York: Firelight Media, 2006).

[15] Reiterman and Jacobs, 47.

[16] *Ibid.*

[17] Lawrence Wright, "Orphans of Jonestown," *New Yorker*, 1993, 71-72.

[18] *Ibid.*

[19] Reiterman and Jacobs, 64.

[20] Stephan Jones, "Like Father, Like Son," The Jonestown Institute, accessed January 25, 2014, http://jonestown.sdsu.edu/?page_id=17018.

[21] *Ibid.*

[22] Reiterman and Jacobs, 122–124.

[23] Jones, "Like Father, Like Son," http://jonestown.sdsu.edu/?page_id=17018.

[24] *Ibid.*

[25] Wright, 75.

[26] Jones, "Like Father, Like Son," http://jonestown.sdsu.edu/?page_id=17018.

[27] California Historical Society, Peoples Temple Collection, Temple interview of Dierdre Renee McMurry, MS3801, box 12, folder 374.

[28] Julia Scheeres, *A Thousand Lives: The Untold Story of Hope, Deception, and Survival at Jonestown* (New York: Free Press, 2011), 61–66; and "Entry to Guyana," http://jonestown.sdsu.edu/?page_id=35655.

[29] Scheeres, 71–72.

[30] *Ibid.*, 73, 107; and "Entry to Guyana," http://jonestown.sdsu.edu/?page_id=35655.

[31] Neva Sly-Hargrave, phone conversation with Judy Bebelaar, March 9, 2010.

[32] Neva Sly-Hargrave, "A Story of Deprogramming," The Jonestown Institute, accessed March 23, 2016, http://jonestown.sdsu.edu/?page_id=17012; and Sly-Hargrave, phone conversation, March 9, 2010.

[33] Linda Mertle, interview with Judy Bebelaar, Berkeley, CA, February 28, 2009, and phone conversation, July 11, 2011.

[34] Marshall Kilduff and Phil Tracy, "Inside Peoples Temple," *New West*, August 1, 1977.

[35] Rebecca Moore, *A Sympathetic History of Jonestown: The Moore Family Involvement in Peoples Temple*. Studies in Religion and Society, vol. 14 (Lewiston, NY: Edwin Mellen Press, 1985), 13.

[36] Mertle interview, February 28, 2009, and phone conversation, July 11, 2011.

[37] Emmanuel Blackwell, interview with Judy Bebelaar and Ron Cabral, San Francisco, CA, September 2007, and email to Judy Bebelaar, June 23, 2013.

[38] Carl Ross and Ronnie Ross, phone conversation with Judy Bebelaar, August 23, 2009.

Chapter 10: Entering the Jungle

[1] Dmitri Allicock, "Some of the Botanical Wonders of Guyana," St. Stanislaus College, accessed March 23, 2016, http://www.st-stanislaus-gy.com/History/Botanical-Wonders-of-Guyana.pdf.

[2] Eugene Smith, interview with Judy Bebelaar, Oakland, CA, September, 2005; and email to Judy Bebelaar, November 2005.

3 "Entry to Guyana," http://jonestown.sdsu.edu/?page_id=35655.

4 *Ibid.*; Rebecca Moore, The Jonestown Institute, "The Demographics of Jonestown," accessed January 19, 2014, http://jonestown.sdsu.edu/?page_id=35666; and Moore, "Jonestown Memorial List," http://jonestown.sdsu.edu/?page_id=690.

5 Angela Miller, senior deputy general counsel, San Francisco Unified School District, letter dated October 15, 2009. The letter cited the Family Education Rights and Privacy Act, as well as the California Public Records Act. Ms. Miller wrote, "Regrettably, the district will not be able to assist you with your research."

6 Layton, 138–139.

7 Smith interview, September, 2005; and email November 2005.

8 *Ibid.*

9 Layton, 138.

10 Michael Touchette, email to Ron Cabral, November 2, 2011.

11 Smith email, November 2005.

12 Layton, 149–150.

13 Eugene Smith, "Moments in Time," The Jonestown Institute, accessed January 19, 2014, http://jonestown.sdsu.edu/?page_id=33207.

14 "Entry to Guyana," http://jonestown.sdsu.edu/?page_id=35655,

15 Wright, 67.

16 Stephan Jones, interview with Judy Bebelaar, San Rafael, CA, January 8, 2015.

17 Wright, 67-68.

18 Denise Stephenson, *Dear People: Remembering Jonestown* (Berkeley, CA: Heyday Books, 2005), 79.

19 Wright, 68-69.

20 Jones interview, January 8, 2015.

21 Wright, 69.

22 Jones interview, January 8, 2015.

23 "Entry to Guyana," http://jonestown.sdsu.edu/?page_id=35655.

24 Wright, 69.

25 *Ibid.*, 78.

26 *Ibid.*, 68.

27 *Ibid.*

28 *Ibid.*, 69.

29 Theodore Taylor (1921-2006), letter to Cornelius Truss and Vance White, dated approximately October 1976.

30 Stephan Jones, "Reunion," The Jonestown Institute, accessed March 10, 2015, http://jonestown.sdsu.edu/?page_id=40173.

31 "Entry to Guyana," http://jonestown.sdsu.edu/?page_id=35655.

32 *Ibid.*

33 "All Residents in Jonestown, ABC Sort — with Residence," The Jonestown Institute, accessed June 23, 2016, http://jonestown.sdsu.edu/wp-content/uploads/2013/10/03b-ResidentsABCRes.pdf.

34 Letter, January 20, 1978, Candace Cordell, MS 3801, California Historical Society, Manuscript Collection.

Chapter 11: Children of Paradise

1 Reiterman and Jacobs, 277.

2 Roller Journals, February 5, 1978, The Jonestown Institute, accessed January 25, 2014, http://jonestown.sdsu.edu/?page_id=35693.

3 "Housing in Jonestown," The Jonestown Institute, accessed January 25, 2014, http://jonestown.sdsu.edu/?page_id=35658.

[4] Reiterman and Jacobs, 186, 347.

[5] "Entry to Guyana," The Jonestown Institute, http://jonestown.sdsu.edu/?page_id=35655.

[6] Deborah Layton, text message to Judy Bebelaar, May 2, 2017.

[7] Reiterman and Jacobs, 278–279.

[8] "Entry to Guyana," http://jonestown.sdsu.edu/?page_id=35655.

[9] Wright, 75.

[10] Stephan Jones, interview with George Stroumboulopoulos, on *The Hour*, Canadian Broadcasting Company, July 11, 2008.

[11] Don Beck, "Rallies," The Jonestown Institute, accessed January 22, 2014, http://jonestown.sdsu.edu/?page_id=35921.

[12] Jordan Vilchez emails to Judy Bebelaar, March 25 and 26, 2013; and Don Beck, "Rallies," The Jonestown Institute, accessed January 22, 2014, http://jonestown.sdsu.edu/?page_id=35921.

[13] Layton, 149.

[14] "Entry to Guyana," http://jonestown.sdsu.edu/?page_id=35655.

[15] *Ibid.*

[16] Reiterman and Jacobs, 389.

[17] Linda Mertle, interview with Judy Bebelaar, Berkeley, CA, February 28, 2009, and phone conversation, July 11, 2011.

[18] "Entry to Guyana," http://jonestown.sdsu.edu/?page_id=35655.

[19] *Ibid.*

[20] *Ibid.*

[21] *Ibid.*

[22] *Ibid.*

[23] California Historical Society, Peoples Temple Collection, Temple interview of Dierdre Renee McMurry, MS 3801, box 12, folder 374.

[24] "Entry to Guyana," http://jonestown.sdsu.edu/?page_id=35655.

[25] *Ibid.*

[26] *Ibid.*

[27] *Ibid.*; and Vernon Gosney, "Remembering Monica," The Jonestown Institute, accessed July 4, 2016, http://jonestown.sdsu.edu/?page_id=40193.

[28] Reiterman and Jacobs, 473.

[29] Roller journals, January 29, 1978, http://jonestown.sdsu.edu/?page_id=35692.

[30] Judy Houston, letter to her mother, September 19, 1977, FBI Collection of Peoples Temple Papers, MS 3801, California Historical Society.

[31] Roller journals, January 29, 1978, http://jonestown.sdsu.edu/?page_id=35692.

[32] Typed report about Jonestown school and proposed changes to get Guyanese accreditation, by Edith Roller, circa February 1978, MS 3800, California Historical Society.

[33] Roller Journals, February 1 and February 15, 1978, http://jonestown.sdsu.edu/?page_id=35693.

[34] Reiterman and Jacobs, 361–363.

[35] Wright, 76.

[36] Reiterman and Jacobs, 364.

[37] Stephan Jones, interview with Judy Bebelaar, San Rafael, CA, January 8, 2015.

[38] Reiterman and Jacobs, 365–367.

[39] Jones interview, January 8, 2015.

[40] Reiterman and Jacobs, 365–367.

[41] *Ibid.*

[42] Stephan Jones, email to Judy Bebelaar, October 19, 2008.

[43] Michael Touchette, email to Ron Cabral, November 2, 2011.

[44] Reiterman and Jacobs, 395.

[45] Layton, 158.

[46] Reiterman and Jacobs, 394.

[47] Roller journals, April 20, 1978, http://jonestown.sdsu.edu/?page_id=35695.

[48] Reiterman and Jacobs, 395.

[49] Roller journals, March 7, 1978, http://jonestown.sdsu.edu/?page_id=35694.

[50] *Ibid.*

[51] *Ibid.*, March 4, 1978.

[52] Reiterman and Jacobs, 449.

[53] Scheeres, 175.

[54] Roller journals, March 10, 1978, http://jonestown.sdsu.edu/?page_id=35694.

[55] *Ibid.*, March 14, 1978.

Chapter 12: "Precious Acts of Treason"

[1] Layton, 151.

[2] *Ibid.*

[3] Wright, 78.

[4] Reiterman and Jacobs, 402; and Stephan Jones, email to Judy Bebelaar, March 18, 2017.

[5] Jones email, March 18, 2017.

[6] "Edith Roller Journals: Transcribed," June 18, 1978, accessed January 25, 2014, http://jonestown.sdsu.edu/?page_id=35697.

[7] Stephan Jones, interview with Judy Bebelaar, San Rafael, CA, June 18, 2015.

[8] Layton, 182; and Jones interview, June 18, 2015.

[9] Roller journals, June 10, 1978, http://jonestown.sdsu.edu/?page_id=35697; and "Residences in Jonestown – ABC Sort," The Jonestown Institute, accessed March 10, 2017, http://jonestown.sdsu.edu/wp-content/uploads/2013/10/03c-ResidencesABC.pdf

[10] Roller journals, March 14, 1978, http://jonestown.sdsu.edu/?page_id=35694

[11] Reiterman and Jacobs, 450; Ricky Johnson, letter to Jim Jones, circa October 1978, FBI Collection of Peoples Temple Papers, MS 3801, Box 28, folder 223, California Historical Society; and "Q265 Transcript," The Jonestown Institute, accessed January 20, 2014, http://jonestown.sdsu.edu/?page_id=27400.

[12] "Q380 Transcript," October 14, 1978, prepared by Vicki Perry, The Jonestown Institute, accessed January 20, 2014, http://jonestown.sdsu.edu/?page_id=27437.

[13] *Ibid.*; and "Q380 Summary," prepared by Fielding M. McGehee III, The Jonestown Institute, accessed, March 10, 2017, http://jonestown.sdsu.edu/?page_id=28143.

[14] "Q265 Transcript," October 17, 1978, prepared by Vicki Perry, The Jonestown Institute, accessed January 20, 2014, http://jonestown.sdsu.edu/?page_id=27400.

[15] Ricky Johnson, letter to Jim Jones, circa October 1978, FBI Collection of Peoples Temple Papers, MS 3801, Box 28, folder 223, California Historical Society.

[16] Scheeres, 76; and Thom Bogue, email to Judy Bebelaar, August 11, 2016.

[17] Scheeres, 108-109; and Bogue email.

[18] Scheeres, 112-113; and Bogue email.

[19] Wright, 80.

[20] Stephan Jones, "Baby Toes," The Jonestown Institute, accessed March 10, 2017, http://jonestown.sdsu.edu/?page_id=34323.

[21] Wright, 80.

[22] *Ibid.*, 80-81.

[23] Jones, "Baby Toes," http://jonestown.sdsu.edu/?page_id=34323.

[24] Roller journals, March 17, 1978, http://jonestown.sdsu.edu/?page_id=35694; Roller journals, June 6, 1978, http://jonestown.sdsu.edu/?page_id=35697; and Stephan Jones, interview with Judy Bebelaar, San Rafael, CA, January 8, 2015.

[25] Jones interview, January 8, 2015.

[26] Roller journals, March 17, 1978, http://jonestown.sdsu.edu/?page_id=35694; and Roller journals, June 6, 1978, http://jonestown.sdsu.edu/?page_id=35697.

[27] Stephan Jones, emails to Judy Bebelaar, July 14 and 17, 2010.

[28] Eugene Smith, "Moments in Time," The Jonestown Institute, accessed January 19, 2014, http://jonestown.sdsu.edu/?page_id=33207.

[29] Roller journals, June 18, 1978, http://jonestown.sdsu.edu/?page_id=35697.

[30] Layton, 216.

[31] Jones interview, January 8, 2015.

[32] Roller journals, June 6 and 16, 1978. http://jonestown.sdsu.edu/?page_id=35697.

[33] Roller letter to Jim Jones 9/9/78, RYMUR 89-4286-1681 B-2, The Jonestown Institute, accessed January 25, 2015, http://jonestown.sdsu.edu/wp-content/uploads/2013/10/24.pdf.

[34] Michael Bellefountaine, "Christine Miller: A Voice of Independence," The Jonestown Institute, accessed January 20, 2014, http://jonestown.sdsu.edu/?page_id=32381.

[35] Stephan Jones, "Ruth's Teeth," The Jonestown Institute, accessed January 20, 2014, http://jonestown.sdsu.edu/?page_id=31395.

[36] Reiterman and Jacobs, 453; and Layton interview with Judy Bebelaar, March 8, 2017.

[37] Wright, 78.

[38] Wright, 78, 80; and Layton interview, March 8, 2017.

[39] Layton interview, March 8, 2017.

[40] Wright, 78.

[41] Wright, 80.

[42] Stephan Jones, email to Judy Bebelaar, March 3, 2010.

[43] Wright, 80.

[44] Reiterman and Jacobs, 454.

[45] Reiterman and Jacobs, 455-456.

[46] Erik H. Erikson, "Youth: Fidelity and Diversity," *Daedalus* 91, no. 1 (1963), 5–27.

[47] Reiterman and Jacobs, 456.

Chapter 13: The Unraveling

The phrase "Things Fall Apart" derives from William Butler Yeats's poem "The Second Coming."

[1] Reiterman and Jacobs, 449.

[2] Fielding McGehee III, "What Are White Nights? How Many of Them Were There?," The Jonestown Institute, accessed January 19, 2014, http://jonestown.sdsu.edu/?page_id=35371.

[3] Reiterman and Jacobs, 294.

[4] *Ibid.*, 294-295.

[5] *Ibid.*, 390-391.

[6] McGehee, http://jonestown.sdsu.edu/?page_id=35371

[7] Reiterman and Jacobs, 294-296.

[8] "Edith Roller Journals: Transcribed," February 17, 1978, The Jonestown Institute, accessed January 19, 2014, http://jonestown.sdsu.edu/?page_id=35693.

[9] Reiterman and Jacobs, 391.

[10] Concerned Relatives [Jim Cobb, Jr., Terri Cobb, Steven Katsaris, Elmer and Deanna Mertle, Howard and Beverly Oliver, Wayne Pietela, Neva Sly, Grace and Tim Stoen, Mickey Touchette, et al.], "Accusation of Human Rights Violations by Rev. James Warren Jones Against Our Children and Relatives at the Peoples Temple Jungle Encampment in Guyana, South America," The Jonestown Institute, accessed January 20, 2014, http://jonestown.sdsu.edu/?page_id=13081.

[11] Layton, 178-181.

[12] Roller journal, April 12, 1978, The Jonestown Institute, accessed January 20, 2014, http://jonestown.sdsu.edu/?page_id=35695.

[13] Layton, 178-181.

[14] Roller journal, April 12, 1978, http://jonestown.sdsu.edu/?page_id=35695.

[15] *Ibid.*, April 13, 1978.

[16] Stephan Jones, email to Judy Bebelaar, August 11, 2011.

[17] Layton, 182.

[18] Layton, 213-268. The statement Deborah Layton signed at the embassy is on page 236.

[19] *Ibid.*, 208.

[20] *Ibid.*

[21] Roller journal, May 13, 1978, http://jonestown.sdsu.edu/?page_id=35696.

[22] *Ibid.*, May 14, 1978.

[23] *Ibid.*, May 15, 1978.

[24] *Ibid.*, May 27, 1978.

[25] Stephan Jones, interview with Judy Bebelaar, San Rafael, CA, January 8, 2015.

[26] Stephan Jones, "Like Father, Like Son," The Jonestown Institute, accessed January 25, 2014, http://jonestown.sdsu.edu/?page_id=17018.

[27] Wright, 77.

[28] Stephan Jones, email to Judy Bebelaar, March 3, 2010.

[29] Reiterman and Jacobs, 448.

[30] Stephan Jones, email to Ron Cabral and Fielding M. McGehee III, April 4, 2009.

Chapter 14: The Last Days

[1] Stephan Jones, email to Judy Bebelaar, March 3, 2010.

[2] "Q352 Transcript," FBI Tape Q352, prepared by Fielding M. McGehee III, The Jonestown Institute, accessed January 26, 2017, http://jonestown.sdsu.edu/?page_id=27428.

[3] "Q400 Transcript," FBI Tape Q400, prepared by Fielding M. McGehee III, The Jonestown Institute, http://jonestown.sdsu.edu/?page_id=27444.

[4] "Q170 Transcript," FBI Tape Q170, prepared by Katherine Hill, The Jonestown Institute, http://jonestown.sdsu.edu/?page_id=27353.

[5] Reiterman and Jacobs, 468.

[6] "Q219 Transcript," FBI Tape Q219, prepared by Fielding M. McGehee III, The Jonestown Institute, http://jonestown.sdsu.edu/?page_id=27381.

[7] "Q161 Transcript," FBI Tape Q161, prepared by Fielding M. McGehee III, The Jonestown Institute, http://jonestown.sdsu.edu/?page_id=27349.

[8] Tim Reiterman, "Peoples Temple and a father's grief," *San Francisco Examiner*, November 13, 1977.

[9] "The Assassination of Representative Leo J. Ryan and the Jonestown, Guyana, Tragedy: Report of a Staff Investigative Group to the Committee on Foreign Affairs, U.S.

House of Representatives," May 15, 1979, 1–2.

[10] Reiterman and Jacobs, 470.

[11] Eugene Smith, interview with Judy Bebelaar, September 2005.

[12] Wright, 81.

[13] "Q175 Transcript," FBI Tape Q175, prepared by Fielding McGehee III, The Jonestown Institute, http://jonestown.sdsu.edu/?page_id=27356.

[14] *Ibid.*

[15] "Jonestown Petition to Block Rep. Ryan," RYMUR 89-4286-571, The Jonestown Institute, accessed January 31, 2017, http://jonestown.sdsu.edu/?page_id=13929.

[16] Scheeres, 185-187.

[17] Vernon Gosney, "Remembering Monica," The Jonestown Institute, accessed January 31, 2017, http://jonestown.sdsu.edu/?page_id=40193..

[18] Reiterman and Jacobs, 474.

[19] Gary Smith, "Escape from Jonestown: How Basketball Gave Life to a Son and Grandson of the Infamous Cult Leader Jim Jones," *SI.com Magazine*, December 24, 2007, accessed January 21, 2014, http://sportsillustrated.cnn.com/2007/magazine/12/24/jonestown1231/index.html.

[20] Stephan Jones, "Baby Toes," The Jonestown Institute, accessed March 10, 2017, http://jonestown.sdsu.edu/?page_id=34323.

[21] Stephan Jones, "Death's Night," The Jonestown Institute, accessed January 25, 2014, http://jonestown.sdsu.edu/?page_id=40172.

[22] Reiterman and Jacobs, 474-75.

[23] "Q313 Transcript," FBI Tape Q313, The Jonestown Institute, accessed January 25, 2017, http://jonestown.sdsu.

edu/?page_id=27417; Tim Reiterman, "Flight to Jonestown: 'relatives' futile ordeal," *San Francisco Sunday Examiner and Chronicle*, A14, November 26, 1978, accessed January 20, 2017, https://stevenwarran.blogspot.com/2013/04/tim-reiterman.html; and Reiterman and Jacobs, 480.

[24] Reiterman and Jacobs, 479-81.

[25] Tim Reiterman, "Ryan, at People's Temple, learns Jones is 'very ill,'" *San Francisco Examiner*, 26, November 16, 1978, accessed January 20, 2017, https://stevenwarran.blogspot.com/2013/04/tim-reiterman.html.

[26] Smith, http://sportsillustrated.cnn.com/2007/magazine/12/24/jonestown1231/index.html.

[27] Stephan Jones, email to Ron Cabral and Fielding M. McGehee III, April 4, 2009.

[28] Ron Javers, "People's Temple Shuts Door on U.S. Visitors," *San Francisco Chronicle*, November 16, 1978, and "Angry Meeting in Guyana," November 17, 1978, *San Francisco Chronicle*, accessed January 20, 2017, https://stevenwarran.blogspot.com/2013/04/2-ron-javers-sec-166.html.

[29] Jones, "Death's Night," http://jonestown.sdsu.edu/?page_id=40172; and Reiterman, "Flight to Jonestown," https://stevenwarran.blogspot.com/2013/04/tim-reiterman.html.

[30] Ron Javers, "People's Temple Mission Gets Through," *San Francisco Chronicle*, November 16, 1978; and Javers, "Angry Meeting in Guyana," https://stevenwarran.blogspot.com/2013/04/2-ron-javers-sec-166.html.

[31] Charles A. Krause with Laurence M. Stern and Richard Harwood, *Guyana Massacre: The Eyewitness Account* (New York: Berkeley Publishing Corporation, 1978), 38-41.

[32] *Ibid.*, 44-45.

[33] "Q048 Transcript," FBI Tape Q048, prepared by Fielding M. McGehee III, The

Jonestown Institute, accessed February 3, 2017, http://jonestown.sdsu.edu/?page_id=27295.

34 Krause, Stern, and Harwood, 46-48; Marshall Kilduff and Ron Javers, *The Suicide Cult: The Inside Story of the Peoples Temple Sect and the Massacre in Guyana* (New York: Bantam Doubleday Dell Publishing Group, 1978), 163; and Stephan Jones, email to Judy Bebelaar, March 18, 2017.

35 Ron Javers, "How Jones Talked Before Tragedy," *San Francisco Chronicle*, November 20, 1978, accessed January 20, 2017, https://stevenwarran.blogspot.com/2013/04/2-ron-javers-sec-166.html.

36 Jones, "Death's Night," http://jonestown.sdsu.edu/?page_id=40172.

37 Krause, Stern, and Harwood, 49-50.

38 Reiterman and Jacobs, 503; and Gosney, http://jonestown.sdsu.edu/?page_id=40193.

39 Reiterman, "Flight to Jonestown," https://stevenwarran.blogspot.com/2013/04/tim-reiterman.html

40 Krause, Stern, and Harwood, 50-51.

Chapter 15: The Last Day

1 Krause, Stern, and Harwood, 65-66.

2 Tim Reiterman, "The cruel collapse of Jim Jones and his dream," *San Francisco Sunday Examiner and Chronicle*, November 21, 1978, accessed January 20, 2017, https://stevenwarran.blogspot.com/2013/04/tim-reiterman.html.

3 Krause, Stern, and Harwood, 66.

4 *Ibid.*, 66-67.

5 *Ibid.*, 66.

6 Reiterman and Jacobs, 507.

7 Krause, Stern, and Harwood, 66-68; Tim Reiterman, "The cruel collapse," https://stevenwarran.blogspot.com/2013/04/tim-reiterman.html; and Kilduff and Javers, *The Suicide Cult*, 158.

8 Reiterman and Jacobs, 510.

9 *Ibid.*, 511.

10 Krause, Stern, and Harwood, 70.

11 Kilduff and Javers, 161-162.

12 *Ibid.*, 163-65.

13 Krause, Stern, and Harwood, 71-73.

14 *Ibid.*

15 Reiterman and Jacobs, 515-18.

16 Vernon Gosney, "Remembering Monica," The Jonestown Institute, http://jonestown.sdsu.edu/?page_id=40193.

17 Reiterman and Jacobs, 515-17, 567.

18 Krause, Stern, and Harwood, 72; and Kilduff and Javers, 168.

19 Krause, Stern, and Harwood, 72-73.

20 Gosney, http://jonestown.sdsu.edu/?page_id=40193.

21 Reiterman and Jacobs, 520-521.

22 Krause, Stern, and Harwood, 81, 85.

23 Krause, Stern, and Harwood, 88-89; and Gosney, http://jonestown.sdsu.edu/?page_id=40193.

24 Kilduff and Javers, 169-174; and Gosney, http://jonestown.sdsu.edu/?page_id=40193.

25 Kilduff and Javers, 173-76.

26 RYMUR 89-4286-1681 B-2, The Jonestown Institute, accessed January 25, 2015, http://jonestown.sdsu.edu/wp-content/uploads/2013/10/24.pdf.

27 Stephan Jones, "Death's Night," The Jonestown Institute, accessed January 25, 2014, http://jonestown.sdsu.edu/?page_id=40172.

[28] Reiterman and Jacobs, 522.

[29] Wright, 82-83.

[30] Jones, "Death's Night," http://jonestown. sdsu.edu/?page_id=40172; and Wright, 83.

[31] Jones, "Death's Night," http://jonestown. sdsu.edu/?page_id=40172.

[32] Reiterman and Jacobs, 546-548.

Chapter 16: The Last White Night

The poems in this chapter, by Dorothy Buckley, Willie Thomas, Joyce Polk, and Mondo Griffith, originally appeared in Opportunity II High's publication of *In Small Dreams*, 1976.

[1] Reiterman and Jacobs, 555.

[2] "Q042 Transcript," prepared by Fielding McGehee III, The Jonestown Institute, of FBI Tape Number Q042, "The Death Tape," accessed January 22, 2014, http:// jonestown.sdsu.edu/?page_id=29079. The majority of the transcript provided in this chapter derives from Fielding McGehee's transcript, with a few alterations based on author interpretation of the audio itself (https://archive.org/details/ptc1978-11-18. flac16). See also "The 'Death Tape,'" http:// jonestown.sdsu.edu/?page_id=29084, for alternate transcripts and related articles.

[3] *Ibid.*

[4] Reiterman and Jacobs, 559.

[5] Scheeres, 229.

[6] "Q042 Transcript," http://jonestown.sdsu. edu/?page_id=29079.

[7] Wright, 88-89.

[8] Wright, 88; and Stephan Jones, interview with Judy Bebelaar, San Rafael, CA, January 8, 2015.

[9] Reiterman and Jacobs, 562.

[10] "Q042 Transcript," http://jonestown.sdsu. edu/?page_id=29079.

[11] Michael Bellefountaine, "Christine Miller: A Voice of Independence," The Jonestown Institute, accessed January 22, 2014, http:// jonestown.sdsu.edu/?page_id=32381.

Chapter 17: Aftermath

[1] Fielding McGehee III, "How Many People Died on November 18?," The Jonestown Institute, http://jonestown.sdsu.edu/?page_ id=35368.

[2] In Dr. Mootoo's sworn statement at the inquest he considered Jones's death to be consistent with suicide "from a right handed person." He felt Ann Moore's injuries were so extensive, made from a high-velocity weapon, they "could not have been self inflicted, she was murdered." Dr. Cyril Leslie Mootoo, "Guyana Inquest (Text)," prepared by Rikke Wittendorf, The Jonestown Institute, accessed January 24, 2014, http:// jonestown.sdsu.edu/?page_id=13675.

Yet the inquest jury found Ann Moore to have committed suicide. "Guyana Inquest," http://jonestown.sdsu.edu/?page_id=13671.

There were seven supposedly more complete autopsies later performed in the United States by the Armed Forces of Pathology; of these it was determined Jones's shot wound entered above his left ear, whereas Dr. Mootoo had specified the entrance to have been above Jones's right ear. As Jones was right-handed, theoretically the U.S. report suggested he did not commit suicide; it only stated the "manner of death" to be "undetermined." Jim Jones autopsy report, The Jonestown Institute, http://jonestown.sdsu. edu/wp-content/uploads/2013/10/JimJones. pdf. All pages accessed January 25, 2014.

[3] Rebecca Moore, *Understanding Jonestown and Peoples Temple* (Westport, CT: Praeger, 2009), 106.

[4] "Autopsies," The Jonestown Institute, accessed January 24, 2014, http://jonestown. sdsu.edu/?page_id=13661.

[5] "Guyana Inquest," The Jonestown Institute, accessed March 30, 2015, http://jonestown.

sdsu.edu/wp-content/uploads/2013/10/GuyanaInquest.pdf.

6 "Guyana Inquest (Text)," The Jonestown Institute, accessed January 24, 2014, http://jonestown.sdsu.edu/?page_id=13675.

7 Stephan Jones, interview with Judy Bebelaar, San Rafael, CA, June 18, 2015.

8 "Who Survived the Jonestown Tragedy?," The Jonestown Institute, http://jonestown.sdsu.edu/?page_id=37978.

9 "Who was in the group that left Jonestown to go on a 'picnic' the morning of November 18th?," The Jonestown Institute, http://jonestown.sdsu.edu/?page_id=35411.

10 Reiterman and Jacobs, 555-56, 560.

11 "How many people survived November 18?" The Jonestown Institute, http://jonestown.sdsu.edu/?page_id=35419; and "Guyana Inquest (Text)," http://jonestown.sdsu.edu/?page_id=13675.

12 "Guyana Inquest (Text)," http://jonestown.sdsu.edu/?page_id=13675.

13 Stephan Jones, "Death's Night," The Jonestown Institute, http://jonestown.sdsu.edu/?page_id=40172.

14 Wright, 83.

15 Jones, "Death's Night," http://jonestown.sdsu.edu/?page_id=40172.

16 Jones interview, June 18, 2015.

17 *Ibid.*

18 Wright, 83.

19 Jones interview, June 18, 2015.

20 Wright, 89.

21 *Ibid.*, 85.

22 Smith, "Escape from Jonestown," *SI.com Magazine*, December 24, 2007, http://sportsillustrated.cnn.com/2007/magazine/12/24/jonestown1231.

23 Wright, 84-86.

24 "Waco siege," *Wikipedia*, accessed October 16, 2016, https://en.wikipedia.org/wiki/Waco_siege.

25 Wright, 86.

26 *Ibid.*, 86-87.

27 *Ibid.*, 84.

28 *Ibid.*, 89.

29 Jones interview, June 18, 2015.

30 *Ibid.*

31 Stephan Jones, "Reunion," The Jonestown Institute, *Alternative Considerations of Jonestown and Peoples Temple*, accessed March 30, 2015, http://jonestown.sdsu.edu/?page_id=40173.

32 Jones interview, June 18, 2015.

33 Carolyn Jones, "Should Jonestown Memorial Include Jim Jones?," *San Francisco Chronicle*, March 1, 2011, accessed January 24, 2014, http://www.sfgate.com/bayarea/article/Should-Jonestown-memorial-include-Jim-Jones-2472696.php.

34 Wright, 88.

35 Stephan Jones, email to Judy Bebelaar, March 5, 2010.

36 Stephan Jones, email to Judy Bebelaar, March 14, 2010.

37 Wright, 84.

38 Stephan Jones, "The Man They Loved," The Jonestown Institute, accessed June 3, 2016, http://jonestown.sdsu.edu/?page_id=64590.

39 Jones, "Reunion," http://jonestown.sdsu.edu/?page_id=40173.

Afterword

[1] Carl Ross, email to Judy Bebelaar August 14, 2009.

[2] Linda Mertle, "From Baby Steps to Long Strides," The Jonestown Institute, accessed January 24, 2014, http://jonestown.sdsu. edu/?page_id=31422. Also posted on the site is a tribute by Linda Mertle, "A Note to My Tiffany": "You will always be my little baby girl, my Tiffany Garcia. I was so blessed to have had the privilege of taking care of you. . . . Leaving you behind when I left the Temple was one of the hardest things I had to do, but you were not mine and I knew I could not have taken you with me. . . . I remember how you used to giggle with your tiny thumb in your mouth, how I would rub your eyebrows to help you drift off to sleep. I loved just holding you in my arms while you slept and tried not to move so I wouldn't wake you." http://jonestown. sdsu.edu/?page_id=40200.

[3] Linda Mertle, interview with Judy Bebelaar, Berkeley, CA, February 28, 2009.

Photo Identification and Credits

Front Cover photos, courtesy of California Historical Society:
    Row 1: Sonje Regina Duncan, Cleveland Garcia, Mondo Griffith
    Row 2: Cindy Cordell, Michelle Touchette, Ricky Johnson, Kimberly Fye
    Row 3: Mark Sly, Rory Bargeman, Stephanie Chacon
    Row 4: Cornelius Truss, Joyce Polk Brown, Willieater Thomas

Back Cover photos, courtesy of California Historical Society:
Lisa Lewis, Wesley Breidenbach, Olli Smith, Christopher Newell

Note: All entries marked with * are courtesy of California Historical Society (CHS), Peoples Temple Collection

viii Peoples Temple building on Geary Avenue, San Francisco, by Nancy Wong, courtesy of Wikimedia Commons

xi   Actors in Leigh Fondakowski's *The People's Temple*, photo by David Allen, with thanks to the Berkeley Repertory Theater

2   Photo collage: Jimi Hendrix poster; "End the War," from *Weebly.com*; "Gay Pride" march, Wikimedia Commons; *Sisterhood is Powerful* book cover; Herb Caen, courtesy of Nancy Wong; "Nixon Resigns," *San Francisco Chronicle*; *Roots* book cover; The Talking Heads album cover.

4   Marcia Perlstein, by Mary Delema

8   Ron Cabral, Yvonne Golden and "Country Joe" Mc Donald, by John Liu-Klein

9   Tina (Kollias) Johns and Hal Abercrombie, by Mary Delema

10   Opportunity II High, by Ron Cabral

11   Cecil Williams and Jim Jones, by Nancy Wong, Wikimedia Commons

12   Dean Marcic, courtesy of Dean Marcic (photographer unknown)

13   Judy Bebelaar and student, by Mary Delema

15   John Liu-Klein (photographer unknown)

16   Judy Bebelaar, by Mary Delema

23   Terry Preston, by Mary Delema

24   Dorothy Buckley, passport photo circa 1974-77*

173 "Shekinah Glory," photo by Elmer Mertle/Al Mills (deceased) from *Six Years With God*, by Deanna Mertle/Jeannie Mills (deceased), courtesy of Linda Mertle

174 Jonestown map, drawn by Ralph Solonitz

181 Stephan Jones on Jonestown basketball court, by unknown photographer, FBI collection, The Jonestown Institute

182 Jonestown's bootleg basketball court, by an unknown photographer, FBI collection, The Jonestown Institute

185 Dancers and drummers, courtesy of San Diego State University Library and Information Access, Special Collections and University Archives

185 "The Cudjoe"*

187 Christine Miller and Ruth Tupper, passport photos circa 1974-77*

189 Ronnie Dennis, passport photo circa 1974-77*

190 Shanda Oliver, passport photo circa 1974-77*

208 Tim Jones (at right) and unknown basketball player, by unknown photographer, FBI collection, The Jonestown Institute (not an FBI photographer)

212 Leo Ryan, public domain

219 Lamaha Gardens*

226 Map of Guyana, drawn by Ralph Solonitz

238 Empty houses in Jonestown, courtesy of *The Jonestown Report*, Jonestown Institute

249 Dorothy Buckley, Willie Thomas, Joyce Polk Brown, and Mondo Griffith, passport photos circa 1974-77*

259 The Jones Brothers: Amy Arbus ©1993: Tim, Jimmy and Stephan

261 Stephan Jones passport photos, courtesy of Stephan Jones

263 Jonestown Memorial, at Evergreen Cemetery, Oakland, courtesy of Wikimedia Commons (photographer Symphony 999). *(A portion of the proceeds of this book will be donated to Evergreen Cemetery in memory of Ollie Smith.)*

270 Ron Cabral and Stephan Jones, courtesy of Ron Cabral

Bibliography

Erikson, Erik H. "Youth, Fidelity and Diversity." *Daedalus* 91, no. 1 (1963), 5–27.

Guinn, Jeff. *The Road to Jonestown: Jim Jones and People's Temple*. NY: Simon & Schuster, 2017.

Hall, John R. *Gone from the Promised Land: Jonestown in American Cultural History*. 2nd ed. Piscataway, NJ: Transaction Publishers, 2004.

Kilduff, Marshall, and Javers, Ron. *The Suicide Cult: The Inside Story of the Peoples Temple Sect and the Massacre in Guyana*. New York: Bantam Doubleday Dell Publishing Group, 1978.

Krause, Charles; Stern, Laurence M.; and, Harwood, Richard. *Guyana Massacre: The Eyewitness Account*. New York: Berkeley Publishing Corporation, 1978.

Layton, Deborah. *Seductive Poison: A Jonestown Survivor's Story of Life and Death in the Peoples Temple*. New York: Doubleday, 1998.

Mills, Jeannie. *Six Years With God: Life Inside Rev. Jim Jones's Peoples Temple*. New York: A & W Publishers, 1979.

Moore, Rebecca. "A Sympathetic History of Jonestown: The Moore Family Involvement in Peoples Temple." *Studies in Religion and Society*, vol. 14. Lewiston, NY: Edwin Mellen Press, 1985.

Moore, Rebecca. *Understanding Jonestown and Peoples Temple*. Westport, CT: Praeger, 2009.

Neihardt, John G. *Black Elk Speaks: Being the Life Story of a Holy Man of the Oglala Sioux*. Lincoln: University of Nebraska Press, 1988.

Reiterman, Tim, with John Jacobs. *Raven: The Untold Story of the Rev. Jim Jones and His People*. New York: E. P. Dutton, 1982. Reissued in paperback, New York: Jeremy P. Tarcher/Penguin, 2008.

Scheeres, Julia. *A Thousand Lives: The Untold Story of Hope, Deception, and Survival at Jonestown*. New York: Free Press, 2011.

Smith, Marcia. *Jonestown: The Life and Death of Peoples Temple*. Directed by Stanley Nelson. New York: Firelight Media, 2006.

Stephenson, Denise. *Dear People*: *Remembering Jonestown*. Berkeley, CA: Heyday Books, 2005.

Urdang, Laurence, ed. *The Timetables of American History*. New York: Simon & Schuster, 1996.

Wessinger, Catherine. *How the Millennium Comes Violently: From Jonestown to Heaven's Gate*. New York: Seven Bridges Press, 2000.

Wright, Lawrence. "Orphans of Jonestown," *The New Yorker*, November 22, 1993.

Yeats, William Butler, "The Second Coming," *Michael Robartes and the Dancer* (Dundrum: Cuala Press, 1921). Reprinted in *Immortal Poems of the English Language*, edited by Oscar Williams. New York: Washington Square Press, 1952.

About the Authors

udy Bebelaar taught English and creative writing for 37 years in public high schools in San Francisco, California. She has received national recognition for her success in helping her students find meaning in writing about their lives. Judy co-hosts a reading series in Berkeley, where she lives, for the Bay Area Writing Project. Her award-winning poetry has been published in dozens of literary magazines; a chapbook, *Walking Across the Pacific* (Finishing Line Press, 2014); and in three anthologies: *Turning a Train of Thought Upside Down* (Scarlet Tanager Books, 2012), *The Widows' Handbook* (Kent State University Press, 2014) and *River of Earth and Sky: Poems for the 21st Century* (Blue Light Press, 2016).

on Cabral, a native of San Francisco, entered teaching in the San Francisco Unified School District in 1965 and became a Middle School principal in 1992. He served 35 years in that capacity, finally retiring in 2002. Ron met Judy Bebelaar, a fellow teacher, in 1969 at Opportunity 1, where he taught Urban Problems, Music Appreciation, Journalism, Drugs and Society, and Radio Production. He also managed and coached the school baseball team. He later transferred to Wilson High School in 1978. Ron is married with three grown children and five grandsons. He lives in Contra Costa County.

Thee do I crave co-partner in that verse
Which I presume on Nature to compose...
Divine one, give my words
Immortal charm.
— Lucretius, 50 BCE, De Rerum Natura

Sugartown Publishing

Based in Crockett, California, home to the famous C&H Sugar plant.

Sugartown Publishing joined a long-established tradition of cooperative publishing in 2012. We are dedicated to bringing into print, electronic and audio media, works of literary merit that have something significant to say.

Current and forthcoming titles include:

- A Stalwart Bends, Poems and Reflections by Ben Slomoff, 2012
- Doing Time With Nehru, memoir by Yin Marsh, 2012
- Among the Shapes that Fold & Fly, poetry by Patricia Nelson, 2013
- Between the Fault Lines: Eight East Bay Poets, edited by Jannie Dresser, 2013
- Workers' Compensation: Poems of Labor & the Working Life by Jannie Dresser, 2013
- Swimming the Sky, poetry by Gail Peterson, 2013
- It Lasts a Moment: New & Collected Poems by Fred Ostrander, 2013
- Falling Home, poetry by Gary Turchin, 2013
- Voices from the Field, poetry by Kimberly Satterfield, 2014
- At My Table, poetry by Judith Yamamoto, 2014
- The Glass Ship, prose-poems by Judy Wells, 2014
- Yew Nork, poetry by Dale Jensen, 2014
- Truchas: Closer to Heaven, poems by Chantal Guillemin, 2015
- Stronger Than I Know: My Story in Poem, poems by Cheri Coleman, 2015
- Sun on the Rind, poems by Bonnie Thomas, 2015
- Joyriding on an Updraft, poems by Deborah Dashow Ruth, 2015
- The Harsh Green World, poems by Robert Coats, 2015
- My Father Believed in Love, poems by Catherine Elizabeth Dana, 2016
- Never Enough, poems by Benjamin Slomoff, 2016
- Storm Camp, poems by John Hart, 2017
- Amateur Mythology, poems by Dale Jensen, 2017
- The Self-Evolution Spa, poems by Bruce Bagnell, 2017
- Mi Tierra: America, Familia, Nicaragua, Amor, poems by Juan Sequeira, 2017
- DUSK, poems by Constance Rowell Mastores, 2017
- And Then They Were Gone: Teenagers of Peoples Temple from High School to Jonestown, by Judy Bebelaar and Ron Cabral, 2018
- The Same River Twice, poems by Lauren Coodley, Spring 2018
- Family Matters, poems by Yvonne Postelle, Spring 2018

1164 Solano Avenue #140
Albany, CA 94706
sugartownpublishing.com
janniedres@att.net

CPSIA information can be obtained
at www.ICGtesting.com
Printed in the USA
BVHW032210250820
587324BV00001B/32

9 781649 218872